AUTOMATING KNOWLEDGE ACQUISITION FOR EXPERT SYSTEMS

**THE KLUWER INTERNATIONAL SERIES
IN ENGINEERING AND COMPUTER SCIENCE**

KNOWLEDGE REPRESENTATION,
LEARNING AND EXPERT SYSTEMS

Consulting Editor

Tom Mitchell
Carnegie Mellon University

Other books in the series:

Universal Subgoaling and Chunking of Goal Hierarchies. J. Laird, P. Rosenbloom, A. Newell.
ISBN 0-89838-213-0.

Machine Learning: A Guide to Current Research. T. Mitchell, J. Carbonell, R. Michalski.
ISBN 0-89838-214-9.

Machine Learning of Inductive Bias. P. Utgoff. ISBN 0-89838-223-8.

A Connectionist Machine for Genetic Hillclimbing. D. H. Ackley. ISBN 0-89838-236-X.

Learning From Good and Bad Data. P. D. Laird. ISBN 0-89838-263-7.

Machine Learning of Robot Assembly Plans. A. M. Segre. ISBN 0-89838-269-6.

AUTOMATING KNOWLEDGE ACQUISITION FOR EXPERT SYSTEMS

edited by

Sandra Marcus
Boeing Computer Services

KLUWER ACADEMIC PUBLISHERS
Boston/Dordrecht/London

Distributors for North America:
Kluwer Academic Publishers
101 Philip Drive
Assinippi Park
Norwell, Massachusetts 02061, USA

Distributors for the UK and Ireland:
Kluwer Academic Publishers
Falcon House, Queen Square
Lancaster LA1 1RN, UNITED KINGDOM

Distributors for all other countries:
Kluwer Academic Publishers Group
Distribution Centre
Post Office Box 322
3300 AH Dordrecht, THE NETHERLANDS

Library of Congress Cataloging-in-Publication Data

Automating knowledge acquisition for expert systems/edited by Sandra
Marcus.
    p. cm.—(The Kluwer international series in engineering and
computer science. Knowledge representation, learning, and expert
systems)
   Includes index.
   ISBN-13: 978-1-4684-7124-3   e-ISBN-13: 978-1-4684-7122-9
   DOI: 10.1007/978-1-4684-7122-9
   1. Expert systems (Computer science)   I. Marcus, Sandra.
II. Series.
QA76.76.E95A97   1988   88–21012
006.3′3—dc19   CIP

Table of Contents

List of Figures

List of Tables

Contributing Authors

Judith Bachant
AI Research Center
Digital Equipment Corporation
290 Donald Lynch Boulevard, DLB5-3/B3
Marlborough, Massachusetts   01752

Larry Eshelman
Philips Laboratories
345 Scarborough Road
Briarcliff Manor, New York   10510

Gary Kahn
Carnegie Group, Inc.
5 PPG Place
Pittsburgh, Pennsylvania   15222

Georg Klinker
Department of Computer Science
Carnegie Mellon University
Pittsburgh, Pennsylvania   15213

Sandra Marcus
Knowledge Systems Laboratory
Advanced Technology Center
Boeing Computer Services
P.O. Box 24346, M/S 7L-64
Seattle, Washington   98124

John McDermott
AI Research Center
Digital Equipment Corporation
290 Donald Lynch Boulevard, DLB5-3/E2
Marlborough, Massachusetts   01752

Daniel Offutt
Electrical Engineering and Computer Science Department
University of Michigan
Ann Arbor, Michigan   48109

Preface

In June of 1983, our expert systems research group at Carnegie Mellon University began to work actively on automating knowledge acquisition for expert systems. In the last five years, we have developed several tools under the pressure and influence of building expert systems for business and industry. These tools include the five described in chapters 2 through 6 -- MORE, MOLE, SALT, KNACK and SIZZLE. One experiment, conducted jointly by developers at Digital Equipment Corporation, the Soar research group at Carnegie Mellon, and members of our group, explored automation of knowledge acquisition and code development for XCON (also known as R1), a production-level expert system for configuring DEC computer systems. This work influenced the development of RIME, a programming methodology developed at Digital which is the subject of chapter 7. This book describes the principles that guided our work, looks in detail at the design and operation of each tool or methodology, and reports some lessons learned from the enterprise.

A common theme of the work, brought out in the introductory chapter, is that much power can be gained by understanding the roles that domain knowledge plays in problem solving. Each tool can exploit such an understanding because it focuses on a well defined problem-solving method used by the expert systems it builds. Each tool chapter describes the basic problem-solving method assumed by the tool and the leverage provided by committing to the method. Where appropriate, the chapter also describes experiments in applying the tool to multiple domains, limitations discovered during the experiments, and modifications growing out of the tests. The RIME methodology, while not focusing on a single problem-solving method, helps programmers define methods and make explicit the ways domain knowledge is used. The RIME chapter describes some mechanisms for doing this and the leverage gained from each. In addition to providing leverage, defining a method for a tool also limits its scope. A final chapter takes steps toward creating a taxonomy of problem-solving methods in terms of the properties of the domains for which they are useful.

During the two years it took to put this book together, the author of the RIME chapter was at Digital and several of the authors in the Carnegie Mellon group moved to other organizations. I would like to thank the authors for their efforts to achieve coherence in the presentation of their work despite the limitations imposed by physical separation and restricted day-to-day communication. I am grateful to Bev Clark and Ed Reading for their editorial assitance and to Linda Green for her help in preparing some of the figures. I would also like to thank the crew that helped proofread: John Boose, Cathy Kitto, Linda Green, Peter Russo, and Dave Shema. I am extremely grateful to my husband, Ric Robinson, for his support throughout this project and to my children, Nate and Emma, for their understanding.

Sandra Marcus

AUTOMATING KNOWLEDGE ACQUISITION FOR EXPERT SYSTEMS

1. Introduction

Sandra Marcus

Expert systems (knowledge-based programs that use a large body of domain facts to solve problems) are coming into widespread use in buisiness and industry. There is a potential for us to learn from our growing experience in building expert systems. Yet the creation of an individual system is often performed as a one-of-a-kind experiment, with costly interviewing of experts and analysis of the problem, resulting in systems that are sometimes difficult to maintain. This book describes a set of studies in automating knowledge acquisition that attempt to capture some of the expertise gained by knowledge engineers. The studies aim for creation of tools or methodologies designed to reduce the cost of building and maintaining expert systems.

Chapters 2 through 6 describe what we will call automated knowledge-acquisition tools: tools that can elicit relevant domain knowledge from experts; maintain that knowledge in a form that makes it accessible for analysis, review or modification; and use the knowledge to perform a specific task. These five tools get much of their power by making a strong assumption about the problem-solving method that will be used by any expert system they create. Chapter 7 describes a programming methodology that, while not focusing on a single problem-solving method, helps programmers define methods and make explicit the ways domain knowledge is used.

Many successful tools for automating knowledge acquisition for expert systems have taken the approach of focusing on one particular problem-solving method to be used by the systems they generate (see, for example, [Davis 79, Boose 84]). The narrow focus simplifies the task of making clear the roles that knowledge plays in finding a solution. Role definition provides several advantages [Clancey 83, Clancey 85, Swartout 83, Neches 84, Chandrasekaran 83, Chandrasekaran 86, McDermott 86, Gruber 87a]:

1. A knowledge-acquisition tool needs a clear understanding of the function of the knowledge required by the system it is building so that it knows what information to ask the expert for. Questions such as "How do you perform your job?" are too undirected to produce useful material for constructing an

expert system.   An understanding of the ways domain
knowledge can be used provides a focus for interrogating
domain experts.

2. A functionally represented knowledge base can be examined
to judge the expert system's adequacy to perform the task for
which it is intended.   For example, a knowledge-acquisition
tool that understands how knowledge will be used can have
strategies for identifying places where knowledge is missing
from the knowledge base and for eliciting remedial knowledge
from experts.

3. Understanding the roles knowledge plays allows the
knowledge-acquisition tool to generate a problem-solving
system that knows how to apply the gathered knowledge when
appropriate.   This is because the knowledge gathered is
identified by role and the problem-solving method itself
specifies when during problem solving each role is applicable.
This also leaves open the possibility of using the same
knowledge base representation with distinct variations in
problem-solving method that use the same knowledge roles
but differ in when they apply the knowledge in those roles.

4. For an expert system to describe to a user how it makes
decisions, its explanation facility must understand the function
of the knowledge used by the system.   The common demands
on knowledge representation from explanation and knowledge
elicitation are not surprising, since in the former the expert
system must "transfer" knowledge to its user, while in the
latter the human domain expert must have the means to
transfer knowledge to the knowledge-acquisition tool.   One
advantage of this relationship is that a function-based
knowledge representation scheme used by a knowledge-
acquisition tool can be incorporated into the expert system it
generates to serve that system's explanation facility.

5. For most expert systems, it is impractical to enumerate all the
potential problems a system will need to solve. However, a
well chosen set of sample problems can be used to help assess
the validity of the system. Establishing selection criteria for
the sample set that take into account how knowledge will be
used can help ensure that the relevant characteristics of the
knowledge base will be tested.

6. An understanding of the roles knowledge plays during problem solving is crucial in mapping a domain expert's description of a problem onto a problem-solving method. The more the AI community understands how to do this for specific problems and problem-solving methods, the better position we will be in to develop methods to match problem-solvers and tools to problems in general.

This last point is an important one. In addition to providing leverage, defining a method for a tool also limits its scope. The final chapter of this book will address this issue.

Each of the tools described in this book has the potential of providing all the advantages listed above. As they have been developed, different tools emphasize different areas.

MORE, for instance, was a groundbreaking experiment in automating knowledge acquisition. It was developed to answer the question, "Can understanding the role knowledge plays in problem solving help a tool pursue useful knowledge the way knowledge engineers do?" The expert systems built by MORE perform a kind of heuristic classification [Clancey 85]. MORE stores domain facts in an event model that represents the relations among occurrences of events and the conditions that affect the relations. From this event model, it generates a rule model of condition/conclusion assertions used to perform diagnosis. Because MORE understands how knowledge is used in diagnosis, it understands what knowledge it needs; it has strategies for detecting errors and for seeking information that will increase the diagnostic power of the knowledge base. MORE demonstrated the feasibility of the approach. MORE's use has been explored in several application areas: diagnosis of drilling-fluid problems, epileptic seizures, disk faults, and manufacturing defects in the wave soldering of circuit boards. MORE's interface was improved in two successors -- TDE, described briefly at the end of the MORE chapter, and MOLE.

A major goal in MOLE's development has been to limit direct questioning of the expert. Like that of MORE, its problem-solver uses a kind of heuristic classification. MOLE acquires the minimal structure of domain facts needed to begin diagnosis, fleshes out the knowledge base by making some intelligent guesses, and refines the knowledge base by assimilating the expert's corrections of its solutions. Gaining knowledge by requesting feedback reduces the amount of questioning MOLE must do and provides the expert with a rich context in which to recall relevant domain facts. MORE has been used to build a number of systems, including systems for diagnosing inefficiencies in a coal-burning power plant, defects in the steel produced by a steel-rolling mill, defects in power supply boards as they come off an assembly line, malfunctions of automobile engines, causes of bad milk on a dairy farm, and communication problems in a large computer network.

A third tool, SALT, is one of a few knowledge-acquisition tools for expert systems that construct, rather than select, solutions. SALT-generated expert systems perform design tasks using a propose-and-revise problem-solving strategy; they propose values for pieces of a design, identify constraints on the design, and use domain knowledge to revise decisions if constraints in the proposal are violated. A critical knowledge-acquisition problem is understanding how to put design decisions together to arrive at a preferred design: while design experts are typically good at detailing constraints that apply to individual design pieces, they are not as good at specifying how they put the pieces together into an overall design that satisfies all the constraints. Thus, SALT takes a piecemeal, bottom-up approach to building the knowledge base, exploiting the knowledge that experts find easiest to provide. SALT analyzes how the pieces fit together and, where necessary, guides the expert in providing knowledge about how to organize design decisions. SALT has been used to develop and maintain an elevator-system designer and to build a flow-shop scheduler.

The fourth tool described in this book, KNACK, is specialized for tasks that require a report as their output. It creates systems that use domain-customized information-gathering techniques to acquire relevant data or descriptions and presents the information in the form of a report. A major part of the development effort has gone into making KNACK's interface easy for domain experts to use. KNACK acquires a domain model that represents the common technical terminology of the domain. This terminology is then used in questioning the expert for knowledge about information-gathering strategies and report construction. KNACK elicits samples from the expert, proposes examples that generalize the samples, and requests feedback on the accuracy of the generalization. KNACK can also acquire the additional knowledge for design and evaluation tasks that need a large amount of knowledge to start with or that require a report as output. KNACK has been used to produce systems that assess and improve the design of an electromechanical system to meet nuclear-hardening requirements, assist with the definition of requirements for a planned software system, and assist in the assessment and report of a project's progress. It is currently being used in the creation of systems to assist a salesperson with the design and configuration of computer networks and to assist an entrepreneur in the preparation of business plans.

The final tool, SIZZLE, builds expert systems that perform quantitative sizing tasks; that is, the systems take descriptions of factors influencing resource demands and recommend the quantities of resources needed. SIZZLE's development is particularly interesting because it explored the appropriateness of distinct problem-solving strategies for sizing. SIZZLE-built sizers reach their solutions by extrapolating from cases validated by experts. The method was chosen both because it is appropriate and efficient for problem solving and because it lends itself to automated knowledge acquisition for sizing domains. This kind of problem-solving strategy is one that sizing experts typically use and find easy to understand. It allows SIZZLE to make localized and well behaved changes to the knowledge base. SIZZLE has been used to build a computer-system sizer that produces an abstract description of the minimal collection of computing hardware needed to satisfy customer requirements. It also appears useful for tasks such as electric-motor sizing, legal-claim sizing, and copier sizing.

Chapter 7 diverges from the other chapters in that it describes a programming methodology, RIME, rather than a knowledge-acquisition tool. RIME provides a way of implementing rule-based systems that makes explicit how they use domain knowledge. RIME's programming guidelines and mechanisms help programmers define problem-solving methods and index domain facts according to how they are used in the method and how they relate to the task. Such an approach makes the system more maintainable and explainable even without a tool; it also has the advantage of laying the groundwork for future automated tool development. The RIME methodology has been used to reimplement XCON (also known as R1), an expert system that configures computer systems and MOLE, the knowledge-acquisition tool described in chapter 3. It is currently being used to reimplement KNACK, described in chapter 5, and to implement an expert system from scratch.

The final chapter of this book is both a summary of some of the individual chapters and an overview of the whole enterprise. Part of what we hope to gain from these studies is an understanding of how to select problem-solving methods and tools according to the demands of a task. Chapter 8 takes steps toward creating a taxonomy of problem-solving methods that identifies discriminating characteristics of the methods in terms of the properties of the domains for which they are useful. The author also expresses his view on the relationship between a problem's need for task-specific control knowledge and the applicability of **role-limiting** methods. It is important to keep in mind when reading this chapter that it describes the tools in their current state; some of the tools are under active development that may extend their scope.

The tools discussed in this book have proved useful in creating and maintaining working expert systems. They are also interesting in that they are applicable to a range of tasks and, thus, can be used to support multiple applications. They further our understanding of how task demands help shape the problem-solving strategies that can apply to them. What is more, our approach to creating these tools is one that can be usefully employed by any programmer of expert systems to make the expert systems more accessible and maintainable.

2. MORE: From Observing Knowledge Engineers to Automating Knowledge Acquisition

Gary Kahn

Abstract

MORE interviews experts for the information they use to solve diagnostic problems, demonstrating that some knowledge-engineering skills can be simulated. These interviews are guided by very specific problem-solving and knowledge-acquisition strategies. As MORE's knowledge base becomes more complete, MORE shows an improved ability to ask relevant questions and to accurately detect errors in the knowledge base. Knowledge elicited by MORE is represented in an event (or qualitative causal) model. This model is used to generate rules and to recognize inconsistencies in the confidence factors assigned to rules by domain experts. MORE applies these rules to solve diagnostic problems.

2.1. Introduction

2.1.1. Goals for MORE

MORE demonstrates that the skills required to elicit knowledge for some diagnostic tasks can be effectively simulated. While not eliminating the knowledge-acquisition bottleneck entirely, MORE's approach promises to greatly reduce the cost of expert system development by eliminating the need for specially trained knowledge engineers. MORE helps domain experts create expert systems by soliciting information and monitoring for suspected errors in the knowledge base. As information is provided in response to MORE's questions, it is mapped into an underlying knowledge base. MORE's problem-solver uses the knowledge base to solve diagnostic problems.

EMYCIN [vanMelle 81] demonstrated that a well designed knowledge-based system should have two components: a domain-independent problem-solver, or inference engine, and a domain-specific knowledge base.

With the availability of a domain-independent problem-solver, expert-systems development is greatly eased, as it becomes focused on knowledge-base specification rather than the more difficult enterprise of creating a problem-solving architecture. However, knowledge acquisition itself is typically a laborious and expensive effort, requiring a set of specialized skills. The task posed by the MORE research program was first to understand the nature of these skills with greater clarity and second to show that they could automated. An earlier step in this direction was taken by Davis [Davis 82].

The knowledge-elicitation procedures represented in MORE were identified, in part, by reviewing the knowledge-engineering techniques used in the development of the MUD system [Kahn 84], a drilling-fluids diagnostic and treatment system. This system was chosen not only because we were intimately familiar with it, but because we had already succeeded in proceduralizing the knowledge-acquisition process in order to facilitate the transfer of the project from the CMU laboratory to the field. Because of the influence of the MUD system on the development of ideas in this paper, examples are drawn from the drilling-fluids domain.

2.1.2. MORE's Problem-Solving Strategy
MORE's problem-solver uses a heuristic or evidential selection method somewhat similar to that introduced by MYCIN [Shortliffe 76] and generalized by EMYCIN. The knowledge base allows developers to represent the diagnostic significance of a pattern of evidence -- that is, the degree to which evidence supports a belief in a particular hypothesis. All possible hypotheses are known at the outset of execution; thus, solutions are said to be selected rather than constructed.

In the MUD domain, for instance, a diagnosis of a problem entails finding the causes for deviant drilling-fluid (or mud) properties. Possible causes include contaminants, high temperatures, high pressures, and inadequate corrective treatments, including the underuse of solids-removal equipment and the unsatisfactory use of chemical additives. Rules express the diagnostic significance of changes in mud properties, such as density, viscosity, and oil/water ratio, among others. The following rule is typical:

> If there is a decrease in density and an
> increase in viscosity, then moderately (7)
> suspect that there has been an influx of
> water. If not, strongly (10) disregard
> the possibility of an influx of water.

Diagnostic significance is represented as a confidence factor ranging from 0 to 10. These weights are assigned subjectively by domain experts, with 0 indicating a lack of significance. In this example, 7 represents a positive confidence factor, used when the rule's conditions are instantiated; 10 represents a negative confidence factor, used as a measure of disbelief when the rule's conditions are not fully instantiated. The positive confidence factor is sometimes referred to as a sufficiency condition, the negative confidence factor as a necessity condition [Fox 83].

In rule-based diagnostic systems, there are typically several rules that can each provide support to the same hypothesis. Such rules express the diagnostic significance, with respect to a particular hypothesis, of observing (or failing to observe) symptoms potentially caused by the hypothesized event. The problem-solver arrives at a measure of belief in each hypothesis by composing the contributions of each relevant rule into an overall measure of belief. For example, in order to determine the likelihood of an influx in water, MORE's problem-solver would consider each rule that could support a belief in this hypothesis. The weights associated with each of these rules would be tallied together, according to a variant of the MYCIN algorithm, and an overall measure of belief in this hypothesis would result. Further details on MORE's problem-solving method are provided in section 2.6.

2.1.3. An Overview
While MORE's problem-solving strategy is built on interpreting rules associating evidence with diagnostic conclusions, MORE's knowledge-acquisition strategy, covered in section 2.2, elicits deeper knowledge about the domain and represents it in an event model as described in section 2.3. There are two reasons for focusing knowledge acquisition on the event model rather than on diagnostic rules. First, in the several cases we explored, domain experts were not good at providing rules -- rules did not correspond to the way they naturally communicated relevant knowledge. Secondly, MORE required a deeper or more explicit representation of the

domain to support the automation of desirable knowledge-acquisition strategies. In short, in order to ask meaningful questions, it is necessary to have a deeper understanding (explicit model) of the domain.

A MORE model is thus composed of a number of interrelated facts:

- Events that could lead to problems and that would constitute explanatory hypotheses for symptomatic observations reported during a diagnostic session.

- Symptomatic observations that could be associated with each of these events.

- Further discriminating attributes of these symptoms, such as a *rapid* increase in a measurable property.

- States or events that could make the occurrence of an observed symptom more or less likely given the occurrence of a hypothesized cause.

- States or events that could make the occurrence of a hypothesized cause more or less likely.

- Tests used to determine the presence of any of the above events or states.

- Conditions that would lead to these tests being more or less accurate.

Facts of these types are represented in a relational network model as they are learned. This model, even when partially complete, is used to generate rules, recognize errors in the confidence factors domain experts assign to rules, and guide further interrogation of the expert. Section 2.4 describes the three types of rules MORE can generate from a domain model, as well as how inconsistencies and errors are detected. The rules are used by MORE's problem-solver to interpret symptomatic evidence, evaluate the reliability of evidence, and take into account the expected likelihood of a hypothesized problem. While MORE generates rule bodies, or condition-conclusion assertions, the developer is responsible for assigning confidence factors to each rule. A confidence factor expresses the certainty of the conclusion given the conditions. This is left to the developer because there is insufficient information in the event model for MORE to infer confidence factors. However, MORE can detect inconsistencies and errors in the assigned confidence factors given constraints implicit in the model.

Section 2.5 describes how MORE uses the event model to identify which of the knowledge-acquisition strategies will most effectively elicit needed information from the domain expert. Although MORE can control the direction of the knowledge-acquisition session, considerable flexibility is provided to the knowledge-base developer or expert. The developer can ask MORE to pursue a strategic line of questioning as soon as MORE recognizes its desirability, or instruct MORE to await a request for guidance. The developer can specify a strategy for MORE to pursue or allow MORE to select the strategy it prefers.

Once the event model has been compiled into rules and the developer has assigned a confidence factor to each rule, diagnostic sessions may be run. During a diagnostic session, the user identifies occurring symptoms; MORE generates hypotheses, asks for further information, and identifies the probable cause of the symptoms. Users may request explanations of MORE's conclusions. MORE's diagnostic procedure is discussed in section 2.6.

Section 2.7 covers lessons learned from MORE and notes how TDE, a subsequent system, addresses some of MORE's inadequacies.

2.2. Strategies for Knowledge Acquisition

Diagnostic problem solving requires a proper assessment of symptomatic evidence. In order to succeed, the problem-solver must recognize that the diagnostic significance of observing or failing to observe symptoms may depend on the context of co-occurring events or background conditions, the reliability of the evidence, and the expected likelihood of hypothesized problems. Successful diagnosis requires the ability to both confirm and disconfirm hypotheses in light of the presence or absence of expected symptoms. In terms of a rule-based problem-solver, confidence factors that express an association between a symptom and a hypothesis will need to vary as the conditions of the rule are refined to include information affecting the diagnostic significance of the symptomatic observation or lack thereof.

Knowledge acquisition thus requires identifying the symptoms associated with diagnosable problems and identifying the co-occurring conditions, events, and expectations in light of which the symptoms must be interpreted. In order to provide an effective knowledge-acquisition tool, it is necessary to recast this broadly specified requirement as interview strategies that will elicit critical information from domain experts.

As a result of observing interview techniques used in the development of MUD, and subsequently understanding the effectiveness of these techniques in terms of MUD's problem-solving behavior, eight interview strategies were identified. These strategies are differentiation, frequency conditionalization, symptom distinction, symptom conditionalization, path division, path differentiation, test differentiation, and test conditionalization. Each strategy elicits domain knowledge that affects the certainty with which the problem-solver can confirm or disconfirm hypotheses during a diagnostic session.

2.2.1. The Genesis of the Strategies

In what follows, we review the critical observations in light of which the knowledge-elicitation strategies were formulated. In order to provide a common thread, all the observations are exemplified in terms of the same set of facts taken from the MUD domain -- facts that also exemplify the kind of domain knowledge acquired by MORE. These are:

- Water, shale, and salt contamination are problems that can explain changes in drilling-fluid properties.

- Symptoms of water contamination are an increase in viscosity, a decrease in density, and an increase in unemulsified water.

- Symptoms of shale contamination are an increase in viscosity, a decrease in density, and an increase in low-specific-gravity solids.

- Symptoms of salt contamination are an increase in viscosity and an increase in chlorides.

- Shale contamination leads to a *gradual* decrease in density, while water contamination leads to a *rapid* decrease in density.

- Salt formations predicted by geological surveys make the problem of salt contamination more likely.

- A high MBT test indicates an increase in low-specific-gravity solids.

Observation: Knowledge engineers press for unique symptoms.

One of the first steps for knowledge engineers in diagnostic domains is to quickly inventory problem areas and determine the symptoms associated with each. Of particular importance are symptoms that uniquely identify an underlying problem. Where similar symptoms are associated with more than one problem, knowledge engineers seek to identify tests or symptoms that will allow these problems to be differentiated. Some observations that constitute differentiating knowledge may not seem significant unless seen against the backdrop of other symptoms.

For instance, both an influx of water and an insufficient use of emulsifier can have the same effects on measurable drilling-fluid properties. However, an increase in volume is usually associated with an influx of water. While this effect can also result from a hydrocarbon influx, other shifts in drilling-fluid properties distinguish hydrocarbon from water influxes. Thus, the problems can be further differentiated by adding the fact that an increase in volume is a confirming observation with respect to a water influx.

Differentiation implies seeking symptoms that provide leverage in distinguishing among diagnosable events. Most powerful in this respect are symptoms that result from a unique diagnosable event.

Observation: Knowledge engineers seek conditions under which a problem would be highly likely or unlikely.

An important intuition, formalized by Bayes as the concept of expected likelihood, is that the assessment of symptomatic evidence should be dependent on the degree to which one already expects the underlying problem to occur. Knowledge engineers exploit this intuition by seeking background conditions under which the occurrence of a particular problem is highly likely or unlikely.

For instance, an increase in viscosity often results from drilling through one of a number of contaminants. Interviews determined that these contaminants may be expected or not, depending on the geology associated with the location being drilled. This suggested the need for rules in which the diagnostic significance of an increase in viscosity was dependent on local knowledge about the likelihood of encountering various contaminants.

Frequency conditionalization is determining if there are background conditions under which a particular cause is more or less likely to occur. The more these conditions lead to the expectation of a particular cause, the greater the confirmatory significance of a related symptom.

Observation: Where underlying problems lead to similar symptoms, knowledge engineers seek out more precise characterizations that would differentiate the causes.

For instance, both an influx of water and shale contamination can cause a decrease in density. However, it was learned that if density decreases *rapidly*, it is more likely to be due to an influx of water.

Symptom distinction thus requires seeking out the special characteristics of a symptom that identify it as having been caused by one rather than another underlying event.

Observation: Knowledge engineers seek background conditions that will increase the likelihood of a symptomatic event given a particular cause.

An important intuition, formalized by the early Greek logicians as *modus tollens*, is that a proposition is false when any proposition it implies is false, so long as the implication is valid. Diagnostic reasoning relies on a similar intuition. If an underlying problem always gives rise to a symptom, the failure to observe this symptom is grounds for believing that the problem is not present. Symptoms, however, are sometimes only partially dependent on a particular problem. In this case, determining which conditions increase the likelihood of observing a symptomatic event, given a cause, can lead to rules that will better justify *modus tollens* reasoning.

For example, viscosity effects are weakly associated with salt contamination of a water-based drilling fluid when the fluid has been pretreated with surfactant thinners. However, if there has not been a pretreatment of this kind, viscosity effects can be expected whenever salt contamination occurs. Thus, when it is known that thinners have not been used, the failure of viscosity symptoms to appear can count as strong evidence against the hypothesis of salt contamination.

Symptom conditionalization refers to the strategy of eliciting conditions in light of which a symptom will be more strongly expected, given a particular problem. If the occurrence of a problem creates strong expectations that a certain symptom will be observed, the failure to observe the symptom will support rejection of the hypothesized problem as an explanation for any observed symptoms.

Observation: Knowledge engineers seek to determine intermediate steps in the causal chain from problem to symptom.

In investigating problems and symptoms, knowledge engineers typically ask if a problem gives rise directly to a symptom or if there are critical intermediate steps. If these steps are observable or testable, the recognition that they have or have not occurred may be more significant than the final symptomatic result.

For example, an increase in bentonite is an intermediate step between the underlying problem of shale collapsing into the bore hole and an observed change in viscosity caused by the bentonite. Because the increase in bentonite is closer to the underlying problem, and consequently more strongly associated with shale contamination, the failure to observe a significant increase in free bentonite through a methylene blue test (MBT) provides stronger disconfirmation than the failure to observe an increase in viscosity.

Path division refers to the strategy of eliciting an intermediate symptomatic event that is produced by an underlying problem and leads to a symptom already associated with the problem by the domain expert. The intermediate symptom selected must be more expected, given the cause, than the less proximal symptom. Knowledge of this relation can lead the system to achieve better diagnostic results at run time, as the failure to observe symptoms closer to a hypothesized problem will provide stronger disconfirmation.

Refinement of the causal path is also used as a means of finding symptoms that will differentiate underlying problems that result in otherwise similar symptoms. For instance, an increase in plastic viscosity in oil mud can result from both shale and water contamination. These underlying problems can be differentiated, however, by understanding the different ways in which they result in viscosity changes. Shale contamination causes an increase in plastic viscosity by increasing the percentage of solids in the drilling-fluid system; water causes an increase by its behavior in a partially emulsified solution. The drilling-fluids engineer can determine which of these mechanisms accounts for increased plastic viscosity through the use of additional tests. These tests measure the amount of unemulsified water and the solids content. Positive results on these tests provide stronger confirmation of the respective causes than does the shared symptom of increased plastic viscosity.

Path differentiation is similar to **path division** in that it seeks to elicit intermediate events on causal pathways. However, it differs in motivation, as the attempt by knowledge engineers, in this case, is to elicit events that differentiate hypothesized events that can result in otherwise similar symptoms.

Observation: Knowledge engineers determine the reliability of information-gathering techniques.

The diagnostic significance of evidence depends on its perceived reliability. Consequently, learning the relative reliability of alternative test procedures can suggest the need for making diagnostic evaluations contingent on the test procedures used. For instance, the significance of observing changes in pH level differs depending on whether pH is measured by litmus paper or the more accurate pH meter.

Similarly, background conditions may affect the reliability of a test procedure. In the MUD domain, cross-test consistency is an important indicator of test reliability. Reliability is also affected by the experience level of the field engineer.

Test differentiation refers to the strategy of distinguishing the reliability of different tests, and **test conditionalization** to that of determining the conditions under which the reliability of a test may vary. The higher the reliability, the more significant the observation. The lower the reliability, the less the results can be used to support a diagnostic conclusion.

2.2.2. Summary

MORE evokes its knowledge-acquisition strategies selectively after first eliciting an initial account of diagnosable problems and related symptoms from the domain expert. Differentiation and path differentiation lead to the knowledge of symptoms or events whose occurrence would better differentiate competing hypotheses entertained during a diagnostic session. Frequency conditionalization and symptom distinction are pursued to more exactly determine the diagnostic significance of an observed symptom. Symptom conditionalization is typically pursued to more exactly determine the diagnostic significance of failing to observe an expected symptom. Path division elicits additional events whose occurrence would have been more strongly expected, given a hypothesized problem, than symptoms farther along the causal path. Finally, test conditionalization and test differentiation bear on the diagnostic significance of observing or failing to observe an expected symptom. The more reliable the observation, the greater its significance. Section 2.5 describes the conditions under which these strategies are evoked.

2.3. Knowledge Representation

MORE employs two forms of knowledge representation that, taken together, enable both diagnostic reasoning and knowledge acquisition. These are an event model of the domain and a rule model of condition/conclusion assertions. The rule model is used to support both diagnostic reasoning and knowledge acquisition, the event model to support only knowledge acquisition. The two are interrelated in that rule bodies -- that is, the condition/conclusion assertions without confidence factors -- are generated from the event model. MORE uses both the domain model and the rule model when recognizing inconsistencies.

2.3.1. The Event Model

As experts are interviewed by MORE, a representation of their responses is built into an event model. Each event model consists of four core representational entities: hypotheses, symptoms, conditions, and links. A **hypothesis** denotes an event whose identification will be the result of a diagnosis. A **symptom** is any event or state consequent to the occurrence of a hypothesis, whose observation disposes toward the acceptance of a hypothesis. A **condition** is an event or state in the environment that is not directly symptomatic of any hypothesis but can affect the diagnostic significance of some other event. **Links** are used to join entities in the model. States or events represented as symptoms may also be hypotheses. MORE is implemented in OPS5 [Forgy 81]; each data type is equivalent to a working memory element class.

The simplest MORE-built models are flat and consist of several hypotheses, or root problems, joined by links to symptoms. In such simple cases, each problem is linked to all the symptomatic events evoked by it. More than one problem may be linked to a particular symptom. Deeper models are also possible, as MORE can represent causal relations between symptomatic events in a causal chain. In addition to the causal relation between root problems and symptoms, a MORE model represents events or states that affect confidence in the observation of a symptom, the expected likelihood of a root problem occurring, and the significance of a symptom with respect to the diagnosis of a hypothesized problem.

Five kinds of conditions may be depicted in a MORE model:

- **Frequency conditions** are used to represent anything that can affect the *a priori* expectation of a given hypothesis. Such conditions are assumed to be independent of observing any particular symptom. Thus, in a MORE model, they are linked directly to an affected hypothesis.

- **Tests** represent procedures or devices used to determine the occurrence of a symptom. Since the expected accuracy of a detection procedure may affect the diagnostic significance of a symptom with respect to any of its explanatory hypotheses, tests are linked directly to their corresponding symptoms.

- **Test conditions** represent events or states that bear on the accurate use of a procedure, device, or visual observation. As test conditions affect confidence in the results or accuracy of a given test with respect to a particular symptom, they are attached to the link joining a test and a symptom.

- **Symptom attributes** are specific characteristics of a symptom that tend to make it more or less likely to be caused by a particular hypothesis. An example is the rapidity with which drilling-fluid density decreases. Symptom attributes provide a way of refining the description of a symptom into one of a number of subclasses, each providing greater discriminating ability among causes of the symptom. Since these conditions refine a symptom's description with respect to the kind of event that could cause it, they are attached to the link connecting the hypothesis and the symptom.

- **Symptom conditions** represent states or events that affect the likelihood of a symptom occurring if the hypothesis has occurred. External events that could, for example, mask or preclude the realization of a symptom even if the hypothesis occurs are represented as symptom conditions. Since these conditions affect the causal link between a hypothesis and symptom, they are attached to the link connecting the hypothesis and the symptom.

2.3.2. An Example Representation

The drilling-fluid facts discussed in section 2.2.1 would be depicted in the manner shown in figure 2-1. Shale contamination, water influx, and salt contamination are each root problems or hypotheses. An increase in low-specific-gravity solids, an increase in viscosity, a decrease in density, an increase in unemulsified water, and an increase in chlorides are shown as symptoms. A *gradual* and a *rapid* decrease of density are depicted as symptom attributes; the use of an oil mud, as a symptom condition; and the expectation of salt formations, as a frequency condition. A single test, MBT, is also shown.

2.4. From Event Model to Rules

While the MORE event model depicts factual considerations relevant to diagnostic problem solving, it does not provide all the information required to carry out a successful diagnosis. Successful diagnosis requires a correct evaluation of evidence provided at the time a problem occurs. It is necessary to know how significant a pattern of evidence is with respect to confirming or disconfirming an entertained hypothesis. The MORE event model does not express sufficient information to support a reasonable evaluation of evidential findings.

For this reason, rules are used to provide an explicit representation of how patterns of evidence should be evaluated with respect to drawing diagnostic conclusions. Rules also provide a mechanism for indicating how the

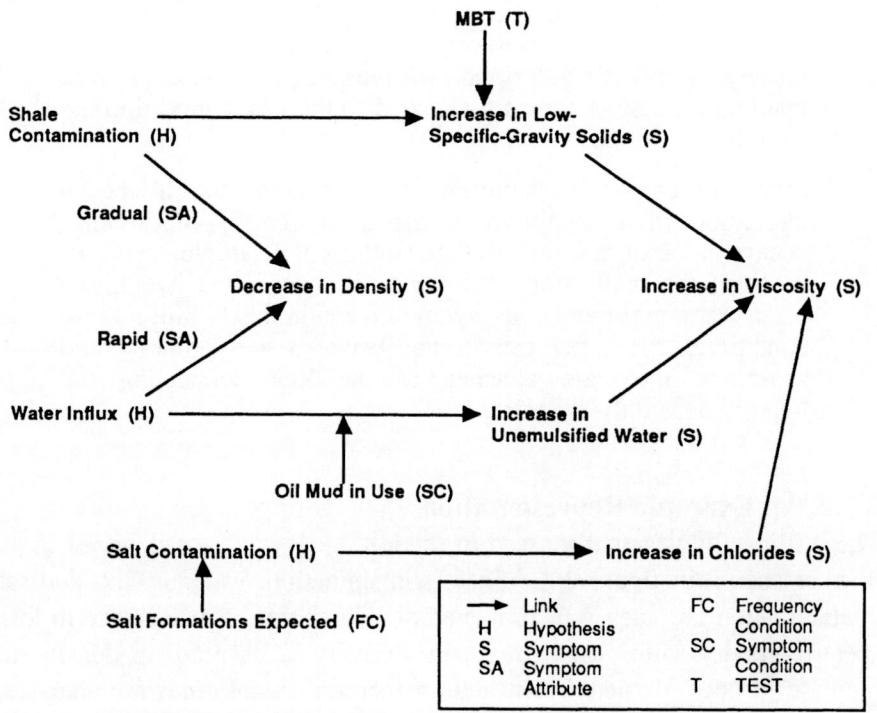

Figure 2-1: Event Model of Drilling-Fluids Facts

reliability of data may vary with the test procedures and conditions under which they become known, as well as a mechanism for representing the effect of background information on the expected likelihood of encountering a problem. In other words, the event model provides the facts that will be taken as evidence during a diagnostic session. The rule model represents the way in which these facts are to be evaluated.

2.4.1. Generating Rules

The event model is used to generate rule bodies, or condition/conclusion assertions, of three kinds. **Diagnostic rules** represent the diagnostic significance of a symptom or set of co-occurring symptoms with respect to a hypothesis. **Symptom-confidence rules** represent the effects of tests and test conditions on the accuracy of a symptomatic observation. **Hypothesis-expectancy rules** represent the effects of frequency conditions on the expected likelihood of a particular hypothesis.

The simplest diagnostic rules represent the evidential significance of a symptom, apart from any known background conditions. For instance,

```
If there is an increase in chlorides <symptom>

then
there is salt contamination.      <hypothesis>
```

For reasons explained below, rules that state a simple association between symptom and hypothesis are called *base rules*.

As the expert specifies new symptom attributes and symptom conditions affecting the evidential or causal relation between a hypothesis and symptom, new rules are created. For instance, the following rule results from the addition of a new condition:

```
If there is an increase in chlorides <symptom>

and the drilling fluid
is undersaturated          <symptom condition>

then
there is salt contamination.      <hypothesis>
```

As conditions are added, rules become more informative. A class of rules that all refer to the same hypothesis/symptom association is referred to as a *rule family*. This concept is important to MORE's problem-solver and advice-giver.

A **symptom-confidence rule** expresses the reliability of a symptomatic observation. For instance,

```
If there is an increase in pH          <symptom>

and this is known
using a pH meter                      <test>

then
the reliability of the symptom
should be treated                     <consequence>
differently than normal.
```

Each time a test or test condition is associated with a symptom in the knowledge base, a new rule is created. Because tests and test conditions affect the reliability of a symptomatic observation independently of its cause, these rules may be applied whenever the evidential effect of the symptom is appraised during a diagnostic session. All symptom-condition rules bearing on the same symptom are considered to be members of the same rule family.

A **hypothesis-expectancy** rule represents the expected likelihood of a hypothesized problem, given frequency conditions expressed in the event model. For instance,

```
If there is the possibility of
salt contamination                    <hypothesis>

and there is
no known geological evidence
for salt formations      <frequency condition>

then
this affects the expectation
of encountering                       <consequence>
salt contamination.
```

Each time a frequency condition is associated with a hypothesis in the knowledge base, a new rule is created. Because frequency conditions affect the interpretation of all the symptomatic evidence associated with a hypothesis, these rules may be applied whenever the evidential effect of any symptom associated with the conditionalized hypothesis is appraised during a diagnostic session. All hypothesis-condition rules bearing on the same hypothesis are considered to be members of the same rule family.

As rules are created, MORE asks the knowledge-base developer, or expert, to assign positive and negative confidence factors to them. For diagnostic rules, the positive confidence factor (0 - 10) represents the degree of diagnostic significance of the symptom with respect to a hypothesis when all the rule's conditions are instantiated. Similarly, the negative confidence factor represents the measure of disbelief contributed by the rule when its condition is not observed.[1]

---

[1]The behavior of rules with condition sets including symptom attributes differs somewhat. The negative factor is contributed when all the symptom attributes are evaluated as false but the symptom is in fact observed.

Symptom-confidence and hypothesis-expectancy rules have only one confidence factor, which is in the range -5 to 5. For symptom-confidence rules, this value is interpreted as a degree of change in the measure of confidence in a reported observation regarding the presence or absence of the symptom. For hypothesis-expectancy rules, this value is interpreted as the degree of change in the expected likelihood of a hypothesis, given the situation described by the condition set of the rule.

Rules with multiple conditions are formulated similarly. Each time MORE learns of a new condition, it creates new single-condition rules, as described above. However it will subsequently add the new condition to the condition set already associated with each rule in the same rule family as the new single-condition rule. For instance, when a new symptom condition is associated with the symptom of increase in chlorides, with respect to the hypothesis of salt contamination, MORE generates a rule that represents the affect of observing both that the drilling fluid is undersaturated (a previously known condition) and that the new condition is present. When a new condition does not plausibly co-occur with other conditions, this may be indicated to the rule generator and a new rule will not be formed. Existing rules to which a new condition is added are called constituent rules. This concept is used in error detection, as discussed in section 2.4.2.

2.4.2. Advice about Confidence Factors

Although confidence factors cannot be inferred from an event model, there is sufficient information to enable expectations to be formed regarding the direction in which factors ought to vary across different rules in the same rule family. When these expectations are violated, MORE warns the knowledge-base developer and explains why it believes there is an inconsistency. The developer is then offered the opportunity of modifying one of the conflicting confidence factors.

MORE monitors for violations of three expectations. First, where one symptom, such as an increase in unemulsified water, leads to another, such as an increase in viscosity, MORE expects that the negative confidence factor for the rule associating increased unemulsified water with a hypothesis, in this case water influx, is greater than the rule that associates increased viscosity with the same hypothesis. In other words, if a symptom (S_1) precedes another symptom (S_2) on a causal chain, it is expected that the negative confidence factor for the more distal symptom (S_2) will be less than or equal to the negative factor of the more proximal symptom (S_1).

This expectation is justified by the intuitive assumption that the causal chain is well modeled as a series of transitional probabilities between events. Thus, if negative confidence factors vary with the degree to which a symptom is expected, given that the hypothesized cause has occurred, the failure to observe symptoms (events) early in the chain should more strongly rule out the hypothesis, other things aside. When this expectation is violated, MORE warns the knowledge-base developer of a possible error.

MORE's second expectation is that the diagnostic significance of observing a symptom will vary inversely with the number of hypotheses that could account for the same symptom. Thus, where symptoms are uniquely indicative of a particular hypothesis, the positive confidence factor associated with the base rule should be maximal. In our example, MORE would expect the diagnostic significance of symptoms indicating shale contamination to be greatest for an increase in low-specific-gravity solids (one explanation) and lowest for an increase in viscosity (three alternative explanations).

Finally MORE has expectations regarding the confidence factors of rules in the same rule family relative to one another. The effect of adding new conditions to constituent rules is expected to be as follows:

- A symptom condition that increases (decreases) the conditional likelihood of a symptom, given a hypothesized event, should result in rules that have greater (lesser) negative confidence factors than their constituent rules.

- A symptom attribute that increases (decreases) the conditional likelihood of a symptom, given a hypothesized event, should result in rules that have greater (lesser) negative and positive confidence factors than their constituent rules.

- A frequency condition that increases (decreases) the expected likelihood of a hypothesized event should result in rules that have greater (lesser) confidence factors than their constituent rules.

- A test or test condition that increases (decreases) the reliability of a symptomatic observation should result in rules that have greater (lesser) confidence factors than their constituent rules.

2.5. Strategy Evocation and Implementation -- Advice for Improving the Knowledge Base

MORE's knowledge-acquisition strategies are pursued on request from the knowledge-base developer. When a request for advice is received, MORE determines which of the eight strategies described in section 2.2 should be pursued. This decision is based on an analysis of the current event model and rule families. For the most part, the strategies attempt to elicit information that will lead to rules with stronger (very high or very low) positive or negative confidence factors. These rules will have more significant diagnostic effect than less informative rules with middling factors. While rules with high factors lead to strong diagnostic conclusions, rules with low factors typically represent the knowledge necessary to avoid erroneous conclusions; that is, false positives or negatives.

MORE pursues the **differentiation** strategy when it identifies a pair or triplet of hypotheses for which there is no differentiating symptom. A symptom (S) is said to differentiate one hypothesis (H_1) from another (H_2) when there is a path over one or more links from H_1 to S and no path from H_2 to S. For triplets, a symptom differentiates H_1 when it is associated with H_1 but not with either of the other two hypotheses.

When MORE finds a pair or triplet without a differentiating symptom, it will ask the knowledge-base developer to provide a symptom associated with one hypothesis but not the others. New differentiating symptoms are easily added to the model by linking their representation to the appropriate hypothesis, as described in section 2.3.

MORE selects **path differentiation** when it identifies a symptom (S) that is directly linked to two hypotheses (H_1,H_2). In this case, MORE attempts to refine the causal path from one of the hypotheses to the symptom. MORE asks the knowledge-base developer for an event caused by H_1 and not H_2 that in turn causes S. Such an event would provide stronger evidence for H_1 than does S. When MORE learns of such an event, it is represented as a symptom with a link to H_1 and to S.

Path division is attempted when a diagnostic-rule family bearing on a particular hypothesis (H) does not contain a rule associating the failure to observe the symptom (S_1) with a high (greater than 7) negative confidence factor. When the lack of such a rule is recognized, MORE seeks an intermediate symptomatic event (S_2) that is caused by H and in turn causes S_1. S_2, as a more proximal symptom, is expected to have a higher probability of occurrence given the hypothesis. Thus, the failure to observe S_2 provides stronger evidence that H has not occurred than does the failure to observe S_1. When MORE learns of S_2, S_2 is represented as a symptom with a link to H and to S_1.

While these strategies lead to new rule families, **symptom conditionalization** and **symptom distinction** refine existing diagnostic-rule families. **Symptom conditionalization** is evoked when there are no rules in a family associated with extreme (less than 4 and greater than 7) negative confidence factors. In this case, MORE attempts to elicit background conditions that decrease or increase the likelihood of the family's symptom occurring given the hypothesis. Knowledge of conditions that decrease the likelihood of observing the symptom helps MORE avoid ruling out real possibilities during a diagnostic session. Knowledge of conditions that increase the likelihood of observing the symptom helps MORE more effectively rule out the hypothesis when the symptom does not occur. When MORE learns of such a condition, it is represented as a symptom condition linked to the path between the family's hypothesis and the symptom. New rules (rule-bodies) are created in the rule family by merging this condition with a copy of the rule-body of each rule in the rule-family.

Symptom distinction is evoked when there is no rule in a diagnostic-rule family with a high (greater than 7) positive confidence factor. In this case, MORE looks for attributes of the family's symptom more likely to be observed when the symptom is due to the family's hypothesis than when it is due to any alternative. As a symptom is distinguished by characteristic attributes, the number of alternative explanatory hypotheses goes down and the positive support contributed by the observation of such a symptom goes up. Like symptom conditions, symptom attributes are represented in MORE's event model as conditions attached to the link joining the hypothesis and the symptom. New rules (rule-bodies) are similarly created in the rule family by merging this condition with a copy of the rule-body of each rule in the rule family.

Test differentiation and **conditionalization** are pursued when there is no rule in a diagnostic-rule family with an extremely high or low positive or negative confidence factor. Again the attempt is to reduce the likelihood of error or indecision that results from using insufficiently informative rules. As MORE learns of new tests and test conditions, the event model is elaborated. Tests are attached by a link directly to the symptom whose diagnostic significance may be affected. Test conditions are attached to the test whose accuracy they modify.

MORE engages in **frequency conditionalization** under similar conditions -- when a diagnostic-rule family for a particular hypothesis (H) has no rules with a high or low positive or negative confidence factor. With this strategy, MORE requests conditions that strongly affect the expected likelihood of H's occurrence. Such conditions are represented as frequency conditions in the event model and are attached directly to the hypothesis they modify. Frequency conditions are mapped into hypothesis-expectancy rules and enhance (or reduce) the measure of belief provided by diagnostic rules.

2.6. The Problem-Solver Revisited

During a diagnostic session, the evaluation of hypotheses occurs in several stages. First, the set of applicable diagnostic rules is identified. Second, the positive or negative confidence factor each of these rules contributes to belief or disbelief in a hypothesis is adjusted in light of applicable symptom-confidence rules. A measure of belief and disbelief is then calculated for each candidate hypothesis. These measures are then adjusted in light of applicable hypothesis-expectancy rules.

Upon the initiation of a diagnostic session, MORE's problem-solver will ask the user to identify observable symptoms that have led to a request for a diagnostic consultation. Hypotheses that could result in these symptoms are considered candidate explanations. For each candidate hypothesis, MORE will determine the set of applicable diagnostic rules. One rule will be selected from each diagnostic-rule family bearing on a candidate hypothesis.

This is done by determining which rules in each family can be instantiated. Thus, the problem-solver needs to query the user about the occurrence of any event referenced in the conditional part of any of the rules in each rule family. The set of instantiated rules is then pruned by eliminating rules whose condition sets are proper subsets of the condition set of another rule.

The most specific, and presumably most accurate, rule is thus selected from each family.

Multiple rules survive this process when there is no rule whose condition set is a superset of every rule in the family. This typically occurs when a diagnostic session is run when the knowledge base has not been completed, and a rule with the combined condition set of the competing rules has not yet been generated. The problem-solver resolves the conflict by selecting the rule with the greatest diagnostic significance; in other words, the rule having the largest positive or negative confidence factor. If there is no such rule, an arbitrary selection is made from the rules having the largest confidence factors.

Prior to applying the rules selected as applicable to a candidate hypothesis, the contribution of each is re-evaluated in light of relevant symptom-confidence rules. The problem-solver will query the user with respect to the conditions referenced by rules in the applicable symptom-confidence rule family. The contribution of the diagnostic rule will be adjusted in proportion to the confidence factor associated with the selected symptom-confidence rule. The maximum adjustment is 40% in one direction or another.[2] A symptom-confidence rule with a factor of -5, for instance, would lead to a 40% decrement in the contribution of the diagnostic rules on which it bore.

After applicable diagnostic rules have had their confidence factors modified by symptom-confidence rules, a measure of belief and a measure of disbelief are calculated for each hypothesis. The measure of belief is calculated as a Bernoulli combination of the positive confidence factors from all candidate diagnostic rules with instantiated conditions. Similarly, the measure of disbelief is a combination of the negative confidence factors of candidate diagnostic rules with noninstantiated conditions. The Bernoulli combination is most typically defined iteratively as $E = E + [(1 - E) * e]$, where E is the total evidence for H so far and e is the contribution of new evidence; $E, e =$

---

[2]This limit was chosen intuitively to reflect the constrained effect of nonsymptomatic considerations. While sufficient for our purposes, we anticipate the need to refine this parameter through controlled experimentation. The same consideration applies to the effect of hypothesis-expectancy rules, discussed below.

{0,1}. The combination must be appropriately normalized when confidence factors {0,10} are used.

Once the measures of belief and disbelief are calculated for each hypothesis, the effects of the hypothesis-expectancy rules are considered. The most salient hypothesis-expectancy rule from each applicable rule family is selected in a manner similar to the selection of other rules. The measure of belief in the candidate hypothesis on which the selected rule bears is then adjusted. The maximum adjustment is 20% in one direction or another. A hypothesis-expectancy rule with a factor of -5, for instance, would lead to a 20% decrement in the measure of belief associated with the candidate hypothesis. The evaluation of the hypothesis is completed by subtracting the measure of disbelief from the measure of belief and using this composite measure, together with certain heuristic strategies for refining the evaluation, as the basis for accepting or rejecting a hypothesis.

2.7. Learning from MORE

MORE's event model provides a structure for representing causal knowledge as it bears specifically on diagnosis. This structure is used not only to elicit information of diagnostic significance but also to generate the rules in terms of which the diagnostic task will be carried out. Much of MORE's acuity comes from using an event model and a rule model together. Each suggests where the other may be incomplete or in error. It is the recognition of gaps and errors in the knowledge base that drives MORE's interactions with a domain expert. For instance, a rule assigning a low diagnostic significance to a symptom will encourage MORE to seek conditions under which the symptom is more likely to occur given the hypothesis in question.

Acquired knowledge leads to improved performance because MORE's knowledge representation and knowledge-acquisition strategies are motivated by a theory of how diagnostic performance can be enhanced. In particular, as MORE's knowledge base becomes more complete, MORE does a better job of selecting questions and warning about potential errors. The more information there is, the easier it is for MORE to identify critical gaps and determine where additional information is likely to be of useful diagnostic significance. For instance, it is only after knowing the extent of overlap between symptoms associated with potentially competing hypotheses that MORE can decide how fruitful it will be to pursue the strategy of symptom distinction. Similarly, MORE's expectations with respect to confidence factors become more accurate with additional information. Since these expectations drive the warning system, unwarranted warnings become less frequent as information about the domain becomes available. Attempting to improve the quality of the knowledge-acquisition process as more becomes known should be the goal of any intelligent knowledge-acquisition system.

MORE was developed as a research prototype and was used in an exploratory fashion on a number of applications. These included diagnosis of drilling-fluid problems, epileptic seizures, disk faults, and manufacturing defects in the wave soldering of circuit boards. While a complete system was never fully developed, the results of MORE's exploratory use pointed to both strengths and weaknesses.

MORE was most effective in its use of well specified knowledge-acquisition strategies to elicit critical information from experts, its identification of a simple but effective model for representing this information, its use of the model to both generate rules and redirect the knowledge-acquisition process, and its ability to effectively monitor for consistency in the assignment of rule weights. It proved weakest in the user interface area, often asking far more questions than experts had patience with (hence the origins of its name). The attempt to correct for this weakness led to work on MOLE, described in chapter 3 of this collection, as well as to the TEST Development Environment discussed in section 2.7.2.

2.7.1. MORE's Problems
As a research prototype, MORE demonstrated the feasibility of our approach. At the same time, it raised several new problems that became critical concerns. Of most importance were issues of control, knowledge-base representation, user interface, and user dependency.

The essential control issue for MORE was knowing when to ask questions. Like the successful knowledge engineer, knowledge-acquisition systems need to not only ask good questions but also conform to the domain expert's desire to provide information as it comes to mind or to skip questions whose answers are unknown. Knowledge-acquisition systems must provide users with the ability to enter information on their own initiative and to easily skip questions they are unprepared to answer. Lacking this capability, MORE struck users as rigid and tedious in its interrogation technique.

Knowledge-base representation in MORE presented several limitations. From a user point of view, the terms in which MORE elicited knowledge were not familiar to all users. For example, the concepts of hypothesis, symptom, and rule were not comfortable for domain experts participating in factory-floor applications, where the operative concepts are failure mode and troubleshooting procedure. From an implementation point of view, MORE's underlying implementation in OPS5, with its simple vector representations, proved laborious to work with for both system and knowledge-base developers.

The hastily erected alphanumeric user interface to MORE proved completely inadequate for even experimental purposes. Knowledge-base development is greatly eased with the use of multiple-window displays and the ability to shift easily between browsing, editing, and execution.

Another problem with MORE was that while it relied on users to its advantage, users would have preferred MORE to ask fewer questions. Was it really necessary to ask for rule weights? Could these have been adequately inferred from the knowledge base?

A later system, MOLE, discussed in chapter 3, answers some of these questions. MOLE addresses the way the event model can be used to generate and tune confidence factors by learning from diagnostic sessions. This lifts a considerable burden from the knowledge-base developers, who no longer need to worry about assigning confidence factors.

2.7.2. Improving on MORE with TDE
The TEST[3] Development Environment (TDE), discussed in detail elsewhere [Kahn 87a, Kahn 87b, Kahn 87c], provides an improved approach to the

---

[3]TEST, Troubleshooting Expert System Tool, is an internal name used at Carnegie Group Inc., where the software was developed.

issues of control, knowledge representation, and user interface raised in connection with MORE.

TDE enables knowledge engineers and trained domain experts to interactively build knowledge bases that can be used by a diagnostic inference engine, TEST. TDE is designed as a mixed-initiative workbench. It enables developers to provide information as they wish, while at the same time offering guidance and direction as it is needed. Almost all user commands are available at the top level, thus avoiding the need to deal with an elaborate nesting of menus. In addition, TEST programs can be run as a separate task, allowing a smooth transition between knowledge-base editing and the running of the diagnostic system. There is no need to compile the knowledge base into a special form, such as rules, prior to execution.

TDE concepts, unlike those of MORE, are familiar within the troubleshooting domain, and, as a result, communication between TDE and system developers is facilitated. In addition, TDE uses a frame-based representation language, CRL, as opposed to the more unwieldy OPS5.

TDE knowledge bases represent the causal consequences of component and functional failures, as well as troubleshooting procedures such as effective ordering of diagnostic tests. The concept most critical to TDE is the **failure mode**. A failure mode represents a deviation of the unit under test from its standard of correct performance. Other conceptual objects are **decision points, tests, test procedures, repair procedures, rules,** and **parts,** among others. Each of these concepts has an obvious mapping into the troubleshooting domain. Rules represent a variety of contingent actions rather than evidence and belief propositions alone, as in MORE. Since knowledge acquisition involves much mapping of the knowledge that supports expert decision making into the representations required by a problem-solving system, the conceptual familiarity of TDE has led to more rapid knowledge-base development than was the case with MORE.

In order to facilitate debugging by nonprogrammers, the TDE/TEST problem-solver is designed to use the knowledge base in much the same way an informed technician would proceed with fault isolation. This again is made possible by structuring problem solving around the high-order concepts represented in the knowledge base. The troubleshooting task proceeds by focusing on an observed or suspected failure mode. An attempt is made to determine whether the failure mode has occurred. If the failure mode has occurred or if its status remains unknown, then the possible causes of the failure mode are investigated to see if they have occurred. The search process is guided by an underlying representation of the order in which diagnostic experts explore possible causes for identified failure modes. Heuristic rules may be inserted in the knowledge base to modify search behavior as runtime information is acquired.

2.7.3. User Interface
TDE provides both system-directed interrogation and graphic-oriented editors for building up the knowledge base. Within a workbench environment, icons representing objects familiar in the domain are easily moved into a representation of the knowledge base. A failure-mode icon, for instance, may be manually linked to another, indicating that it is a cause of the latter problem.

Novice users of TDE rely heavily on the interrogation techniques, while experienced users tend to use direct manipulation of graphic items as the preferred method. These methods support each other. For the novice user, a graphic map of the knowledge base is displayed and incrementally augmented as TDE's questions are answered. The experienced user can directly manipulate the graphic representation, as well as activate the interrogator by selecting menu options and clicking on relevant portions of the graphics display with the mouse. Developers may move freely between system- and user-directed modes of operation. Figure 2-2 provides an example of TDE's multiwindow display.

2.8. Conclusion
MORE demonstrates that the skills required to elicit knowledge for some diagnostic tasks can be effectively simulated. In order to support the goals of MORE, the knowledge representation strategy had to be sufficiently rich to capture domain knowledge, support the generation of rules, enable the evocation of knowledge-acquisition strategies, and permit MORE to evaluate the consistency of confidence factors assigned to rules. This required two forms of interrelated representation: the event model and the rule model.

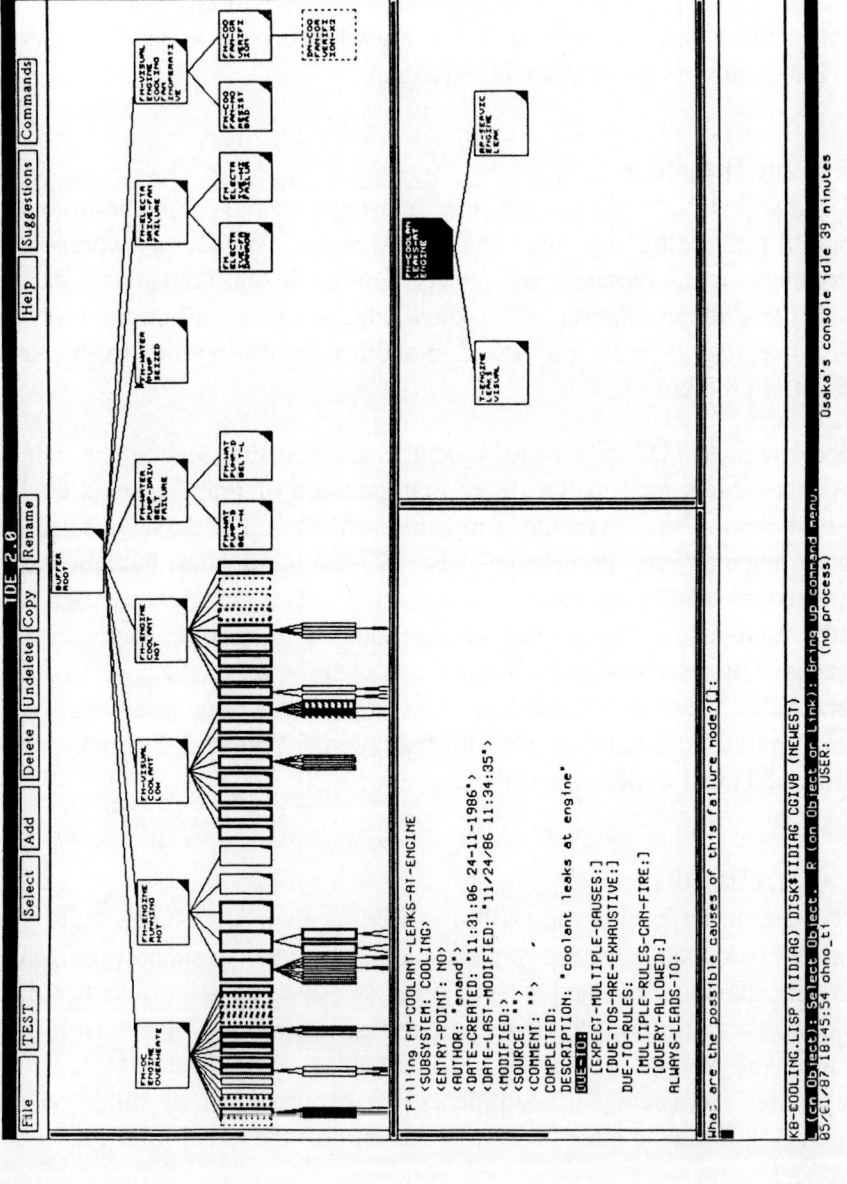

Figure 2-2: Example of TDE's Multiwindow Display

As a research prototype, MORE demonstrated the feasibility of our approach. At the same time, however, it raised several new problems. Most significant were issues of control, knowledge-base representation, user interface, and user-dependency. Subsequent systems, MOLE and TDE, address these problems.

Acknowledgements

MORE was developed in collaboration with John McDermott and Steve Nowlan while the author was at Carnegie Mellon University. TDE and TEST were developed at Carnegie Group, Inc. in collaboration with Edwin H. Breaux, Rajiv Enand, Peter DeKlerk, Robert L. Joseph, Al Kepner, Jeff Pepper, and Bill Richer. Sandy Marcus's insightful editorial assistance resulted in a much more readable manuscript.

3. MOLE: A Knowledge-Acquisition Tool for Cover-and-Differentiate Systems

Larry Eshelman

Abstract

MOLE is a knowledge-acquisition tool for generating expert systems that do heuristic classification. More specifically, MOLE assumes that the task can be performed using a cover-and-differentiate problem-solving method. Using this method, the expert system generated by MOLE proposes a set of candidate explanations for the events or states that need to be explained (or covered) and then differentiates among the candidates, picking the candidates that best explain the specified events or states. The problem-solving method presupposed by MOLE makes several heuristic assumptions about the space of covering hypotheses that MOLE is able to exploit when acquiring knowledge. In particular, by distinguishing between covering and differentiating knowledge and by using this distinction to help it refine the expert's preferences, MOLE is able to disambiguate an under-specified knowledge base and to interactively refine an incomplete knowledge base.

3.1. Introduction

MOLE [Eshelman 86, Eshelman 87a, Eshelman 87b] is an expert system shell that can be used in building systems that use a specialized form of heuristic classification to diagnose problems. MOLE is both a performance system ($MOLE_p$) that interprets a domain-dependent knowledge base and a knowledge-acquisition tool ($MOLE_{KA}$) for building and refining this knowledge base. $MOLE_p$ presupposes that the task can be represented as a classification problem: some solution object is selected from a set of enumerable candidates (for example, faults, diseases, components) on the basis of evidential considerations (for example, cues, symptoms, requirements) [Clancey 84, Clancey 85, Buchanan 84]. $MOLE_{KA}$ builds a knowledge base by eliciting knowledge from the domain expert, guided by its understanding of how to represent the knowledge required by its problem-solving method. In the process, it identifies missing knowledge and refines the knowledge base, guided by its understanding of how to determine what knowledge the problem-solving method might be missing.

MOLE belongs to a family of knowledge-acquisition tools that get their power by paying close attention to the problem-solving method used by their performance systems [McDermott 86, Gruber 87a]. Examples of such systems are TEIRESIAS [Davis 82], ETS [Boose 84], AQUINAS [Boose 87], MORE [Kahn 85a, Kahn 85b], KNACK [Klinker 87a, Klinker 87b, Klinker 87c], and SALT [Marcus 85, Marcus 87]. The first four of these systems, like MOLE, presuppose heuristic classification as the underlying problem-solving method. The main difference between these systems and MOLE is that MOLE$_p$'s interpretation of its evidential associations (or rules) is much more structured. For example, ETS and its successor, AQUINAS, look for correlations between various attributes but, unlike MOLE, have no presuppositions about the nature of these correlations. Similarly, MYCIN, an exemplar of the system that TEIRESIAS can build, views its rules essentially as arbitrary implications among arbitrary facts about the world [Szolovits 78].

MOLE is closer to classification systems such as INTERNIST [Miller 82, Pople 82] and CASNET [Weiss 78] that provide a much more specific interpretation -- a causal interpretation -- of the network of rules or associations connecting their facts. MOLE's assumption that every abnormal finding has a cause, its preference for a single (parsimonious) explanation, and its technique of differentiation are similar to the heuristic principles that underlie INTERNIST and its successor, CADUCEUS. MOLE's forward and backward reasoning within a network representing Bayesian-type relationships resembles CASNET.

MOLE's immediate predecessor is MORE. Unlike MORE, INTERNIST and CASNET, MOLE avoids using numeric representations of certainty. In this respect, MOLE accepts the spirit of Cohen's argument that numeric representations of uncertainty are not needed [Cohen 83]. But in contrast to the approach of Cohen, MOLE tries to exploit certain heuristics for combining knowledge and resorts to asking the expert how evidence is to be combined only when its default method fails. Even then, MOLE seeks to elicit from the expert preferences [Doyle 85] that can be used for inferring combining functions, rather than explicitly asking for such functions.

The goal of the project has been to make MOLE smart; that is, to enable it to build a reasonable knowledge base with a minimal amount of information elicited from the expert. The underlying research strategy has been to restrict the information that MOLE can elicit from the expert and to search for heuristics that will enable it to build from this limited information a knowledge base that can perform the task reasonably well. MOLE can then refine the knowledge base in response to feedback about its performance. This chapter describes the results of this strategy. Section 3.2 describes the problem-solving method presupposed by MOLE and the set of knowledge roles imposed by the problem-solving method. Section 3.3 describes the initial generation of a knowledge base during an interview session with the expert. Section 3.4 explains how MOLE handles uncertainty. Section 3.5 describes how MOLE refines its knowledge base. Section 3.6 discusses MOLE's scope. Section 3.7 offers some concluding remarks.

3.2. MOLE's Problem-Solving Method and Knowledge Roles

$MOLE_{KA}$ gets its power from its knowledge of the problem-solving method of $MOLE_P$. This section describes the method used by $MOLE_P$ to perform diagnostic tasks. The first part of the section describes $MOLE_P$'s problem-solving method and the knowledge roles presupposed by this method. The second part provides an example of how $MOLE_P$ puts these together in diagnosing a problem. It should be noted that although $MOLE_{KA}$ is not strictly limited to building diagnostic systems, all the systems built by $MOLE_{KA}$ have been diagnostic systems. Section 3.6 discusses the reasons MOLE's applications have been limited to diagnosis.

3.2.1. The Cover-and-Differentiate Problem-Solving Method

$MOLE_P$ uses a cover-and-differentiate problem-solving method, which is a form of heuristic classification. It diagnoses a problem by first proposing candidates that will cover or explain the symptoms or complaints specified by the user and then seeking information that will differentiate the candidates. This cover-and-differentiate process is iterative. Often, some of the evidence used to differentiate the candidates needs to be explained. Furthermore, once a candidate is accepted, it may need to be explained by some higher-level candidate hypothesis. Throughout this process, MOLE eliminates redundant candidates and strives to combine the viable local explanations into a coherent, parsimonious, global explanation.

MOLE's problem-solving method can be summarized in terms of two fundamental knowledge roles -- covering knowledge and differentiating knowledge:

- For each symptom or abnormal event propose a set of **covering** alternatives or explanations.

- Seek information that will help **differentiate** these alternatives.

This problem-solving method determines how domain facts are represented; that is, their representation makes clear how they can be used to identify explanations that cover observed symptoms and to differentiate candidate explanations in order to select a solution. Some symptoms are readily noticed by the nonexpert and prompt the nonexpert to seek diagnostic help. These will be referred to as the initial symptoms or complaints. $MOLE_p$ searches the space of possible explanations of these initial symptoms to find a solution. Other symptoms are more subtle manifestations of the underlying problem that the diagnostician uses to help determine the cause of the initially recognized complaints. The root nodes represent the ultimate or final explanations. Usually these are the causes that can be treated or modified to correct the symptoms.

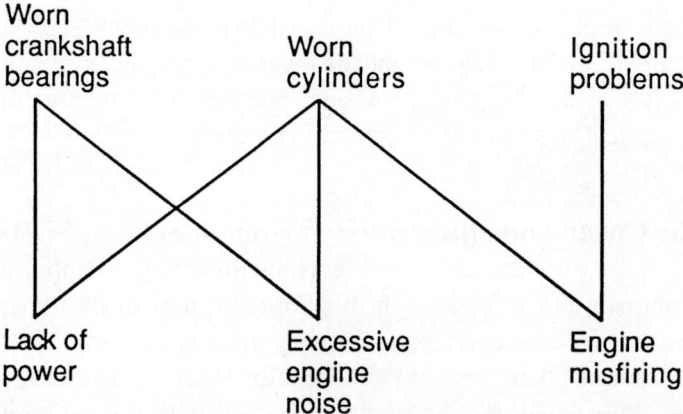

Figure 3-1: Network Representation of a MOLE Knowledge Base

Figure 3-1 illustrates a small part of a knowledge base built by $MOLE_{KA}$ for diagnosing automobile engine problems. There are three symptoms: lack of power, excessive engine noise, and engine misfiring. There are also three explanations: worn crankshaft bearings, worn cylinders, and ignition problems. This example is flat; it could be expanded to include higher-level explanations of the explanations shown. In such an expanded example, interior nodes represent intermediate explanations. They explain the nodes "below" them and are explained by the nodes "above" them.

Three constraints -- one strong and two weak -- guide and confine MOLE's search toward its goal of producing a consistent and parsimonious explanation. MOLE's search for an explanation must meet the following strong constraint:

- If an event has at least one potential explanation, the final diagnosis must include at least one of these potential explanations.

This constraint can be recast in terms of the assumption of **exhaustivity**: Assume that every abnormal finding has an explanation; that is, some candidate hypothesis will account for it. Interpreting the exhaustivity assumption causally is equivalent to saying that every symptom has a cause. MOLE assumes that it knows about the causes of the symptoms or abnormal findings that it is attempting to diagnose. If a symptom is not explained by one of its covering hypotheses, MOLE assumes that it must be explained by one of the symptom's other covering hypotheses. This knowledge of the potential explanations for an event constitutes covering knowledge.

Whereas the strong constraint confines the search within strict bounds, the weak constraints serve only as guides. MOLE's search is guided by the following two weak constraints:

- For any abnormal event or state, a single pathway leading to a top-level explanation is preferred.

- It is preferable that the various pathways leading from the bottom-level abnormal events should converge on as few top-level explanations as possible.

Whereas the strong constraint states that there must be a viable explanatory pathway from each activated symptom to some ultimate explanation, the weak constraints attempt to keep the explanation simple; they state that the final subgraph of pathways should, ideally, form a tree with all activated symptoms connected to a single root hypothesis.

The exhaustivity assumption makes it possible to differentiate competing hypotheses via pruning. Because a symptom must be explained by at least one hypothesis according to exhaustivity, a candidate hypothesis can be confirmed by eliminating or ruling out all of its competitors. Although the elimination of pathways by pruning provides an indirect way of shaping the initial graph into a tree-like structure, MOLE relies upon another assumption, **exclusivity**, that enables it to do this more directly.

Basically, the exclusivity assumption provides the foundation for the maxim that when diagnosing a problem one should not accept two explanations if one will do. Interpreted causally, the exhaustivity assumption is a version of Occam's razor: All other things being equal, parsimonious explanations should be favored. From a practical point of view, the exclusivity assumption captures the rule of thumb that the types of events represented by competing hypotheses are fairly rare, so it is unlikely that several occur simultaneously.

MOLE uses exclusivity by assuming that if there is independent evidence for preferring some pathway (explanation) and there is no independent evidence for competing explanations, then the competing explanations can be eliminated. In effect, MOLE is assuming that the alternative explanations for a symptom are mutually **exclusive**, although only in a weak sense. Two competing candidates can both be accepted, but only if there is independent evidence for both. Otherwise, once a hypothesis is accepted, often by establishing that a node is needed to explain something else and thus cannot be eliminated, its competitors are rejected.

The exhaustivity and exclusivity assumptions can be combined into a single rule: Accept the candidate hypothesis that is best relative to its competitors. Because a symptom must be explained by some hypothesis (exhaustivity), a candidate hypothesis can be confirmed by ruling out its competitors. And because only one hypothesis is likely to be true (exclusivity), a candidate hypothesis can be disconfirmed if there is independent evidence for one or more of its competitors but not for it. Evidence that independently supports or rules out a hypothesis covering some symptom, thereby differentiating it from its competitors, constitutes differentiating knowledge.

So far, two knowledge roles have been explicitly identified: covering knowledge and differentiating knowledge. However, it should be clear by now that there are several kinds of differentiating knowledge. Differentiating knowledge enables MOLE to evaluate the relative covering or explanatory value of the hypotheses explaining the same symptom. The value of an explanation depends on two considerations:

1. The independent acceptability (likelihood) or unacceptabilty of the covering event or state (that is, independent of what is being explained).

2. The dependability of the covering connection (for example, the strength of the causal connection).

In diagnosis, these considerations can typically be interpreted as the prior belief in the hypothesis and the conditional belief in the symptom given the hypothesis. In practice, this means that a candidate explanation can be ruled out by providing reasons for rejecting the explanatory event or for doubting that the connection between the explaining and explained event holds. Differentiating knowledge concerning the independent acceptability or unacceptability of a state or event will be called **event-qualifying** knowledge; that qualifying the connectivity between two events will be called **connection-qualifying** knowledge.

As an illustration, suppose that the event to be explained is someone's death, and one of the possible explanations is that the person was stung by a bee. This hypothesis could be ruled out by the fact that it is winter and, thus, there are no bees. This would be an event-qualifying piece of evidence. The hypothesis could also be ruled out by the fact that the person in question was not allergic to bees. This would be a connection-qualifying piece of evidence. This fact does not rule out that the person was stung by a bee, but does rule out a bee sting as the cause of death.

Figure 3-2 builds on the knowledge base presented in figure 3-1. There is one event-qualifying piece of evidence, new bearings, which rules out worn crankshaft bearings (ruling out is indicated by the negation sign). There is also one connection-qualifying piece of evidence, air conditioner on, which qualifies worn crankshaft bearings as an explanation for lack of power. It can easily be seen from this example that the effect of event-qualifying evidence is more global than that of connection-qualifying evidence. If the air conditioner is not on, then the hypothesis that there are worn crankshaft bearings is ruled out as the explanation for lack of power, but it is not ruled out for excessive engine noise. On the other hand, the fact that the bearings

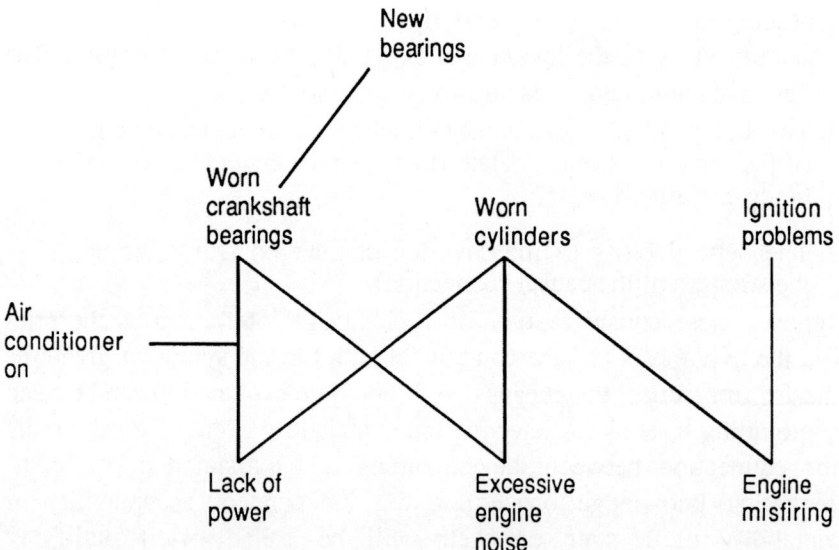

Figure 3-2: Diagnosing Engine Problems

are new rules out worn crankshaft bearings as the explanation for both symptoms.

This example also illustrates how a covering association for one symptom can be used to differentiate the explanations covering another symptom. If MOLE is trying to differentiate between the two explanations for excessive engine noise, then the fact that the engine is misfiring will provide evidence for preferring worn cylinders over worn crankshaft bearings as the explanation for excessive engine noise, since only the former explains both symptoms. The case will be substantially improved if, in addition, it can be shown that the cause of the engine misfiring cannot be ignition problems.

3.2.2. Diagnosing Inefficiencies in a Power Plant

The following interaction shows $MOLE_p$ diagnosing a problem with a coal-burning power plant. $MOLE_{KA}$ was used to generate a knowledge base for this domain. All subsequent examples will be drawn from this domain and will be concerned with problems with the boiler, the central unit in such a power plant. The problems encountered rarely prevent the boiler from functioning, but they are a major source of inefficiency. A boiler that is functioning inefficiently can waste millions of dollars of fuel as well as dump tons of pollutants into the atmosphere.

$MOLE_p$ begins by asking the user to identify what is wrong from a list of possible complaints.

```
Indicate whether LOSS-IN-GAS
>> YES NO [ NO ] yes

Indicate whether HIGH-FLY-ASH-FLOW
>> YES NO [ NO ] <cr>

Indicate whether DARK-ASH
>> YES NO [ NO ] <cr>

Indicate whether HIGH-BOTTOM-ASH-FLOW
>> YES NO [ NO ] <cr>
```

In the example, $MOLE_p$ has asked the user about four initial symptoms or complaints. The underlined expressions are the users responses. The prompt (>>) is followed by the acceptable responses. (In addition, the user can always indicate "unknown.") The bracketed words are default responses that the user can enter using carriage return (<cr>). The symptoms typically range over the values "yes" and "no," although any set of discrete values is allowed. In the example, the user indicates that the problem to be explained is LOSS-IN-GAS.

Once MOLE has determined what the initial complaints are, it asks about evidence that will help differentiate the possible explanations. For example, LOSS-IN-GAS is potentially explained by LOW-HEAT-TRANSFER and by HIGH EXCESS-AIR. In order to differentiate between the two, MOLE asks about the OXYGEN-READING (an indicator of HIGH EXCESS-AIR).

```
Indicate whether OXYGEN-READING
>> HIGH NORMAL LOW [ NORMAL ] <cr>

Indicate whether RADIATION-INTENSITY-READING
>> HIGH NORMAL LOW [ NORMAL ] low

Indicate whether SMALL-RED-FLAME
>> YES NO [ NO ] <cr>
```

The user's response to OXYGEN-READING enables MOLE to favor LOW-HEAT-TRANSFER over HIGH EXCESS-AIR as the explanation for LOSS-IN-GAS. LOW-HEAT-TRANSFER then needs to be explained.

MOLE proceeds to ask about evidence that will differentiate explanations for LOW-HEAT-TRANSFER (RADIATION-INTENSITY-READING and SMALL-RED-FLAME). When MOLE has differentiated the potential explanations enough to find a unique pathway from the initial complaint (LOSS-IN-GAS) to the top-level explanations or it has no more relevant differentiating knowledge, it displays its diagnosis to the user.

```
LOSS-IN-GAS is explained by
   HIGH-MOISTURE-CONTENT or
   LARGE-PARTICLES.

Do you want a more detailed account?
>> [ YES ] <cr>

LOSS-IN-GAS is explained as follows:
   1  LOSS-IN-GAS is explained by
         LOW-HEAT-TRANSFER
   2  LOW-HEAT-TRANSFER is explained by
         LOW-RADIATION
   3  LOW-RADIATION is explained by
         HIGH-MOISTURE-CONTENT or
         LARGE-PARTICLES.
```

MOLE diagnoses that either HIGH-MOISTURE-CONTENT or LARGE-PARTICLES is the ultimate cause of LOSS-IN-GAS. As was explained earlier, MOLE tries to differentiate explanations until it can settle on a single cause. However, as this case illustrates, MOLE is not always successful in narrowing the field of candidates to a single explanation.

After MOLE's diagnosis has been presented, the user can ask for an explanation for any step in the diagnosis.

```
>> why 3

LOW-RADIATION can be explained by
   LOW-FLAME-TEMPERATURE or
   LOW-MOISTURE-CONTENT or
   LARGE-PARTICLES.

   4 LOW-FLAME-TEMPERATURE was ruled out because
     NO SMALL-RED-FLAME.
```

```
5 There is not sufficient information to
  differentiate between
     LOW-MOISTURE-CONTENT and
     LARGE-PARTICLES.
```

Here the user asks MOLE for an account of its explanation for LOW-RADIATION. The user can ask for a still deeper account of this explanation by typing, for example, "why 5."

This section has described MOLE$_p$'s problem-solving method. MOLE seeks to explain all the symptoms that are present. Covering knowledge specifies the set of viable alternative explanations. Differentiating knowledge is used to determine the preferred alternative. MOLE differentiates hypotheses both in a negative, passive fashion by eliminating all but one alternative, and in a positive, active fashion by providing independent evidence for some hypothesis, eliminating the others by default. Active differentiation favors parsimonious explanations. Section 3.3 describes how covering and differentiating knowledge are acquired.

3.3. Acquiring the Knowledge Base

Usually it is not hard to elicit knowledge from an expert. The problem is eliciting the right sort of knowledge. Knowledge needs to be in a form that can be applied to the problem in the right way at the right time. The first step is to explicitly identify the appropriate problem-solving method for the task and the types of knowledge roles relevant for this method. Once this is done, it is fairly easy to build a knowledge collector. However, if the goal is to replace the knowledge engineer with an automated system, rather than to provide the knowledge engineer with a programming tool, then two troublesome features of the knowledge-acquisition process need to be addressed:

- Indeterminateness: When specifying associations between events, the expert is likely to be fairly vague about the nature of these associations and events.

- Incompleteness: The expert will probably forget to specify certain pieces of knowledge.

Indeterminateness reflects the fact that experts are not accustomed to talking about associations between events in a way that precisely fits the problem-solving method's predefined knowledge roles. Since the goal is to develop a tool that replaces the knowledge engineer, the burden is upon the knowledge-acquisition system to make sense of whatever information the domain expert is willing or able to provide. Although the expert can be encouraged to be as specific as possible, a smart knowledge-acquisition tool must be able to tolerate ambiguity and indeterminateness.

Incompleteness is the problem of identifying missing or incorrect knowledge. The expert, no matter how qualified or thorough, will forget to mention certain special circumstances. Sometimes the expert will make mistakes. Thus, a smart knowledge-acquisition tool needs to be able to add knowledge incrementally to the knowledge base, refine existing knowledge, and sometimes correct existing knowledge.

The problems of indeterminateness and incompleteness dominate the two phases of knowledge acquisition: (1) the gathering of information for constructing the initial knowledge base and (2) the iterative refinement of this knowledge base. During the first phase, $MOLE_{KA}$ relies mainly on static techniques of analysis. MOLE examines associations and events in the context provided by the surrounding structures and how they might be used by cover-and-differentiate problem solving. MOLE tries to recognize areas where the knowledge is obviously incomplete and tries to disambiguate the information provided by the expert. During the second, dynamic phase, MOLE and the expert interact to refine the knowledge base. The expert gives MOLE a test case, $MOLE_p$ makes the diagnosis, and the expert confirms or corrects the diagnosis. If $MOLE_p$ makes an incorrect diagnosis, $MOLE_{KA}$ tries to determine the source of the error and recommends possible remedies. Typically, this means adding knowledge or qualifying existing knowledge, but sometimes the interpretation provided in the previous phase needs to be revised. In the remainder of this section the first phase -- the initial generation of the knowledge base -- will be described. The second, dynamic phase will be described in section 3.5.

Our experience with human diagnosticians is that usually they have little trouble identifying an initial set of complaints and providing candidate explanations. In addition, they usually can provide higher-level explanations of these candidate explanations. The acquisition of differentiating knowledge, on the other hand, is much more problematic.

Although experts typically have no trouble providing information that is relevant for differentiating several hypotheses, they often have trouble specifying precisely how it helps differentiate. For example, does it support a hypothesis directly or does it support a hypothesis by ruling out a competing hypothesis? And if the latter, does it qualify an explanatory connection or rule out the occurrence of an event? As the examples in the remainder of this section illustrate, $MOLE_{KA}$ avoids confronting the expert with such matters. The following three subsections illustrate how MOLE is able to elicit from an expert the initial symptoms, covering knowledge, and differentiating knowledge without requiring the expert to have a deep understanding of its method or the underlying knowledge roles.

3.3.1. Acquiring the Initial Symptoms

$MOLE_{KA}$ begins a new knowledge-acquisition session by asking the expert to list some of the complaints or symptoms that would tell a potential user there is a problem to be diagnosed. The following sample interaction uses examples from the initial knowledge-acquisition session for the expert system that diagnoses problems associated with a coal-burning power plant.

```
List possible complaints or symptoms that
might need to be diagnosed:

Complaint:
>> [ NONE ] loss-in-gas
   LOSS-IN-GAS [ YES NO ]
   Status:              NEW
   Method:              ASK
   Default Value:       NONE
>> Confirm (Yes, No): [ YES ] <cr>

Complaint:
>> [ DONE ] high-fly-ash-flow
   HIGH-FLY-ASH-FLOW [ YES NO ]
   Status:              NEW
   Method:              ASK
   Default Value:       NONE
>> Confirm (Yes, No): [ YES ] <cr>
```

```
Complaint:
>> [ DONE ] high-bottom-ash-flow
   HIGH-BOTTOM-ASH-FLOW [ YES NO ]
   Status:                NEW
   Method:                ASK
   Default Value:         NONE
>> Confirm (Yes, No): [ YES ] <cr>

Complaint:
>> [ DONE ] dark-ash
   DARK-ASH [ YES NO ]
   Status:                NEW
   Method:                ASK
   Default Value:         NONE
>> Confirm (Yes, No): [ YES ] <cr>

Complaint:
>> [ DONE ] <cr>
```

In this example the expert has entered four complaints that require diagnosis. After each complaint is entered, MOLE redisplays the name of the complaint followed by what MOLE assumes to be the values it can have (for example, "yes" and "no"). On the next three lines MOLE indicates the settings for various parameters. The expert can either confirm or disconfirm this information. The first line indicates whether this is the first time that MOLE has seen this event or state (for example, the status is "new" rather than "old"). MOLE also displays the default method for ascertaining the value of the event (that is, ask the user or infer the value). In the case of complaints MOLE assumes the value is ascertained by asking the user. Finally, MOLE indicates whether any of these values is to be the default value. $MOLE_{KA}$ gives the expert the option of designating one of the possible values to be a default value; $MOLE_p$ assumes the default value holds unless there is evidence to the contrary.

3.3.2. Acquiring Covering Knowledge
After the expert is finished entering complaints, MOLE asks for states or events that will explain or cover them.

```
List possible explanations for
LOSS-IN-GAS:

Possible explanation for LOSS-IN-GAS:
>> [ NONE ] low-heat-transfer
   LOW-HEAT-TRANSFER [ YES NO ]
   Status:              NEW
   Method:              INFER
   Default Value:       NONE
>> Confirm (Yes, No): [ YES ] <cr>

Possible explanation for LOSS-IN-GAS:
>> [ DONE ] excess-air high
   EXCESS-AIR HIGH [ HIGH NORMAL LOW ]
   Status:              NEW
   Method:              INFER
   Default Value:       NONE
>> Confirm (Yes, No):  [ YES ] <cr>

Possible explanation for LOSS-IN-GAS:
>> [ DONE ] <cr>
```

The format for each of the possible explanations is the same as it is for complaints. The default method for ascertaining the value of an explanatory event or state is "infer." At this point, MOLE does not care how it is to be inferred, but only knows that it should obtain its value indirectly rather than by asking the user for its value.

Note that for the second explanation the user specified not only the piece of evidence but the relevant value ("high"). The default value for any event is "yes," but other values can be specified. MOLE knows that "high" often goes with "normal" and "low" and suggests these three values as the possible values for EXCESS-AIR. The user confirms this.

MOLE continues in this fashion, acquiring possible explanations for each of the complaints, until all complaints have potential explanations.

```
List possible explanations for
HIGH-FLY-ASH-FLOW:
```

```
Possible explanation for HIGH-FLY-ASH-FLOW:
>> [ NONE ] exc high
   EXCESS-AIR HIGH [ HIGH NORMAL LOW ]
   Status:              OLD
   Method:              INFER
   Default Value:       NONE
>> Confirm (Yes, No): [ YES ] <cr>

Possible explanation for HIGH-FLY-ASH-FLOW:
>> [ DONE ] <cr>
```

MOLE always checks whether the entered name is a truncated version of a name that it already knows about. In the latter example, MOLE infers from "exc high" that the user means "HIGH EXCESS-AIR." (If there are several possibilities, MOLE lists them and asks the user to choose which one is meant.) Since this is an event or state that MOLE already knows about, its status is "old."

Once MOLE has acquired possible explanations for all the complaints, it seeks higher-level explanations.

```
List possible explanations for
LOW-HEAT-TRANSFER:

Possible explanation for LOW-HEAT-TRANSFER:
>> [ NONE ] misbalance-of-convection
   MISBALANCE-OF-CONVECTION
   Status:              NEW
   Method:              INFER
   Default Value:       NONE
>> Confirm (Yes, No): [ YES ] <cr>

Possible explanation for LOW-HEAT-TRANSFER:
>> [ DONE ] low-radiation
   LOW-RADIATION
   Status:              NEW
   Method:              INFER
   Default Value:       NONE
>> Confirm (Yes, No): [ YES ] <cr>

Possible explanation for LOW-HEAT-TRANSFER:
>> [ DONE ] <cr>
```

```
List possible explanations for
MISBALANCE-OF-CONVECTION

Possible explanation for
MISBALANCE-OF-CONVECTION:
>> [ NONE ] fouling
     FOULING
     Status:               NEW
     Method:               INFER
     Default Value:        NONE
>> Confirm (Yes, No):  [ YES ] no


Options:                          Current Value:

1 Change Name:                    FOULING
2 Possible Values:                YES NO
3 Change Method (ask infer):      INFER
4 Change Default Value:           NONE
5 Done
>> [ 3 ] <cr>


Options:                          Current Value:

1 Change Name:                    FOULING
2 Possible Values:                YES NO
3 Change Method (ask infer):      ASK
4 Change Default Value:           NONE
5 Done
>> [ 5 ] <cr>
```

The expert indicates that even though FOULING is a possible explanation
for MISBALANCE-OF-CONVECTION, its value can be ascertained by
directly asking the user. However, if, during diagnosis, the user should
indicate that its value is "unknown," $MOLE_p$ can try to infer its value.

As the events or states and their explanations are entered, $MOLE_{KA}$ builds a
network of nodes and links. The nodes represent states or events and the
links represent covering (explanatory) relations between the nodes. This
network constitutes the initial explanation space (cf. figure 3-3).

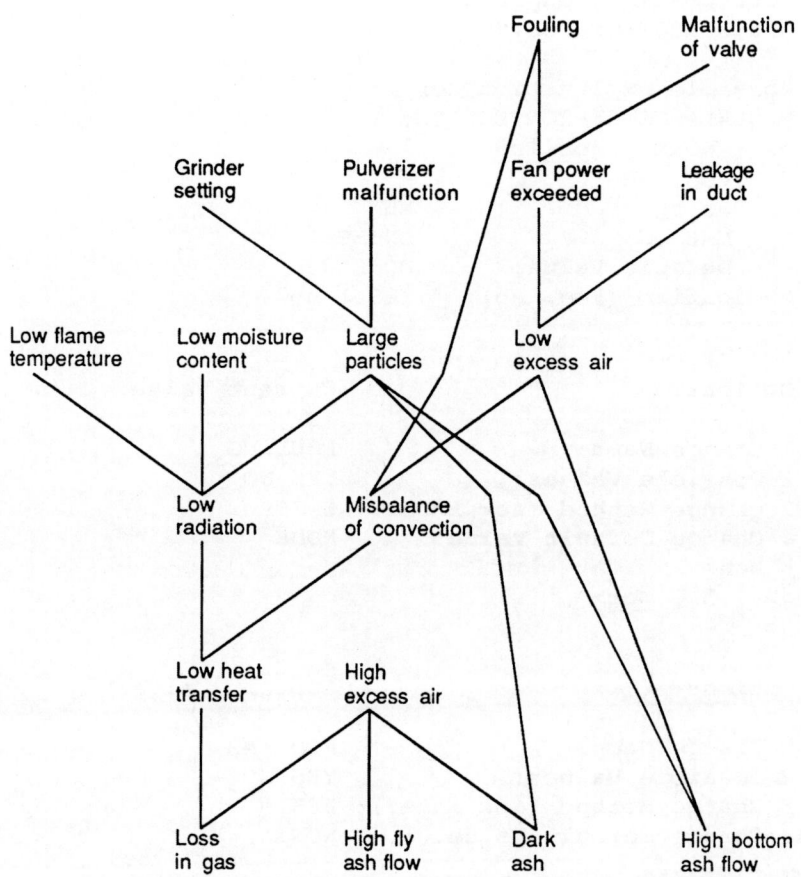

Figure 3-3: The Initial Explanation Space for the Power Plant Domain

3.3.3. Acquiring Differentiating Knowledge

Once the initial explanation space has been built, MOLE$_{KA}$ tries to determine what information will help differentiate the candidate explanations. MOLE seeks only enough information to differentiate each hypothesis in principle. As we shall see, such differentiating knowledge may not be enough in practice. However, during this initial, static phase of knowledge acquisition, MOLE has no way of determining this.

Sometimes no additional knowledge is required to differentiate among the hypotheses explaining a symptom. In the simplest case, the values of some of the competing hypotheses are directly ascertainable. For example, a MISBALANCE-OF-CONVECTION is explained by either FOULING or LOW EXCESS-AIR. Since MOLE has been told that the presence of FOULING can be ascertained by asking, MOLE has enough knowledge to differentiate between FOULING and LOW EXCESS-AIR. If during a diagnostic session the user answers that there is FOULING, then FOULING will be accepted as the explanation of MISBALANCE-OF-CONVECTION. On the other hand, if the user indicates that there is no FOULING, then the only other alternative, LOW EXCESS-AIR, will be accepted as the explanation because of MOLE's exhaustivity assumption.

Typically the values of covering events cannot be ascertained by asking. In such cases, MOLE needs a less direct way of differentiating among them. Before eliciting new information, however, MOLE attempts to make use of existing knowledge. Often, hypotheses can be differentiated by some combination of covering knowledge. For example, the only explanation that MOLE initially knows about for HIGH-FLY-ASH-FLOW is HIGH EXCESS-AIR. Thus, if LOSS-IN-GAS is the problem, the presence of HIGH-FLY-ASH-FLOW will provide a reason for choosing HIGH EXCESS-AIR over LOW-HEAT-TRANSFER. This is because there is independent evidence for HIGH EXCESS-AIR -- it is needed to explain HIGH-FLY-ASH-FLOW.

Even when MOLE needs to acquire new knowledge in order to differentiate hypotheses, this new knowledge does not always require MOLE to learn about a new state or event. The relevant new knowledge may consist of learning about an additional relationship between events or states already in the knowledge base. MOLE always prefers to exploit existing knowledge to adding completely new knowledge. Differentiating knowledge may be correlated with covering knowledge.

Covering knowledge says that a hypothesized event might be a cause of a symptom. Anticipatory knowledge says that a hypothesized event, if it occurs, almost always causes a particular symptom to be present. Covering knowledge sanctions inferences from symptoms to hypotheses. Anticipatory knowledge sanctions inferences from hypotheses to symptoms or, conversely, from the absence of symptoms to the falsehood of hypotheses. An anticipatory relationship is a covering relationship of a special type. Given the covering knowledge that event E_1 explains event E_2, anticipatory knowledge is the additional information that the presence of E_1 is likely to lead to E_2, or alternatively, that the absence of E_2 tends to rule out E_1.

Not every covering relationship is anticipatory. Anticipatory knowledge depends upon the strength of the causal connection between a hypothesis and a symptom. In a covering relationship, the causal connection between the hypothesis and the symptom may be tenuous. Perhaps certain enabling (that is, connection-qualifying) conditions must be present before the symptom can be caused by the hypothesized event. In the absence of an anticipatory relationship, the fact that a hypothesized event (sometimes) causes a symptom does not mean that the symptom is likely to be present if the hypothesized event occurs.

In the following example, MOLE seeks to discover information that will differentiate between two explanations for LOSS-IN-GAS by determining whether certain covering associations also provide anticipatory knowledge. MOLE notes that HIGH-FLY-ASH-FLOW and DARK-ASH are explained by HIGH EXCESS-AIR, and hypothesizes that the absence of either of these states may rule out HIGH EXCESS-AIR.

```
Indicate which of the following
tends to rule out EXCESS-AIR HIGH
as the explanation for LOSS-IN-GAS?
   1   HIGH-FLY-ASH-FLOW
   2   DARK-ASH
>> [ NONE ] 1 2
```

The user's response confirms that both associations are anticipatory. MOLE now knows of evidence that can enable it to prefer LOW-HEAT-TRANSFER over HIGH EXCESS-AIR as an explanation for LOSS-IN-GAS (that is, the absence of HIGH-FLY-ASH-FLOW and DARK-ASH). This is enough information to discriminate between these two hypotheses, and so MOLE, at this point in the interview, does not seek any additional differentiating information.

In the example, MOLE hypothesized that the absence of a symptom might rule out a hypothesis, and thus enable it to discriminate in favor of a competing hypothesis. MOLE reasons in a similar fashion with regard to higher-level explanations. In the following example, MOLE asks whether the presence of a higher-level explanation is a good reason to anticipate a lower-level event and, thus, favor it as the explanation for an even lower-level event.

```
LOW-HEAT-TRANSFER is explained by
the following possible explanations:
    LOW-RADIATION
    MISBALANCE-OF-CONVECTION.

Which of the following would be relevant
evidence for preferring one of the
explanations over the others:
1 LARGE-PARTICLES favoring LOW-RADIATION
2 FOULING favoring MISBALANCE-OF-CONVECTION
3 EXCESS-AIR LOW favoring
        MISBALANCE-OF-CONVECTION

List the relevant responses:
>> [ NONE ] 2 3
```

Knowing that LARGE-PARTICLES is a potential explanation for LOW-RADIATION, and that FOULING and LOW EXCESS-AIR are potential explanations for MISBALANCE-OF-CONVECTION, MOLE hypothesizes that these relationships might be anticipatory as as well as explanatory. The expert confirms that FOULING and LOW EXCESS-AIR do typically cause MISBALANCE-OF-CONVECTION. MOLE now knows that one way of proving that MISBALANCE-OF-CONVECTION is a likely explanation for LOW-HEAT-TRANSFER is to show that there is either FOULING or LOW EXCESS-AIR. In addition, MOLE infers that if a MISBALANCE-OF-CONVECTION is unlikely, it can rule out FOULING and LOW EXCESS-AIR.

It is interesting that in trying to differentiate between LOW-RADIATION and MISBALANCE-OF-CONVECTION, MOLE ignored two possible explanations for LOW-RADIATION -- LOW-FLAME-TEMPERATURE and LOW-MOISTURE-CONTENT -- as potential anticipatory associations. The reason is that although LOW-FLAME-TEMPERATURE and LOW-MOISTURE-CONTENT are potential explanations for LOW-RADIATION, it wouldn't be useful to the diagnosis even if they were anticipatory. That is because MOLE does not know at this point of any independent way of proving them, unlike the case with LARGE-PARTICLES.

In the following example, MOLE has no information that may be relevant for differentiating between two explanations and so has to ask for new information.

```
List any evidence that might be relevant for
discriminating among the following possible
explanations for LARGE-PARTICLES:
    LOW-GRINDABILITY-RELATIVE-TO-SETTING
    PULVERIZER-MALFUNCTION

Evidence:
>> [ NONE ] low-pulverizer-current
    LOW-PULVERIZER-CURRENT
    Status:              NEW
    Method:              ASK
    Default Value:       NONE
>> Confirm (Yes, No): [ YES ] <cr>

Evidence:
>> [ DONE ] <cr>

Does LOW-PULVERIZER-CURRENT
need to be explained?
>> [ YES ] <cr>

List possible explanations for
LOW-PULVERIZER-CURRENT:

Possible explanation for
LOW-PULVERIZER-CURRENT:
>> [ NONE ] pulverizer-mal
    PULVERIZER-MALFUNCTION
    Status:              OLD
    Method:              INFER
    Default Value:       NONE
>> Confirm (Yes, No): [ YES ] <cr>

Possible explanation for
LOW-PULVERIZER-CURRENT:
>> [ NONE ] <cr>
```

Although the reader might be able to guess that LOW-PULVERIZER-CURRENT is related to the hypothesis PULVERIZER-MALFUNCTION, MOLE does not know what any of these events or states mean. However, when MOLE learns about a new node, it always asks the expert whether it needs to be explained. In the previous example, MOLE learns that LOW-PULVERIZER-CURRENT   is   only   explained   by   PULVERIZER-MALFUNCTION.   This tells MOLE not only that it constitutes event-qualifying knowledge, but also that LOW-PULVERIZER-CURRENT is explained by PULVERIZER-MALFUNCTION and only that event.

In this example, it is fairly easy to determine what role a particular piece of differentiating knowledge played.   Usually, things are not this simple. Fortunately, it is often not that important how a piece of differentiating knowledge is classified.   For example, if the hypotheses explaining a symptom do not explain any other symptoms, then it does not make any operational difference whether a reason supporting one hypothesis over another is treated as event-qualifying or connection-qualifying knowledge. MOLE treats such reasons as generic differentiating knowledge -- that is, simply as reasons for preferring one hypothesis over another in the context of the symptom that is to be explained.

In the next example, there are three hypotheses for LOW-RADIATION and one of them explains several other events.   MOLE handles this more complex situation by explicitly eliciting knowledge that would affect the expert's preference among the hypotheses.

```
List any evidence that might be relevant for
discriminating among the following possible
explanations for LOW-RADIATION:
     LOW-FLAME-TEMPERATURE
     LOW-MOISTURE-CONTENT
     LARGE-PARTICLES

Evidence:
>> [ NONE ] small-red-flame
     SMALL-RED-FLAME [ YES NO ]
     Status:              NEW
     Method:              ASK
     Default Value:       NONE
>> Confirm (Yes, No): [ YES ]   <cr>

Evidence:
>> [ DONE ] <cr>

Does SMALL-RED-FLAME
need to be explained?
>> [ YES ] no
```

In answering the last question, it did not occur to the expert that SMALL-RED-FLAME is a symptom that is explained by LOW-FLAME-TEMPERATURE. Fortunately, MOLE does not need to know this. All MOLE needs to know is that SMALL-RED-FLAME is a reason for favoring LOW-FLAME-TEMPERATURE over its competitors. MOLE finds this out by asking what hypothesis the expert would prefer in light of SMALL-RED-FLAME.

```
Given the presence of
SMALL-RED-FLAME,
rank the following explanations of
LOW-RADIATION:
    LOW-FLAME-TEMPERATURE         [ 1 ] <cr>
    LOW-MOISTURE-CONTENT          [ 1 ] 2
    LARGE-PARTICLES               [ 1 ] 2
```

Here the expert indicates his preference, given some piece of evidence, by dividing the possible explanations into those that are more favored (1) and those that are less favored (2). In principle, an expert can divide the explanations into any number of equivalence classes, although in practice experts tend to divide the explanations into only two or three groups: those that the expert (1) favors, (2) is neutral about, or (3) disfavors. If the expert uses only two equivalence classes, and if the number of candidates in one class is smaller than in the other, MOLE takes this as suggesting that the evidence is directly acting on the smaller set and indirectly on the large set. Thus, in the above example, the fact that the favored category is the smaller (has only one member) is taken to indicate that SMALL-RED-FLAME directly supports LOW-FLAME-TEMPERATURE and thus indirectly tends to rule out, by the exclusivity principle, LOW-MOISTURE-CONTENT and LARGE-PARTICLES.

MOLE continues in this fashion until all competing hypotheses can be differentiated, at least in principle. There is no presumption that the resulting knowledge base will be complete. In fact, at this point MOLE does not even try for completeness. Its goal is to build up an explanation space of covering knowledge as quickly as possible and to make sure it has enough information to differentiate among candidate explanations. MOLE has no way of determining from the structure of the knowledge base whether this information will be adequate in practice. It is only during the dynamic refinement phase that MOLE is able to determine whether the knowledge base is adequate. But before describing the dynamic knowledge-acquisition process, something needs to be said about an important knowledge structure that was briefly mentioned in this section but has not been described in detail: preferences.

3.4. Handling Uncertainty

Nothing has been said so far about certainty factors or support values. This is because MOLE dispenses with cardinal measures of support or belief and uses ordinal preferences instead. For instance, in the last example MOLE elicited an ordinal ranking of competing hypotheses in light of the evidence that there was a SMALL-RED-FLAME. Preferences, unlike cardinal measures of support, do not measure how strongly one hypothesis is favored over another. They simply indicate a ranking. Preferences are not restricted to binary relationships. They partition competing hypotheses or conflicting differentiating knowledge into ranked equivalence classes. Preferences usually reflect the relative likelihood of their objects, but they can take into account other factors such as cost. Preferences are context-specific and can be qualified by conditions. The fact that H_1 is preferred over H_2 in one context does not mean that it is preferred in another context. Preferences do not just apply to hypotheses. They apply to any situation where there can be conflicting reasons -- for example, reasons for and against the same hypothesis. There can also be higher-order preferences -- that is, preferences about preferences.

The advantage of preferences over certainty factors is that they are much easier for the expert to provide. In order to differentiate among hypotheses, $MOLE_{KA}$ only needs to elicit from the expert information that will enable it to know when to favor one hypothesis over others. However, preferences have one critical shortcoming that needs to be addressed: Although it may be easy to elicit a specific preference, it would seem that a lot of them need to be acquired. The expert needs to rank the hypotheses for every viable combination of evidence. The elicitation of preferences may be simple, but it is also likely to be long and tedious.

Another problem with any ordinal ranking of hypotheses, as opposed to a cardinal measure of support, is that it does not provide any mechanism for combining evidence. When cardinal measures of support are used, the expert indicates not only that he is more confident in one hypothesis than another but by how much -- for example, twice as confident. Furthermore, not only is it possible that these measures of certainty can be combined, there are reasonably good theories available for doing this -- for example, Bayesean theory, Dempster-Shafer theory [Shafer 76]. The fact that the application of these theories is often computationally intractable means only that in practice certain heuristic shortcuts may be necessary. MYCIN-style certainty factors, for example, can be interpreted as one method of simplifying Bayesian theory for use in practical applications [Charniak 83].

As theoretically appealing as these numeric approaches may be there are two fundamental problems with incorporating them into expert systems. First, it has been our experience that experts are not very good at specifying their degree of certainty in a way that can be consistently captured by these cardinal representations. An earlier version of MOLE tried to elicit certainty factors from the experts. Typically, when an expert was asked to indicate the degree of support of some piece of evidence by selecting a number within a fixed range, the expert would think about the question for a while and then choose some number near the middle of the range. This may not be simply a problem in communication. It has been questioned whether experts use explicit degrees of belief in their own reasoning [Harman 86]. On the other hand, experts have little trouble ranking the hypotheses that may explain a particular symptom under various evidential conditions. Furthermore, what we are concerned about is behavior -- the diagnostic performance of the system -- not getting the numbers right. The only practical way of getting the numbers right is by fitting them to the desired behavior.

Secondly, even if the expert could provide a cardinal indication of his degree of confidence, it is not likely that any single method for combining evidence would be applicable [Cohen 83, Gruber 87b]. Evidence has a structure and cannot be reduced to a single numeric measure that can be manipulated by a combination function. This is not to say that emphasis on structure is incompatible with a numeric approach. In fact, the "belief networks" built by MOLE structurally resemble those of Pearl's approach [Pearl 86]. This should not be too surprising. As pointed out in section 3.2.1, MOLE's distinction between event-qualifying and connection-qualifying evidence is analogous to the Bayesian distinction between prior and conditional probabilities. However, instead of propagating numbers representing probabilities through a tree-like network, MOLE makes categorical decisions at each node in light of the evidence of the surrounding nodes. These decisions are always tentative, however, and are often made on the basis of default assumptions. MOLE makes use of dependency-directed backtracking in order to maintain a consistent network [Doyle 79].

Of course, pointing out the limitations of cardinal measures of uncertainty does not make any less real the threat of a combinatorial explosion of ordinal preferences. Fortunately, MOLE is able to avoid needing a preference for every combination of evidence that might help differentiate a set of hypotheses because it is able to generalize many of its local preferences so they can be integrated into a richer set of evidential structures. For instance, if a new piece of evidence favoring one hypothesis over another can be identified as event-qualifying knowledge that rules out some event, then this evidence can be used for ruling out the same hypothesis when it is a candidate for explaining some other symptom. For example, evidence that rules out the possibility of HIGH EXCESS-AIR as an explanation for LOSS-IN-GAS will also be likely to rule out HIGH EXCESS-AIR as the explanation for DARK-ASH.

To avoid eliciting preferences for every combination of evidence, $MOLE_{KA}$ could attempt to generalize all local preferences. However, generalization also requires some effort on the part of MOLE and the expert in refining the knowledge structure. When $MOLE_{KA}$ encounters a new piece of information, it must decide whether to treat the new information as a simple, local preference or try to refine it. MOLE bases its decision on the principle that there is no point in trying to refine knowledge beyond its operational significance. For example, suppose symptom S is explained by two hypotheses, H_1 and H_2, and no other symptoms are explained by these hypotheses. Suppose also that the only differentiating knowledge is a preference for H_1 in the presence of E and a preference for H_2 in its absence. Then it will not be worth trying to figure out whether E is an event-qualifying or connection-qualifying reason. The information will have no effect on the diagnosis. As a rule, the more connections there are among covering associations differentiated by a set of preferences, the more useful it is to try to refine the preferences.

When MOLE$_{KA}$ decides to attempt a refinement, it proceeds by forming a proposal for how a preference can be refined (and thus generalized). It then tests the proposal by asking the expert a few questions. If the proposal is confirmed, MOLE replaces the preference with a richer knowledge structure. Otherwise MOLE considers alternative proposals. If there are no more testable proposals, MOLE will abandon the attempt at refinement of the preference.

In forming proposed refinements, MOLE$_{KA}$ uses some heuristics to try to reduce the number of questions it asks the expert. Preferences partition competing hypotheses or reasons into equivalence classes, the preference categories. As illustrated in the SMALL-RED-FLAME example, one of the clues that MOLE$_{KA}$ uses to form proposals is the relative sizes of the equivalence classes. If, for example, some piece of information partitions the set of hypotheses explaining some symptom into two equivalence classes -- those that are to be rejected and those that are viable -- and if one set is considerably larger, MOLE will assume the reason directly qualifies the hypotheses in the smaller set. That is, if R is a reason for favoring H_1 and H_2 over H_3, then MOLE first proposes that the reason directly provides evidence against H_3.

MOLE$_{KA}$ also is guided by the structure of the network when generating proposed refinements. The schematic network in figure 3-4 can be used to illustrate how MOLE generates and tests proposals. Symptoms S_1, S_2 and S_3 can be explained by the hypotheses (H_1, H_2, H_3, H_4) connected to them. Suppose the expert indicates that R (not shown) is a reason for preferring H_2 over H_3 as an explanation for S_2. MOLE will consider three proposed refinements:

1. R directly supports H_2.

2. R directly rules out H_3.

3. R is a condition that cuts the link from H_3 to S_2.

MOLE tests the event-qualifying proposals first since they are usually easier to confirm. In this case, the candidate explanations (H_2 and H_3) are partitioned into two equivalence classes of equal sizes, so MOLE does not have any reason to suppose R directly supports H_2 rather than directly rules out H_3 or vice versa. MOLE arbitrarily picks one of the potential

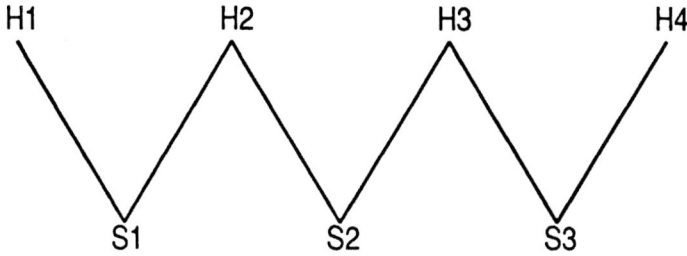

Figure 3-4: Symptoms and Hypotheses

refinements and tests it by asking the expert hypothetical questions. For example, to test the first proposal (that R directly supports H_2), MOLE presents the expert with a situation in which the presence of S_1 must be explained and asks whether R would be a reason for favoring H_2 over H_1. If the experts reply is affirmative, then MOLE concludes that R is a reason for favoring H_2 as the explanation not only of S_1 and S_2 but other symptoms that it might potentially explain.

The conditions for confirming each of the three proposed refinements are summarized below:

1. If R is also a reason for preferring H_2 over H_1 when S_1 is present, then R is assumed to directly support H_2.

2. If R is also a reason for preferring H_4 over H_3 when S_3 is present, then R is assumed to be directly ruling out H_3.

3. If there is an independent reason for believing in H_3, but because of R, H_2 is preferred over H_3 as an explanation for S_2, then R is assumed to be a condition that cuts or disables the connection from H_3 to S_2.

If none of these proposals is confirmed, MOLE will continue to treat R as a local preference favoring H_2 over H_3 as an explanation for S_2. These rules for generating and testing proposed refinements will be illustrated in section 3.5 in the discussion of the dynamic acquisition of differentiating knowledge.

3.5. Identifying Weaknesses in the Knowledge Base

Section 3.3 described how MOLE checks to make sure that competing explanations can **in principle** be differentiated. If there is no information for differentiating competing hypotheses MOLE tries to elicit knowledge from the expert that will enable it to differentiate them. In order to discover whether the knowledge base is missing relevant knowledge, the system must either ask the expert for missing knowledge (the static approach) or ask the expert to present the knowledge-based system with cases and evaluate the system's performance (the dynamic approach). However, static techniques of refinement are quite limited.

The static approach is too unconstrained. There are an indefinite number of ways that knowledge can be missing. To exhaustively query the expert about these possibilities is not practical. To ask the expert to suggest what knowledge might be missing is to shift the burden onto the expert. Although MOLE does allow the expert to add whatever knowledge he feels is appropriate, the goal is to make MOLE an active acquirer rather than a passive receptacle of knowledge. Furthermore, experts often overlook knowledge that is missing until they are reminded of it in a situation where it is needed.

Instead of relying solely on the static approach and exhaustively querying the expert, $MOLE_{KA}$ uses dynamic refinement of the knowledge base in the context of providing diagnoses. The expert gives MOLE a test case and tells MOLE the correct diagnosis. If $MOLE_P$ makes an incorrect diagnosis, $MOLE_{KA}$ tries to determine the source of the errors and recommends possible remedies. This provides the expert with a richer context to recall missing knowledge than is provided by static analysis and gives MOLE a richer context to distinguish a wider range of association types. The context is provided by feedback from the expert during dynamic analysis. In the remainder of this section MOLE's techniques for refining its knowledge base dynamically will be discussed.

3.5.1. Refining Covering Knowledge

If $MOLE_P$'s diagnosis does not match that supplied by the expert, $MOLE_{KA}$ first determines whether the diagnosis would have been attainable if the hypotheses had been differentiated differently. If the problem is not a failure to differentiate hypotheses, then $MOLE_{KA}$ looks for missing covering knowledge. There are two possible cases:

1. The expert says a hypotheses should be accepted, but $MOLE_p$ rejects it because it is not needed to explain any symptom.

2. The expert says a hypothesis should be rejected but $MOLE_p$ cannot reject it be because it is needed to explain some otherwise unexplained symptom.

If a hypothesis is mistakenly rejected because it is not needed to explain anything, then $MOLE_{KA}$ asks the expert if there is some symptom that is present in the test case context that can be explained by this hypothesis. In the following example, $MOLE_p$'s diagnosis is correct but incomplete. There is a symptom, HIGH-OTHER-LOSS, that MOLE does not know about.

```
DARK-ASH is explained by
  PULVERIZER-MALFUNCTION.

Is this correct?
>> [ YES ] <cr>

Is the diagnosis complete?
>> [ YES ] no

Is there some explanation that
should have been accepted?
>> [ YES ] <cr>

What is that explanation?
>> [ NONE ] low-heat
     LOW-HEAT-TRANSFER [ YES NO ]
     Status:            OLD
     Method:            INFER
     Default Value:     NONE
>> Confirm (Yes, No): [ YES ] <cr>

LOW-HEAT-TRANSFER is only needed
to explain LOSS-IN-GAS.
But you indicated that there was
no LOSS-IN-GAS.
```

```
Indicate whether
1  There was LOSS-IN-GAS.
2  There is some other symptom that
   LOW-HEAT-TRANSFER is needed to explain.
>> [ NONE ] 2

Indicate the symptom that
LOW-HEAT-TRANSFER explains:
>> [ NONE ] high-other-loss
   HIGH-OTHER-LOSS
   Status:            NEW
   Method:            ASK
   Default Value:     NONE
>> Confirm (Yes, No): [ YES ] <cr>

List any other possible explanations for
HIGH-OTHER-LOSS
besides LOW-HEAT-TRANSFER:

Possible explanation for HIGH-OTHER-LOSS:
>> [ NONE ] <cr>
```

This example illustrates the case where a known hypothesis failed to be accepted because MOLE does not know about some symptom it was needed to explain. The next example illustrates the other case of a missing hypothesis. If a hypothesis fails to be rejected because it is needed to explain some symptom, then MOLE asks the expert for an alternative explanation for the symptom.

```
DARK-ASH is explained by
   LOW-GRINDABILITY-RELATIVE-TO-SETTING.

Is this correct?
>> [ YES ] no

DARK-ASH is explained as follows:
   1  DARK-ASH is explained by
         LARGE-PARTICLES
   2  LARGE-PARTICLES is explained by
         LOW-GRINDABILITY-RELATIVE-TO-SETTING
Indicate the first incorrect step:
>> [ NONE ] 1
```

```
What is the correct explanation for
DARK-ASH:
    1   LARGE-PARTICLES
    2   EXCESS-AIR HIGH
 >> (NONE) [ 2 ] none

In order to explain DARK-ASH
some hypothesis must be accepted.

Enter the explanation for DARK-ASH:
 >> [ NONE ] excess low
      EXCESS-AIR LOW [ HIGH NORMAL LOW ]
      Status:            OLD
      Method:            INFER
      Default value:     NONE
 >> Confirm (Yes, No): [ YES ] <cr>
```

Here MOLE discovers that LOW EXCESS-AIR is a possible explanation of DARK-ASH after being told in a test case that both hypotheses considered as possible explanations for DARK-ASH should be rejected. MOLE reasons that DARK-ASH must have an explanation that it does not know about, and asks the expert for this explanation.

This case would have been less straightforward if the expert had told MOLE that there is no alternative explanation, yet informed MOLE that the two explanations that it knows about are incorrect. In such a situation, MOLE would consider two possibilities: (1) the report or observation of the symptom is mistaken; (2) the event in question is not really a symptom -- that is, it does not need to be explained. MOLE would first inquire whether it is possible that the reported observation that there is DARK-ASH could be mistaken. If it can be, MOLE notes this, and the next time MOLE is in this situation, it will ask the user whether he is sure about the occurrence of this symptom. However, if the expert is quite certain about this reported event, then MOLE would examine how it came to believe that this event was a symptom. If it learned about this "symptom" during the piecemeal differentiating or refinement phases, rather than during the initial, systematic acquisition of covering knowledge, then there is a fairly good chance that it ¦; really differentiating evidence, such as a connection-qualifying reason, rather than covering knowledge.

3.5.2. Refining Differentiating Knowledge

If MOLE$_p$'s diagnosis is different from that of the expert but it would be possible to reach that diagnosis if the hypotheses had been differentiated differently, then MOLE$_{KA}$ looks for missing differentiating knowledge that will result in the correct hypothesis being selected. The principles for adding differentiating knowledge dynamically are basically the same as those for adding it statically. The only difference is that it is done in the context of some actual or hypothetical example. Since the static stage of knowledge acquisition made sure that all hypotheses can be differentiated in principle, the failure to correctly differentiate means either that some of the differentiating knowledge is not active and needs to be supplemented, or that it is active and needs to be overridden or qualified by additional differentiating knowledge.

As in the case of the static phase of knowledge acquisition, MOLE tries to make use of existing structures -- especially covering knowledge. When there is no usable covering knowledge to exploit, MOLE's task is more difficult. It must decide whether to treat the new information as a simple, local preference or try to refine it. As was discussed in section 3.3, MOLE's guiding principle is that there is no point in trying to refine knowledge beyond its operational significance. Differentiating knowledge needs to be refined into either event-qualifying or connection-qualifying knowledge only if at least one of the hypotheses being differentiated potentially explains other symptoms.

In the following example MOLE$_p$ needs to explain two symptoms: LOSS-IN-GAS and HIGH-FLY-ASH-FLOW. MOLE knows that LOSS-IN-GAS is explained by either LOW-HEAT-TRANSFER or HIGH EXCESS-AIR, and that HIGH-FLY-ASH-FLOW is explained by either SMALL-PARTICLES or HIGH EXCESS-AIR. Not having any information to prefer one hypothesis over another, MOLE$_p$ accepts HIGH EXCESS-AIR as the explanation for both symptoms and rejects the other two hypotheses (LOW-HEAT-TRANSFER and SMALL-PARTICLES). MOLE$_p$'s reasoning is that since it does not have any reason to favor the other two hypotheses, HIGH EXCESS-AIR is the best choice because it alone can explain both symptoms. However, the expert informs MOLE$_{KA}$ that its diagnosis of LOSS-IN-GAS is mistaken.

```
LOSS-IN-GAS is explained as follows:
  1  LOSS-IN-GAS is explained by
       EXCESS-AIR HIGH
Indicate the first incorrect step:
>> [ NONE ] 1

What is the correct explanation for
LOSS-IN-GAS?
  1  LOW-HEAT-TRANSFER
  2  EXCESS-AIR HIGH
>> (NONE) [ 1 ] <cr>

Indicate any evidence for preferring
LOW-HEAT-TRANSFER over
EXCESS-AIR HIGH:

Evidence:
>> [ NONE ] oxygen-reading low
     OXYGEN-READING LOW [ LOW NORMAL HIGH ]
     Status:              NEW
     Method:              ASK
     Default Value:       NONE
>> Confirm (Yes, No): [ YES ] <cr>

Evidence:
>> [ NONE ] <cr>

Does OXYGEN-READING LOW
need to be explained?
>> [ YES ] no
```

If the expert had answered that LOW OXYGEN-READING needs to be explained, and that it is explained by LOW EXCESS-AIR, then MOLE$_{KA}$ would realize that LOW OXYGEN-READING rules out HIGH EXCESS-AIR. However, at this point the expert did not think of LOW OXYGEN-READING as a symptom of LOW EXCESS-AIR, so MOLE has to make use of less direct means in order to determine how LOW OXYGEN-READING differentiates between the explanations for LOSS-IN-GAS.

MOLE observes that it also accepted HIGH EXCESS-AIR as the explanation for HIGH-FLY-ASH-FLOW and checks to see whether this new piece of evidence will upset this evaluation as well.

```
Is HIGH-FLY-ASH-FLOW explained by
  HIGH EXCESS-AIR?
>> [ NO ] <cr>

Given OXYGEN-READING LOW,
should SMALL-PARTICLES
be favored over
EXCESS-AIR HIGH
as the explanation for
HIGH-FLY-ASH-FLOW?
>> [ YES ] <cr>
```

MOLE$_{KA}$ concludes that since LOW OXYGEN-READING rules out HIGH EXCESS-AIR as an explanation for both LOSS-IN-GAS and HIGH-FLY-ASH-FLOW, it must be an event-qualifying piece of knowledge that negatively qualifies, or rules out, HIGH EXCESS-AIR. If the symptom HIGH-FLY-ASH-FLOW had not been present in this case, MOLE$_{KA}$ would have tested this hypothesis by asking the expert a "what if" question.

```
Suppose HIGH-FLY-ASH-FLOW
needs to be explained.

Given OXYGEN-READING LOW,
should SMALL-PARTICLES
be favored over
EXCESS-AIR HIGH
as the explanation for
HIGH-FLY-ASH-FLOW?
>> [ YES ] <cr>
```

The next example is a case where connection-qualifying knowledge is acquired. In this example MOLE$_p$ accepts FOULING as the explanation for FAN-POWER-IS-EXCEEDED because it has learned from a previous test case to prefer FOULING over MALFUNCTION-OF-VALVE, all other things being equal. However, the expert tells MOLE$_{KA}$ that this is the wrong choice. MOLE responds by describing its diagnosis.

```
HIGH-BOTTOM-ASH-FLOW is explained as follows:
    1   HIGH-BOTTOM-ASH-FLOW is explained by
          EXCESS-AIR LOW
    2   EXCESS-AIR LOW is explained by
          FAN-POWER-IS-EXCEEDED
    3   FAN-POWER-IS-EXCEEDED is explained by
          FOULING
Indicate the first incorrect step:
>> [ NONE ] 3

What is the correct explanation for
FAN-POWER-IS-EXCEEDED
    1   FOULING
    2   MALFUNCTION-OF-VALVE
>> (NONE) [ 2 ] <cr>

Indicate any evidence for preferring
MALFUNCTION-OF-VALVE
over FOULING
as the explanation for
FAN-POWER-IS-EXCEEDED:

Evidence:
>> [ NONE ] light-load
      LIGHT-LOAD [ YES NO ]
      Status:           NEW
      Method:           ASK
      Default Value:    NONE
>> Confirm (Yes, No): [ YES ] no
```

The expert tells MOLE that LIGHT-LOAD is the reason for preferring MALFUNCTION-OF-VALVE over FOULING as the explanation for FAN-POWER-IS-EXCEEDED. Note that in this case the expert does not confirm the default "parameters" for LIGHT-LOAD. MOLE displays a menu that the expert can use to make any corrections that need to be made.

```
Options:                             Current Value:

1 Change Name:                       LIGHT-LOAD
2 Possible Values:                   YES NO
3 Change Method (ask infer):         ASK
4 Change Default Value:              NONE
5 Done
>> [ 3 ] 4 no


Options:                             Current Value:

1 Change Name:                       LIGHT-LOAD
2 Possible Values:                   YES NO
3 Change Method (ask infer):         ASK
4 Change Default Value:              NO
5 Done
>> [ 5 ] <cr>
```

The expert specifies a default value of "no" for LIGHT-LOAD. In other words, $MOLE_p$ is to assume this value unless otherwise specified. The knowledge that a certain piece of evidence usually has some designated value saves $MOLE_p$ from asking the user needless questions. However, whenever $MOLE_p$ reaches an impass in its reasoning -- for example, it does not have enough information to differentiate several candidates, or it has ruled out all the viable candidates -- $MOLE_p$ can examine its default assumptions, asking the user to verify those values that might be the cause of the impass.

Having been told that LIGHT-LOAD is a reason for preferring MALFUNCTION-OF-VALVE over FOULING as the explanation for FAN-POWER-IS-EXCEEDED, $MOLE_{KA}$ next tries to determine more precisely its role. It hypothesizes that LIGHT-LOAD is event-qualifying evidence which rules out FOULING no matter what symptom needs to be explained MOLE tests this by asking a "what if" question involving a symptom different from the test case's FAN-POWER-IS-EXCEEDED.

```
Suppose MISBALANCE-OF-CONVECTION
needs to be explained.

Given LIGHT-LOAD,
should EXCESS-AIR LOW
be favored over
FOULING
as the explanation for
MISBALANCE-OF-CONVECTION
>> [ YES ] no
```

The expert's response disconfirms MOLE$_{KA}$'s proposed knowledge structure refinement. MOLE next tests the proposal that LIGHT-LOAD is connection-qualifying evidence. MOLE knows that FOULING can lead to FAN-POWER-IS-EXCEEDED. Since FOULING doesn't lead to FAN-POWER-IS-EXCEEDED in the test case, MOLE hypothesizes that NO LIGHT-LOAD might be a condition that is necessary for the explanatory relation to hold. MOLE tests with a counterexample; it asks if FOULING can lead to FAN-POWER-IS-EXCEEDED when there is a LIGHT-LOAD.

```
Suppose there is strong evidence that
FOULING.

Given LIGHT-LOAD
should MALFUNCTION-OF-VALVE
be favored over
FOULING
as the explanation for
FAN-POWER-IS-EXCEEDED.
>> [ YES ] no
```

Because the counterexample is not confirmed, MOLE interprets the expert's response as evidence for its proposal. Normally, independent evidence for FOULING would make FOULING the preferred explanation for FAN-POWER-IS-EXCEEDED. MOLE reasons that since this is not the case when there is a LIGHT-LOAD, NO LIGHT-LOAD is a background condition that must hold in order for FOULING to explain FAN-POWER-IS-EXCEEDED.

As these examples illustrate, MOLE$_{KA}$'s refinement of differentiating knowledge relies heavily upon the structure of the knowledge base's covering knowledge. There is always the danger that the weight of the differentiating process is more than the structure of covering knowledge can bear. However, as these examples have also illustrated, during the dynamic refinement of the knowledge base, $MOLE_{KA}$ acquires not only differentiating knowledge but also covering knowledge. This means that as it acquires more preferences it also acquires more covering structure it can use as a context to refine the preferences into event-qualifying and connection-qualifying differentiating knowledge. It can use the richer context to acquire connection-qualifying conditions for event-qualifying knowledge (including anticipatory knowledge) and even connection-qualifying conditions for other connection-qualifying associations. It can also use the richer context to acquire preferences about its preferences. MOLE can manage a rich collection of differentiating knowledge, provided it is built upon a solid enough structure of covering knowledge. The critical role that covering knowledge plays in the success and failures of $MOLE_{KA}$ will be discussed in section 3.6.

3.6. MOLE's Scope

$MOLE_{KA}$ has been used to build a number of diagnostic systems or prototypes. These include systems for diagnosing (1) inefficiencies in a coal-burning power plant (used as an illustration in this paper), (2) defects in the steel produced by a steel-rolling mill, (3) defects in power supply boards as they come off an assembly line, (4) malfunctions of automobile engines, (5) causes of bad milk (for example, high bacteria or cell count) on a dairy farm, and (6) communication problems in a large computer network. There have also been several domains for which an attempt was made to use $MOLE_{KA}$, but $MOLE_{KA}$ was found to be inappropriate: (1) the selection of computer components given a set of generic specifications, (2) diagnosing problems in an oil refinery, and (3) debugging OPS5 programs.

Probably more can be learned about MOLE's scope from its failures than its successes. The first failure -- the selection of computer components -- may look like an obvious mismatch given that MOLE was designed with diagnostic problems in mind. On the other hand, given that $MOLE_p$'s problem-solving method is a variant of heuristic classification, it might be assumed that it should be easy to adapt MOLE to nondiagnostic tasks that rely mainly upon selecting a solution. Its adaptability, however, is limited by two important restrictions:

1. It must be practical to pre-enumerate the hypotheses or solutions that are to be selected.

2. It must be practical to cast the problem in terms of covering knowledge.

The computer component selection problem failed to meet either condition. Although the problem was one of selection -- the selection of components -- the solutions were often not individual components but combinations of components. For example, several different kinds of disk drives might be needed to meet the computer system's storage requirements as well as take into account such considerations as portability and speed. If the solution requires several disk drives, it is likely that the choices will be interdependent. MOLE could only handle this problem by treating each viable combination as a solution, but it was not practical to pre-enumerate all these combinations.

Of course, the same problem can occur when the task is diagnosis. Symptoms sometimes have multiple, interacting causes. In so far as this is typical for a domain, MOLE is probably not the appropriate knowledge-acquisition tool. Often, however, what appears to be a case of multiple causes is really a case where there are intermediate causes. As we have seen, MOLE can handle multiple levels of explanation.

Whereas the first restriction follows from the nature of the problem-solving method used by the performance system, the second follows from the nature of the knowledge-acquisition process. For $MOLE_{KA}$ knowledge-acquisition is driven by covering knowledge. If the initially acquired covering knowledge does not provide much structure, then MOLE will have trouble acquiring the knowledge needed to differentiate among the explanations. The sparser the explanations for any event, the easier it is to acquire the information needed to differentiate among the explanations. Generally speaking, sparseness can be bought at the price of increasing the number of intermediate levels in the explanation space. The challenge, then, is getting the expert to provide the intermediate levels. This is the major snag when using $MOLE_{KA}$. On the first pass, experts tend to describe a flat network, explaining the initial symptoms in terms of the final causes. However, diagnostic experts usually have no trouble grasping that intermediate explanations are needed and soon become proficient at supplying them.

Nondiagnostic domains (or more generally, tasks for which explanation is not the central goal) are difficult for $MOLE_{KA}$ to handle because the experts have more difficulty systematically providing the initial covering associations. This is not to say that the equivalent of covering knowledge cannot be identified for nondiagnostic domains. For example, if the task is component selection, covering knowledge might link the components (hypotheses) with requirements that must be met (symptoms). Differentiating knowledge could be information indicating what tradeoffs can be made between various components. Components would be ruled out either because they are unacceptable for independent reasons (for example, too costly) or because they inadequately meet the requirements. The problem is that any such nondiagnostic counterpart to covering knowledge is rather forced and, thus, difficult for the expert to grasp.

$MOLE_{KA}$ failed in part, on the component selection problem because there was not enough easily recognizable structure to the problem. In the oil refinery diagnosis and OPS5 debugging problems, there is too much structure, or much of the structure cannot be exploited by MOLE. $MOLE_{KA}$ needs to elicit from the expert all the potentially abnormal events (complaints) and their potential explanations. MOLE has no way of exploiting other regularities in the problem. For example, MOLE could not make direct use of the structure of the oil refinery (in terms of conduits and components) to diagnose problems. Such structural information was used implicitly, but it had to be represented indirectly in terms of covering knowledge.[4]

It should be noted that there is nothing about MOLE's approach that precludes making use of a more descriptive model of the system being diagnosed. One possibility we are exploring is the use of KNACK's techniques for exploiting a domain model to aid $MOLE_{KA}$'s knowledge-acquisition process. Experts' schematic accounts of how various problems are diagnosed could serve as sample reports. $MOLE_{KA}$ could then use a

---

[4]YAKA, a knowledge-acquisition tool developed at Carnegie Mellon University by Herve Lambert that builds diagnostic systems that make use of qualitative reasoning, is very effective for this domain. All YAKA needs in order to diagnose refinery problems is a structural model of the refinery plus knowledge as to how the relatively few different kinds of constituent components (for example, valves, pumps, tanks) function. (See chapter 8.)

model of the domain to help it generalize the report fragments in much the way that KNACK does.

3.7. Conclusion

$MOLE_{KA}$ illustrates how much power a knowledge-acquisition tool can obtain from a relatively simple problem-solving method. Although the previous section has focused on the difficulties MOLE has in handling certain types of problems, the surprising thing is that MOLE has been useful for such a diverse set of domains. Provided the expert can identify the initial set of abnormal events and supply explanations for these events, $MOLE_{KA}$ can guide the expert in the acquisition of the initial knowledge base. As we have seen, there is always the danger when differentiating among these explanations that MOLE and the expert will become bogged down in a combinatorial explosion of preferences. However, to the extent that the expert is initially able to provide a multileveled explanation space, there is not much danger of this in practice. In short, the knowledge-acquisition process is driven by covering knowledge. It stands or falls with the quality of the initial set of covering knowledge. Differentiating knowledge, although more diverse than covering knowledge, is acquired in the context of covering knowledge. The expert does not have to understand the various subroles that $MOLE_{KA}$ assigns to various pieces of differentiating knowledge.

Given the importance of covering knowledge, $MOLE_{KA}$ could benefit from any technique that would help it guide the expert in the acquisition of the explanation space. In the previous section the use of richer domain models was suggested as one possibility. Another possibility would to be to make use of the repertory grid techniques exploited by AQUINAS [Boose 87]. As we apply MOLE to new domains, we hope to explore some of these possibilities.

Acknowledgements

This research effort is supported by Digital Equipment Corporation. The views and conclusions contained in this document are those of the author and should not be interpreted as representing the official policies, either expressed or implied, of Digital Equipment Corporation.

Many people have made important contributions to MOLE. Foremost is John McDermott who helped shape the direction of the project from its inception. Damien Ehret, Mike Goss, Marc Green, Jim Park, Isabelle Paoli, Linda Rodi, Jos Schreinemakers, and Ming Tan have contributed to the project. I have benefited from discussions with Gary Kahn, Georg Klinker, Herve Lambert, Sandy Marcus, and Dan Offutt.

4. SALT: A Knowledge-Acquisition Tool for Propose-and-Revise Systems[5]

Sandra Marcus

Abstract

SALT[6] is a knowledge-acquisition tool for generating expert systems that use a propose-and-revise problem-solving strategy. The SALT-assumed method constructs a design incrementally by proposing values for design parameters, identifying constraints on design parameters as the design develops, and revising decisions in response to constraint violations in the proposal. This problem-solving strategy provides the basis for SALT's knowledge representation. SALT uses its knowledge of the intended problem-solving strategy in identifying relevant domain knowledge, in detecting weaknesses in the knowledge base in order to guide its interrogation of the domain expert, in generating an expert system that performs the task and explains its line of reasoning, and in analyzing test case coverage. The strong commitment to problem-solving strategy that gives SALT its power also defines its scope.

4.1. Introduction

SALT is one of few knowledge-acquisition tools for systems that construct, rather than select, a solution. (See [Mitchell 85] and [van de Brug 86] for descriptions of two others.) SALT is intended for use by domain experts to create and maintain systems that perform constraint-satisfaction tasks such as designing an artifact or constructing a schedule. It acquires knowledge from an expert and generates a domain-specific knowledge base compiled into rules. It then combines this compiled knowledge base with a problem-solving shell to create an expert system. SALT maintains a permanent,

---

[5]This material, first published in **Artificial Intelligence,** an international journal of Elsevier Publishers B.V. (North-Holland), Amsterdam, is reprinted here by the permission of the publisher.

[6]*kNowledge ACquisition Language.*

declarative store of the knowledge base, which is updated during interviews with the domain expert and is the input to the compiler/rule-generator. Like other tools in this book, SALT gets much of its power by making a strong assumption about the problem-solving strategy used by the expert systems it creates; it uses this focus in representing, analyzing and applying the knowledge it acquires.

A SALT-generated system uses a *propose-and-revise* method. The expert system constructs an approximate plan or design by proposing a value for one parameter of the design at a time and checking to see whether each parameter satisfies all constraints on it. Whenever constraint violations are detected, the system revises past decisions, for example, by changing a parameter value in some way that is dependent on the constraint violated.

This problem-solving strategy defines multiple roles that knowledge can play in the system. The high degree of interaction among pieces of knowledge in different roles means that it is sometimes difficult to understand how each piece of knowledge added to the system will fit with what is already in the knowledge base. SALT uses its assessment of the completeness, consistency and adequacy of the knowledge base to guide its interrogation of the user.

SALT represents knowledge according to the role it will play in the problem-solving strategy it assumes. A representation language that identifies domain knowledge by its function in problem solving has the following desired properties [Clancey 83, Clancey 85, Swartout 83, Neches 84, Chandrasekaran 83, Chandrasekaran 86, McDermott 86, Gruber 87a]:

- The language provides the basis for well-motivated knowledge-elicitation strategies. It allows SALT to help the user identify relevant domain knowledge.

- Analyses run on the intermediate store of the knowledge base can help determine the adequacy of the knowledge base.

- Because language identifies knowledge by its function in problem solving, it is a good key to how and when the knowledge should be used by the problem-solver.

- The language provides the basis for an explanation facility that describes what is in the knowledge base and can justify the generated system's reasoning.

- The knowledge base representation identifies important features of the program that should be tested in any validation study. The generated expert system can analyze a set of test cases for their coverage of these features.

Section 4.2 describes how knowledge roles define the relevant pieces of knowledge that must be acquired by SALT. Section 4.3 describes the knowledge base built up from these pieces during an interview and the analyses used to identify and respond to gaps and inadequacies in the knowledge base. Section 4.4 describes SALT's compilation procedure to create an expert system. The SALT-generated explanation capability is discussed in section 4.5. Section 4.6 looks at a SALT-generated facility for assessing the coverage of test problem sets. Section 4.7 briefly describes our explorations in understanding SALT's applicability.

4.2. Acquiring Relevant Knowledge Pieces
A functional knowledge representation helps identify what knowledge is relevant to acquire; that is, it identifies what domain knowledge is required by the problem-solver in order to solve the problem. A SALT-generated problem-solver creates a design by proposing values for design parameters, checking constraints on those parameters, and revising values if constraints on proposed parameters are violated. There are three roles that knowledge can play in such a problem-solving strategy:

1. PROPOSE-A-DESIGN-EXTENSION

2. IDENTIFY-A-CONSTRAINT on a part of the design

3. PROPOSE-A-FIX for a constraint violation

These are the relevant kinds of knowledge that SALT needs to acquire in order to serve the problem-solver.

In acquiring this knowledge, SALT follows a piecemeal, bottom-up strategy of elicitation, where the grain size and identification of the pieces is determined by these knowledge roles. Our experience with human designers and schedulers is that they are fairly good at describing individual considerations for constructing a solution for their domain. They can extemporaneously list many of the constraints that the solution needs to satisfy. They can consult manuals of formulas and tables for producing values for individual design parameters. But they are less clear on how the individual steps should fit together. In addition, domain experts need help in organizing pieces into a system when later pieces are added as a system evolves over time or when a system must represent expertise from multiple experts. SALT aids users by allowing them to enter knowledge piecemeal, starting at any point. SALT then cues for appropriate links, keeps track of how the pieces are fitting together and warns the user of places where pieces might be missing or creating inconsistencies.

In order to illustrate what it looks like to supply pieces of knowledge through SALT, we will use examples based on knowledge acquired in building VT.   VT [Marcus 88a] is a SALT-generated expert system currently in use at Westinghouse Elevator Company to custom-design elevator systems. VT takes as input customer requirements, such as how fast the elevator should travel and what its carrying capacity should be, as well as architectural details about the building it will service, such as floor heights and wall-to-wall dimensions in the elevator shaft. VT must produce a list of quantities, ordering codes and other parameters for all equipment required, including some routine modifications of standard equipment, and an equipment layout customized to the elevator shaft.

When a SALT interview is initiated, the user is shown a menu like the one below for indicating the type of knowledge to be entered or viewed. These knowledge types correspond to the knowledge roles identified earlier. PROCEDURE is used to describe a procedure for determining the value for a proposed design extension. CONSTRAINT is used to identify a constraint and supply a procedure for determining its value. FIX is used for specifying potential remedies for specific constraint violations. The user may begin the interview by entering any of these types of knowledge.

```
1. PROCEDURE       Enter a procedure for a value
2. CONSTRAINT      Enter constraints on a value
3. FIX             Enter remedies for a
                     constraint violation
4. EXIT            Exit interviewer

Enter your command [ EXIT ]:
```

The knowledge role identifications assumed by SALT force domain experts to carve their knowledge into these pieces in return for the guidance SALT provides in putting the pieces together. SALT users are given the following guidelines to help them fit their knowledge into the SALT schema: A PROCEDURE must be given for every design parameter needed to describe the completed design.[7] The PROCEDURE should, as far as possible, take into account all of the considerations, or constraints, that affect the specification of a value. When this is not possible, as, for example, in the case of under-constrained parameters, the user should use PROCEDURE to specify a preferred choice given the considerations available. CONSTRAINT is used to identify limits on the value of a design parameter that are not captured in the specification of the PROCEDURE but should be explicitly checked before a solution can be reached by the generated expert system. FIX must be used to suggest revisions to decisions in response to a violation of tests expressed by CONSTRAINT knowledge. Revisions may change the values of inputs, design parameters or constraints. Users get the maximum benefit of SALT's analytic capabilities if they do not enter FIXes until the other pieces are in place.

Each piece of knowledge must be associated with a value name. For PROCEDURE, it is the name of the value that will be determined by the procedure. For CONSTRAINT, it is the name of the value that is constrained. For FIX, it is the name of the violated constraint. These value names are relevant in tying the pieces of knowledge together as described in section 4.3.

Once a user selects a knowledge type and supplies the desired value name, SALT displays a schema of prompts for information associated with the knowledge role selected. The identification of what responses to the prompts are allowed, or interpretable by SALT, is somewhat application-dependent (see section 4.7). A default schema for supplying a procedure for determining the value of CAR-JAMB-RETURN is shown next.

---

[7]PROCEDUREs may also be entered for determining intermediate values that are used to determine design parameters. The user may mention such intermediate values the first time by directly entering a PROCEDURE for them or by using them in a PROCEDURE for some other value. If not otherwise supplied, SALT will prompt for PROCEDUREs for the intermediate values.

```
1 Name:                  CAR-JAMB-RETURN
2 Precondition:          NONE
3 Procedure:             CALCULATION
4 Formula:
5 Justification:

Enter your command [ EXIT ]:
```

SALT's prompts for information are given on the left. Users fill in the schema by indicating the number of the prompt and then typing the knowledge requested by the prompt. A completed schema is shown below:

```
1 Name:                  CAR-JAMB-RETURN
2 Precondition:          DOOR-OPENING = CENTER
3 Procedure:             CALCULATION
4 Formula:               [ PLATFORM-WIDTH -
                           OPENING-WIDTH ] / 2
5 Justification:         CENTER-OPENING DOORS LOOK
                           BEST WHEN CENTERED ON
                           THE PLATFORM.
```

The precondition specifies that this procedure should only be used on cases in which the value assigned to DOOR-OPENING is CENTER. The type of procedure is a calculation using the formula given on line 4. (Information on how DOOR-OPENING, PLATFORM-WIDTH and OPENING-WIDTH receive values must be supplied by the user through separate PROCEDUREs.) In this case, the value of CAR-JAMB-RETURN is under-constrained by the limits placed on it; this procedure supplies a preferred value. The justification states why this value is preferred.

A second example will illustrate a PROCEDURE screen that uses a method other than CALCULATION. A completed screen for a PROCEDURE for MACHINE-MODEL is shown next.

```
 1  Name:              MACHINE-MODEL
 2  Precondition:      NONE
 3  Procedure:         DATABASE-LOOKUP
 4  Table name:        MACHINE
 5  Column with
        needed value:  MODEL
 6  Parameter test:    MAX-LOAD >=
                       SUSPENDED-LOAD
 7  Parameter test:    DONE
 8  Ordering column:   HEIGHT
 9  Optimal:           SMALLEST
10  Justification:     THIS PROCEDURE IS TAKEN
                       FROM STANDARDS MANUAL
                       IIIA, P. 139.
```

When the procedure DATABASE-LOOKUP is selected, the user is presented with a set of subprompts asking for details for locating the value to be retrieved. In the example, the name of the table and column from which the value is retrieved are SALT-generated defaults. Each parameter test lists a test to be performed on table entries (rows) to decide which are viable candidates for retrieval. In this case the entry must have a listing under the column MAX-LOAD that is greater than or equal to SUSPENDED-LOAD, a separately generated value. Finally, if more than one entry under MODEL meets this test, ORDERING-COLUMN and OPTIMAL are used to determine a preferred candidate. Here the user indicates that the entry with the SMALLEST HEIGHT is the most desirable.

The crucial information needed to use a constraint is an indication of what value it constrains[8] and the nature of the limit it places on that value. This information is conveyed in response to the first two prompts in the two examples that follow. In addition, the user must give a procedure for specifying a value for the constraint; prompts for this information are identical to those on the PROCEDURE screen.

---

[8]The CONSTRAINT schema requests the user to supply a single name of a value that is constrained. This imposes some conventions on how constraint knowledge is expressed when a constraint affects more than one value. If x and y are parts of the solution whose sum is constrained to be less than z, the SALT user must define an intermediate value, *sumxy*, that is constrained by z. If z is a maximum for x and a maximum for y, the user can enter two different names for z, such as *maximum-x* and *maximum-y*, with the same value.

```
1 Constrained value:    CAR-JAMB-RETURN
2 Constraint type:      MAXIMUM
3 Constraint name:      MAXIMUM-CAR-JAMB-RETURN
4 Precondition:         DOOR-OPENING = SIDE
5 Procedure:            CALCULATION
6 Formula:              PANEL-WIDTH *
                          STRINGER-QUANTITY
7 Justification:        THIS PROCEDURE IS TAKEN
                          FROM INSTALLATION
                          MANUAL I, P. 12b.
```

```
 1 Constrained value:   MOTOR-MODEL
 2 Constraint type:     CHOICE-SET
 3 Constraint name:     CHOICE-SET-MOTOR-MODEL
 4 Precondition:        NONE
 5 Procedure:           DATABASE-LOOKUP
 6 Table name:          MACHINE
 7 Column with
       needed value:    COMPATIBLE-MOTORS
 8 Parameter test:      MODEL = MACHINE-MODEL
 9 Parameter test:      DONE
10 Ordering column:     NONE
11 Justification:       THIS PROCEDURE IS TAKEN
                          FROM STANDARDS MANUAL
                          IIIA, P. 154.
```

In the generated system, whenever a constraint violation is detected, the problem-solver considers ways to revise decisions it has made in order to make the design fit the constraint. The crucial domain information the problem-solver needs is an identification of the value to change, how to change it and some idea of the expert's preference for this revision over others that might be tried.

```
1 Violated constraint:  CHOICE-SET-MOTOR-MODEL
2 Value to change:      MOTOR-MODEL
3 Change type:          UPGRADE
4 Preference rating:    8
5 Reason for
     preference:        Changes major
                          equipment sizing
```

This suggested fix for a violation of CHOICE-SET-MOTOR-MODEL would upgrade the value of MOTOR-MODEL, that is, would select a model using the criteria of the table lookup for MOTOR-MODEL, but choose the next less preferred (more costly) model. The user may suggest more than one potential fix for the same constraint violation. For example, an upgrade of MACHINE-MODEL might also fix a violation of CHOICE-SET-MOTOR-MODEL. The preference rating is used to compare the current fix to other proposed fixes that have been or might be entered. Specifying what revisions should be made in response to a constraint violation is one of the most difficult tasks of a domain expert supplying knowledge. We will describe how SALT aides the user in filling in such a knowledge piece in the next section.

4.3. Analyzing How the Pieces Fit Together

In representing the knowledge pieces, SALT must make clear how these pieces interact during problem solving. An understanding of decision interaction is needed particularly for analyzing the completeness of the knowledge base, its compilability and its adequacy in converging on a solution. For this purpose, connections represented in the knowledge base express how decisions based on one piece of knowledge affect decisions based on others, where the observable effect of a decision on the solution is the assignment of a value to an input, design parameter or constraint.

SALT's representational scheme is built around the framework of a dependency network. For SALT, each node in the network is the name of a value the expert system must acquire or generate; this can be the name of an input, a design parameter or the name of a constraint. There are three kinds of directed links that represent relations between nodes: (1) "Contributes-to" links A to B if the value of A is used in a procedure to specify a value for B. (2) "Constrains" links A to B if A is the name of a constraint and B is the name of a design parameter and the value of A places some restriction on the value of B. (3) "Suggests-revision-of" links A to B if A is the name of a constraint and a violation of A suggests a change to the currently proposed value of B.

Each of these links is derived from a knowledge piece. One of the anchors of the link is the value name asked for when the SALT user enters a piece of knowledge; the other is extracted from the knowledge supplied. (SALT users can enter synonym lists for each value name. The synonyms help the user establish appropriate connections and browse the knowledge base.) Each knowledge piece supports the links derived from it with more refined knowledge describing the nature of the link: (1) "Contributes-to" links are supported by PROCEDUREs and the procedure parts of CONSTRAINTs that tell how contributors are combined to specify the value of the node pointed to. (2) "Constrains" links are supported by a specification of the nature of the restriction taken from CONSTRAINT knowledge pieces. (3) "Suggests-revision-of" links are supported by a declaration of the nature of the proposed revision (for example, direction and amount of change) and its relative preference, specified in FIX knowledge pieces.

Examples of the connections that would be generated from the knowledge pieces given in section 4.2 are shown in figure 4-1. "Contributes-to" links are shown as solid-line arrows, "constrains" by dotted-line links, and "suggests-revision-of" by broken-line.

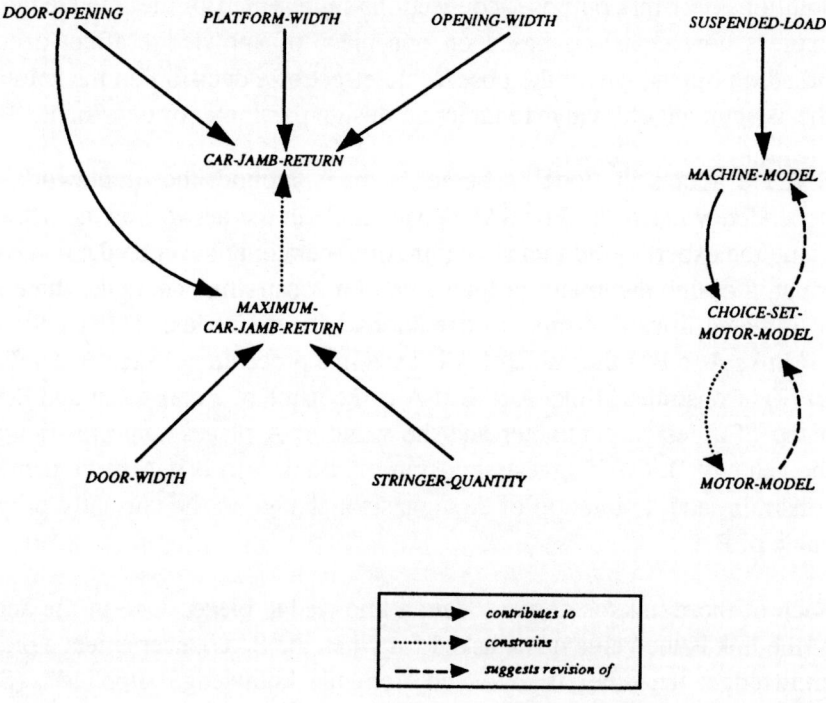

Figure 4-1: SALT's Representation of the Links among Knowledge Pieces

Once the user enters some knowledge, SALT guides the elicitation of further knowledge by using its understanding of how the problem-solver will use the knowledge. Some interrogation is driven by a rather broad notion of completeness checking. Other interactions amount to delivering a kind of compile-error warning combined with guidance in how to correct the error by redefining knowledge roles or adding knowledge. Finally, some guidance is aimed at making sure that the knowledge given will be adequate to converge on a solution.

4.3.1. General Completeness
When a piece of knowledge is added to the knowledge base store, it may create new nodes in the network. When a node is added, SALT checks for the existence of other links that may point to or from that node. SALT expects "contributes-to" links to every node in the network unless the node represents a "ground," that is, an input or a constant. It therefore checks to make sure that all nodes have procedures associated with them that will either supply "contributes-to" links or identify the node as an input or constant. If a procedure is not stored for a node, SALT will ask the user for one. SALT also considers potential "constrains" and "suggests-revision-of" links that might emanate from a node. SALT requests the user to supply constraints for any nonconstraint value and fixes for a violation of any constraint identified in the course of the interview.

4.3.2. Compilability
The task of the problem-solver is to find a path through the network, assigning values at each node, that leads to quiescence, a state in which all constraints have been checked and satisfied. The compiler proceduralizes these paths. Most of the compilability issues enter into checking whether a unique and complete path can be found through the dependency network for a set of inputs.

Uniqueness and Connectedness.

SALT checks for the uniqueness and connectedness of paths by analyzing the coverage of sets of preconditions on multiple procedures that might be used to contribute to the same node. For example, an overlap in preconditions would exist if there were one formula for CAR-JAMB-

RETURN when DOOR-OPENING = CENTER and another when [DOOR-OPENING = CENTER AND DOOR-SPEED = SINGLE]. Similarly, there would be no unique path to MOTOR-TORQUE for a speed of 250 if one procedure was applicable for speeds less than 300 and another for speeds greater than 200. The user is warned of such overlaps in preconditions. In addition, SALT checks to see whether preconditions on procedures allow at least one path to be followed for the values checked in the preconditions. If a user requested precondition checking on the knowledge base shown in figure 4-1, the following warning messages would be issued:

```
SIDE was mentioned as a legal value for
DOOR-OPENING but the case:
   [ DOOR-OPENING  =  SIDE ]
is not considered in preconditions for
CAR-JAMB-RETURN.

CENTER was entered as a legal value for
DOOR-OPENING but the case:
   [ DOOR-OPENING  =  CENTER ]
is not considered in preconditions for
MAXIMUM-CAR-JAMB-RETURN.
```

It is not necessary for a user to address all precondition warnings. The cause of a warning is sometimes intentional. The warnings are given to remind the user that knowledge may have been left out inadvertently. Failure to address a problem with uniqueness will result in the problem-solver's selecting randomly between alternative paths. Failure to address a warning of a missing link will mean that no value will be assigned at that node on the identified cases.

Acyclicity in Dependency.

If each step in the path in assigning values that the problem-solver follows includes all relevant considerations, the resulting expert system will be a least-commitment system, in the sense that, like MOLGEN [Stefik 81a, Stefik 81b], it will not make a decision until all necessary information is available. In supplying procedures to propose design extensions, SALT users are asked to include all relevant considerations needed to determine a value. The most basic compilation strategy, the one SALT uses, tries to create a least-commitment system by compiling each procedure with data-driven control. A procedure to determine a value will be eligible for use when all values that contribute to it have been specified. If, however, there is a cycle in the dependency network, this eligibility requirement will never be met for the procedures on the loop. SALT detects loops in the dependency network and will guide the expert in setting up the knowledge base for propose-and-revise to get values for all nodes on the loop.

Figure 4-2 shows a section of the knowledge base after the following procedures have been added:

```
HOIST-CABLE-QUANTITY    =
    SUSPENDED-LOAD / HOIST-CABLE-STRENGTH

HOIST-CABLE-WEIGHT      =
    HOIST-CABLE-UNIT-WEIGHT *
    HOIST-CABLE-QUANTITY * HOIST-CABLE-LENGTH

CABLE-WEIGHT            =
    HOIST-CABLE-WEIGHT + COMP-CABLE-WEIGHT

SUSPENDED-LOAD          =
    CABLE-WEIGHT + CAR-WEIGHT
```

It is clear from this representation that the procedures cannot be applied in a strict forwardchain. When the problem-solver reaches the loop, it will become stuck, since it cannot have all the information needed to apply any procedure without having the results of applying the procedure itself. When SALT detects such a loop,[9] it delivers the following message:

---

[9]Sometimes loops are detected at this level of analysis that would never occur at runtime because of preconditions on the steps. For example, one set of procedures may say "If DOOR-OPENING = CENTER, A= 3 and B = A + C" and another "If DOOR-OPENING = SIDE, B = 3 and A = B + C." Based on potential dependency, A contributes to B and B contributes to A, but both of these contributions will not be active on a given run. If such a case were detected, SALT would ask the user if this in fact is the case; that is, if it is true that DOOR-OPENING will not be CENTER and SIDE at the same time. If that is the case, the loop is ignored.

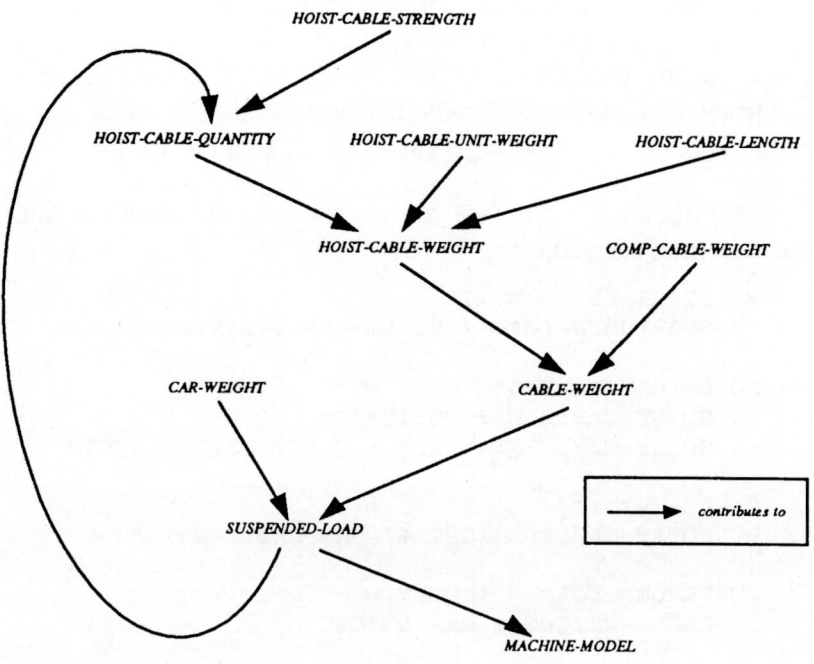

Figure 4-2: Knowledge Base Showing Cyclicity in Dependency

In the procedures I have been given, there is
a loop. The list below shows the values on the
loop; each value uses the one below it and the
last uses the first:

    1 HOIST-CABLE-QUANTITY
    2 SUSPENDED-LOAD
    3 CABLE-WEIGHT
    4 HOIST-CABLE-WEIGHT

In order to use any procedure, I need some way
of getting a first estimate for one of the
names on the list. Which one do you wish to
estimate?

In supplying a new procedure for proposing a value for one of the nodes on
the loop, SALT users are coached to provide a way of determining the most
preferred value given what the problem-solver could know at that point.

This means that users can use any information that predicts the quality and success of the choice as long as the new procedure does not create additional cyclicities in the dependency network. In this example, the user elected to estimate HOIST-CABLE-QUANTITY. The procedure uses CAR-WEIGHT to rule out values of HOIST-CABLE-QUANTITY the expert knows cannot be used and then selects the smallest HOIST-CABLE-QUANTITY that might be used since this incurs the lowest dollar cost.

```
1  Name:                 HOIST-CABLE-QUANTITY
2  Precondition:         NONE
3  Procedure:            DATABASE-LOOKUP
4  Table name:           HOIST-CABLE
5  Column with
      needed value:      QUANTITY
6  Parameter test:       MAX-LOAD > CAR-WEIGHT
7  Parameter test:       DONE
8  Ordering column:      QUANTITY
9  Optimal:              SMALLEST
10 Justification:        THIS ESTIMATE IS THE
                         SMALLEST HOIST CABLE
                         QUANTITY THAT CAN BE
                         USED ON ANY JOB.
```

SALT does not need to be told that this procedure to propose a design extension does not contain all of the information that should go into making the decision; that information was contained in the original procedure. Therefore, SALT proposes to change the role of the original procedure for HOIST-CABLE-QUANTITY as identifying a constraint that must be explicitly checked after the value for HOIST-CABLE-QUANTITY is proposed. SALT tells the user this and asks for the additional information required by that role, namely a specification of what kind of constraint the value is:

```
The procedure you originally gave for
HOIST-CABLE-QUANTITY will be used as a check
of the estimate. How does the value arrived at
by that procedure limit the estimate?
[ MINIMUM ]: <cr>
```

MINIMUM contained in brackets is SALT's suggested default, which in this example the user accepts by typing a carriage return (<cr>). The knowledge base, shown in figure 4-3, now contains a knowledge piece for a new constraint, MINIMUM-HOIST-CABLE-QUANTITY.

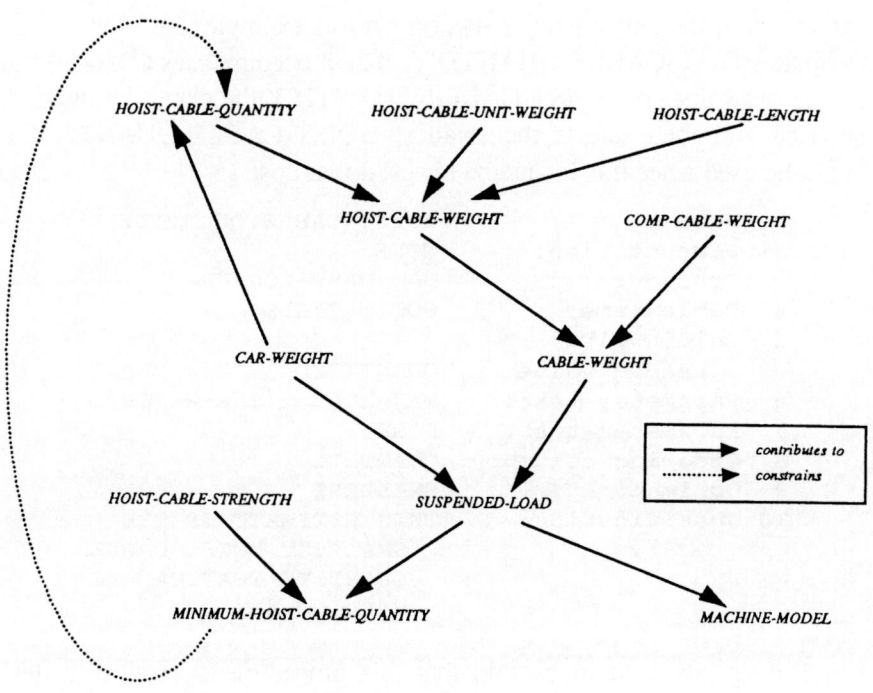

Figure 4-3: Knowledge Base Modified to Remove Cyclicity

Now that SALT has knowledge of a new constraint, checks for general completeness will require the user to supply a suggested fix the problem-solver can use if the constraint is violated. If the user now exits from the interview, SALT will issue the following request:

```
I have no knowledge of fixes for
MINIMUM-HOIST-CABLE-QUANTITY.  Do you wish to
specify any now? [ SAVE ]:
```

The completed screen for the proposed fix is shown next. According to this fix, the problem-solver should consider increasing HOIST-CABLE-QUANTITY by the same amount that it fell below the minimum. Figure 4-4 shows the knowledge base after the addition of this piece of fix knowledge.

```
1 Violated constraint:    MINIMUM-HOIST-CABLE-
                             QUANTITY
2 Value to change:        HOIST-CABLE-QUANTITY
3 Change type:            INCREASE
4 Step type:              SAME
5 Preference rating:      4
6 Reason for
     preference:          Changes minor
                             equipment sizing
```

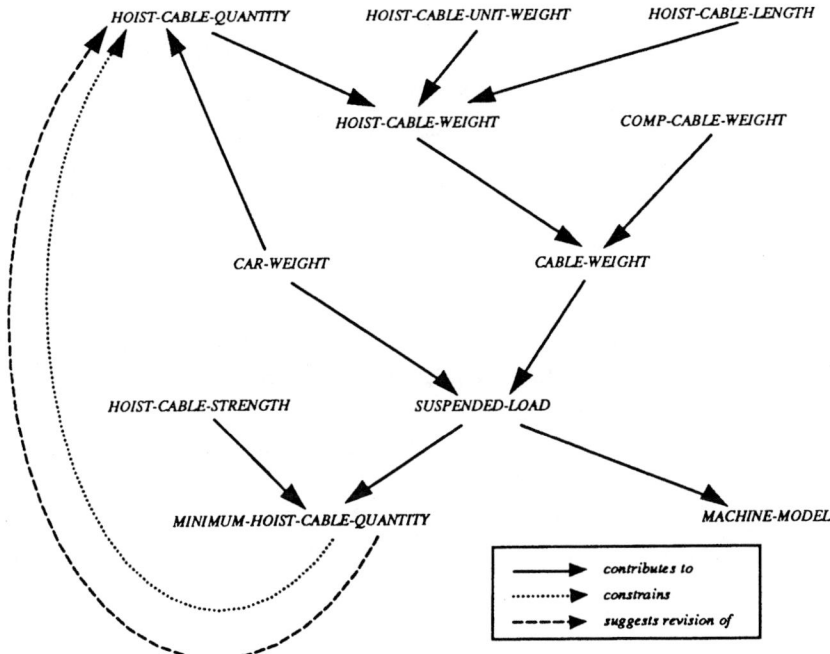

Figure 4-4: Knowledge Base Prepared for a Propose-and-Revise Treatment
of Cyclicity

One final piece of SALT advice is the prompt for a ceiling on the increase of
HOIST-CABLE-QUANTITY.

```
I have no knowledge of a procedure for
MAXIMUM-HOIST-CABLE-QUANTITY which could bound
the increase of HOIST-CABLE-QUANTITY called
for by a fix for MINIMUM-HOIST-CABLE-QUANTITY.
Would you like to specify one now? [ SAVE ]:
```

The knowledge base now calls for the problem-solver to start with the smallest quantity of hoist cables possible and to use that estimate to make other equipment selection and sizing decisions. It will then use the results of those decisions to calculate the smallest quantity of hoist cables that would be required using that estimate. If the estimate is equal to or greater than this calculated minimum, the current design is fine. If it is less, hoist cable quantity will be increased by the amount that it fell below the minimum, and the process is repeated using this new estimate for hoist cable quantity. If the calculated minimum ever exceeds the specified maximum, the problem-solver will stop increasing hoist cable quantity and reach a dead end; it will then declare that no solution is possible for this over-constrained job.

Filling in a knowledge piece for a fix for MINIMUM-HOIST-CABLE-QUANTITY creates a propose-and-revise treatment for the original cycle in the dependency network. Revision itself will explicitly introduce a cycle into the problem-solver's path through the network. Spotting how a cycle like increasing HOIST-CABLE-QUANTITY in the small knowledge base shown in figure 4-4 could go awry is fairly simple. The next section deals with problems with convergence caused by interactions among revisions for different constraints.

4.3.3. Convergence

In order for a propose-and-revise problem-solver to move toward a solution, it needs control knowledge identifying what revision is appropriate to make when a proposed design does not meet a constraint. In addition to trying to converge on a solution if one is possible, the problem-solver must also attempt to optimize the solution. In general, there is not enough knowledge contained in procedures to extend a design and identify constraints to figure out how to achieve this second goal. Domain knowledge is required to specify what revisions are feasible and which are preferable.

SALT starts acquiring a knowledge piece for a fix by asking the user to consider one constraint violation at a time. As with SALT's elicitation of procedures to propose a design extension, the idea is to get the user to express every local consideration that relates to the decision. Then SALT uses analyses of the knowledge base to figure out if this is a sound approach for the problem-solver to take; that is, does the knowledge base have enough knowledge for the problem-solver to converge on a solution? The basic pieces of fix knowledge -- what to change, how to change it and its relative preference -- can be used to predict convergence and could be used to help the user understand what additional knowledge might help guide the search. This section describes how the basic fix knowledge piece is acquired and the analyses that use the knowledge.

In many cases, deciding what parts of the proposed design to revise in order to remedy an individual constraint violation can be nontrivial. In principle, any value that contributes to the constraint or its constrained value might serve as potentially helpful revisions. If the dependency network is very dense, the user may have difficulty recalling all contributors. SALT helps by reading out the relevant part of the network on request as shown here:

```
Contributors to HOIST-CABLE-QUANTITY:

1    CAR-WEIGHT


Contributors to MINIMUM-HOIST-CABLE-QUANTITY

2    HOIST-CABLE-STRENGTH
3    SUSPENDED-LOAD
        CAR-WEIGHT
4       CABLE-WEIGHT
5         HOIST-CABLE-WEIGHT
6           HOIST-CABLE-UNIT-WEIGHT
7           HOIST-CABLE-QUANTITY
              CAR-WEIGHT
8           HOIST-CABLE-LENGTH
9         COMP-CABLE-WEIGHT

Give the number of the one you want to work on
(0 for new) [ 0 ]: 7
```

The level of contribution is represented by indentation. The leftmost values contribute directly to MINIMUM-HOIST-CABLE-QUANTITY. The values indented one level below SUSPENDED-LOAD contribute directly to it and so on. In this case, the user suggests a revision of HOIST-CABLE-QUANTITY as a potential remedy for a violation of MINIMUM-HOIST-CABLE-QUANTITY. The user might suggest a change to some other value as well, for example, to CAR-WEIGHT.

Given that procedures used in proposing a value for a design extension are the ones the expert would prefer in an under-constrained case, potential fixes must be less preferred than the value originally proposed. What the problem-solver needs from the expert is some indication of the relative preference of a change to one design parameter, for example, to HOIST-CABLE-QUANTITY, compared to some other change it might make, for example, to CAR-WEIGHT. SALT allows the domain expert to supply a list of reasons why revisions could be less preferred than the value originally proposed. (This list can be modified by the domain expert.) The list used for VT is shown below:

```
1.  Causes no problem
2.  Increases maintenance requirements
3.  Makes installation difficult
4.  Changes minor equipment sizing
5.  Violates minor equipment constraint
6.  Changes minor contract specifications
7.  Requires special part design
8.  Changes major equipment sizing
9.  Changes the building dimensions
10. Changes major contract specifications
11. Increases maintenance costs
12. Compromises system performance
```

These effects are ordered from most to least preferred. The reasons mainly reflect concerns for safety and customer satisfaction as well as dollar cost to the elevator company. Because of the dissimilarity in the nature of the negative effects, relative position on this scale is significant but absolute position is not. For example, an increase of HOIST-CABLE-QUANTITY changes minor equipment sizing. This cost can be measured directly in dollars. It is preferred to a decrease in CAR-WEIGHT, which changes major contract specifications. This is associated with a cost measured in less concrete terms of additional effort required for contract negotiations with a probable loss in customer satisfaction.

The information provided in a fix piece gives the problem-solver what it needs to start a revision. As a default strategy, the problem-solver might begin revision as soon as a single constraint violation is detected and start by trying the most preferred fix associated with that constraint, then the next less preferred fix, and so on until the constraint no longer registers as violated. If fixes for one constraint violation have no effect on other constraint violations, this strategy guarantees that the first solution found will be the most preferred. However, it is possible that remedies selected for one constraint violation may aggravate constraint violations that occur elsewhere in the network.

For example, figure 4-5 shows a section of a knowledge base containing antagonistic constraints. These two constraints are connected to the values they constrain by dotted-line arrows at the bottom. Above these is the portion of the dependency network that links the constraint-constrained pairs to their potential fix values. In order to make the figure more readable, not all contributors are shown. In addition, "suggests-revision-of" links have been omitted. Instead, suggested revisions in response to a violation of MAXIMUM-MACHINE-GROOVE-PRESSURE are surrounded by rectangles while suggested revisions for violations of MAXIMUM-TRACTION-RATIO are enclosed in ovals.

Based on the knowledge in this part of the knowledge base, SALT can detect the possibility of a problem-solving scenario involving thrashing such as this one: The problem-solver derives values for MACHINE-GROOVE-PRESSURE and MAXIMUM-MACHINE-GROOVE-PRESSURE and finds that MACHINE-GROOVE-PRESSURE is greater than the maximum. The problem-solver responds by decreasing CAR-SUPPLEMENT-WEIGHT. This decreases CAR-WEIGHT which in turn decreases SUSPENDED-LOAD. This decreases MACHINE-GROOVE-PRESSURE, the desired effect, but also increases TRACTION-RATIO. An increase in TRACTION-RATIO makes it more likely for it to exceed its maximum. A violation of MAXIMUM-TRACTION-RATIO calls for an increase of COMP-CABLE-UNIT-WEIGHT which in turn increases COMP-CABLE-WEIGHT, CABLE-WEIGHT and SUSPENDED-LOAD. Increasing SUSPENDED-LOAD increases MACHINE-GROOVE-PRESSURE making it more likely to violate MAXIMUM-MACHINE-GROOVE-PRESSURE. At this point, the scenario could repeat itself.

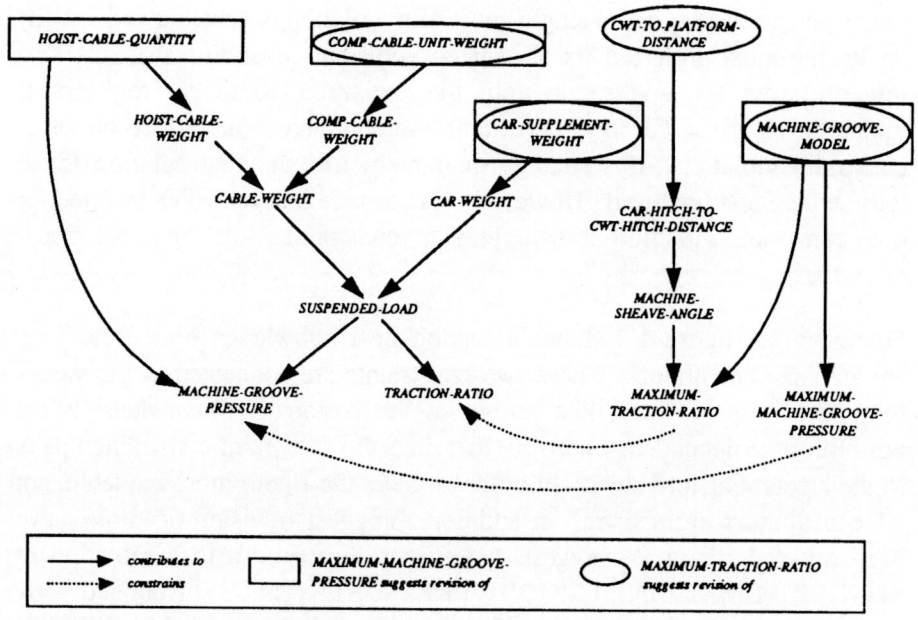

Figure 4-5: Knowledge Base with Antagonistic Constraints

In order to alert the user to the possibility of thrashing caused by interacting fixes, SALT produces a listing of chains of interacting fixes such as the one shown in the next example. Each chain originates from a constraint whose fixes make other constraints more likely to be violated. Fixes are shown in parentheses under the constraint they address and give the value to change and the direction of change. Embedded beneath each fix is a list of constraints that they might aggravate. If fixes for any of the constraints in this second tier make other constraints more likely to be violated, these are added to the chain and so on. Loops are flagged when a constraint recurs in the chain.

The following message represents SALT's report on the fix interaction in the knowledge base in figure 4-5:

```
*
MAXIMUM-TRACTION-RATIO --------------------|
*                                          |
   (CWT-TO-PLATFORM-DISTANCE, Down)        |
                                           |
   (COMP-CABLE-UNIT-WEIGHT, Up)            |
      MAXIMUM-MACHINE-GROOVE-PRESSURE      |
         (MACHINE-GROOVE-MODEL, Down)---*LOOP*-|
         (HOIST-CABLE-QUANTITY, Up)       |
         (COMP-CABLE-UNIT-WEIGHT, Down)-*LOOP*-|
         (CAR-SUPPLEMENT-WEIGHT, Down)--*LOOP*-|
                                           |
   (CAR-SUPPLEMENT-WEIGHT, Up)             |
      MAXIMUM-MACHINE-GROOVE-PRESSURE      |
         (MACHINE-GROOVE-MODEL, Down)---*LOOP*-|
         (HOIST-CABLE-QUANTITY, Up)       |
         (COMP-CABLE-UNIT-WEIGHT, Down)-*LOOP*-|
         (CAR-SUPPLEMENT-WEIGHT, Down)--*LOOP*-|
                                           |
   (MACHINE-GROOVE-MODEL, Up)              |
      MAXIMUM-MACHINE-GROOVE-PRESSURE      |
         (MACHINE-GROOVE-MODEL, Down)---*LOOP*-|
         (HOIST-CABLE-QUANTITY, Up)       |
         (COMP-CABLE-UNIT-WEIGHT, Down)-*LOOP*-|
         (CAR-SUPPLEMENT-WEIGHT, Down)--*LOOP*-|
```

This display indicates to the SALT user that three suggested fixes for a violation of MAXIMUM-TRACTION-RATIO make a violation of MAXIMUM-MACHINE-GROOVE-PRESSURE more likely, while three proposed fixes for a violation of MAXIMUM-MACHINE-GROOVE-PRESSURE also make a violation of MAXIMUM-TRACTION-RATIO more likely. Lack of embedding under the fix CWT-TO-PLATFORM-DISTANCE and lack of embedding or looping from the fix HOIST-CABLE-QUANTITY indicate that the proposed changes to these values do not hinder ability to satisfy constraints elsewhere in the network.

On the basis of SALT's identification of potential loops among revisions for different constraint violations, the SALT user can specify that these constraints should be treated as antagonistic. SALT stores knowledge about constraint antagonism with the knowledge to identify a constraint. The problem-solver then knows to deal with these constraints as a set in order to keep track of what combinations of revisions for this set it has tried. The additional information that SALT then asks for is very sparse. For every set of antagonistic constraints, SALT asks the user to order the constraints according to how important they are to fix. Then, if the problem-solver can't fix all constraint violations, it at least knows the best place to stop. This is a somewhat brute force approach to prevent thrashing. How to more effectively elicit domain knowledge about what tradeoffs should be made and how to compile the information to achieve tradeoffs efficiently is still an open research issue not addressed by this study.

4.4. Compiling the Knowledge Base

A functional knowledge base representation provides the key to how and when the knowledge should be used during problem solving. SALT proceduralizes the domain-specific knowledge base into rules written in OPS5 [Forgy 81]. These are combined with a problem-solving control shell, also written in OPS5. In providing SALT with this rule-generation capability, our goal was to demonstrate the feasibility of this approach. We wanted to show that a compiler could be written that could go from a declarative representation of the knowledge base that supports effective knowledge-elicitation strategies to a functional expert system.

An outline of the activities of the problem-solver during a run will make it easier to understand the SALT rule-generation procedure. The problem-solving control shell shifts control between the phases of problem solving and uses domain-specific knowledge to decide what other domain-specific knowledge to apply next. The flow of control of the problem-solving strategy as it makes use of the pieces of knowledge is as follows: The expert system starts with a forwardchaining phase in which procedures to propose design extensions and identify constraints are eligible to apply. The control in this constructive phase is data-driven; any step can be taken as soon as the information called for by the procedure associated with the step is available. As it extends the design, the expert system also builds a dependency network that, for each fact, records which other facts were used to derive it.

Demons are used to check for constraint violations; when a constraint and the value it constrains are known, they are compared. When the system detects a constraint violation, it selects alternatives in order of decreasing preference from a pre-enumerated set of possible fixes. Combinations of changes may also be tried, where fixes are selected to be combined in order of preference.

The problem-solver then investigates the success of the revision. The expert system first verifies that no constraints on the revised value itself are violated by the change. It then makes the proposed change and works through the implications according to its knowledge for proposing design extensions and identifying constraints. If the constraint is not identified as antagonistic to others, the problem-solver explores revision implications until it has enough knowledge to evaluate the originally violated constraint. If a proposed change violates the constraints, it is rejected, and another selection is made. This lookahead is limited because it only considers constraints on the revised value and the originally violated constraint. If the constraint is identified as belonging to an antagonistic set, lookahead is extended to include evaluation of the other constraints in the set. If others in the set are violated, the problem-solver will keep track of combinations of revisions for the set it has tried and not repeat any. The purpose of this lookahead is to limit the work done in exploring the implications of a proposed guess until the system has reason to believe it is a good guess.

Once a good guess has been identified, the system applies a truth-maintenance system; that is, it uses the dependency network constructed during the forwardchaining phase to identify and remove any values that might be inconsistent with the changed value. This includes removing the effects of previous fixes if the current change will cause a re-evaluation of the constraint that they remedied. The expert system then re-enters the data-driven constructive phase for extending the design with the new data.

To describe the generation of the domain-specific rules used in a problem-solving episode, we will detail how knowledge in each of the three main knowledge roles is proceduralized by SALT. We will describe the six main types of rules in roughly the order in which the rule type first appears during a run. The exact order of firing is defined by the control described in each rule.

For PROPOSE-A-DESIGN-EXTENSION, the knowledge the user provides consists of a description of a procedure. A completed screen of knowledge is shown next.

```
Knowledge Piece 1:

1 Name:              CAR-JAMB-RETURN
2 Precondition:      DOOR-OPENING = CENTER
3 Procedure:         CALCULATION
4 Formula:           [ PLATFORM-WIDTH -
                       OPENING-WIDTH ] / 2
5 Justification:     CENTER-OPENING DOORS LOOK
                     BEST WHEN CENTERED ON
                     THE PLATFORM.
```

An example of an English translation of an OPS5 rule for a "constructive" PROPOSE-A-DESIGN-EXTENSION is shown below:

```
Rule 1:

IF      values are available for DOOR-OPENING,
        PLATFORM-WIDTH and OPENING-WIDTH, and

        the value of DOOR-OPENING is CENTER, and

        there is no value for CAR-JAMB-RETURN,

THEN    Calculate the result of the formula
        [ PLATFORM-WIDTH - OPENING-WIDTH ] / 2.

        Assign the result of this calculation as
        the value of CAR-JAMB-RETURN.

        Leave a trace that DOOR-OPENING,
        PLATFORM-WIDTH and OPENING-WIDTH
        contributed to CAR-JAMB-RETURN.

        Leave a declarative representation of
        the details of the precondition and
        calculation and its justification.
```

Leaving a trace of contributions builds up the dependency network used by the truth-maintenance system and explanation. A declarative representation of the knowledge base is used by the explanation facility.

While the problem-solver is building a description of the proposed design, it is specifying constraints that apply to parts of the design. A completed screen from an interview is shown next.

```
Knowledge Piece 2:

1 Constrained value:    CAR-JAMB-RETURN
2 Constraint type:      MAXIMUM
3 Constraint name:      MAXIMUM-CAR-JAMB-RETURN
4 Precondition:         DOOR-OPENING = SIDE
5 Procedure:            CALCULATION
6 Formula:              PANEL-WIDTH *
                          STRINGER-QUANTITY
7 Justification:        THIS PROCEDURE IS TAKEN
                          FROM INSTALLATION
                          MANUAL I, P. 12b.
```

For every piece of IDENTIFY-A-CONSTRAINT knowledge, a rule is generated that both supplies a procedure for specifying a value for the constraint and provides the crucial identifying information to the problem-solver.

```
Rule 2:

IF     values are available for DOOR-OPENING,
       PANEL-WIDTH, and STRINGER-QUANTITY, and

       the value of DOOR-OPENING is SIDE, and

       there is no value for MAXIMUM-CAR-JAMB-
       RETURN,

THEN   Calculate the result of the formula
       PANEL-WIDTH * STRINGER-QUANTITY.

       Assign the result of this calculation
       as the value of MAXIMUM-CAR-JAMB-RETURN.

       Identify this value as a constraint of
       type MAXIMUM on CAR-JAMB-RETURN.

       Leave a trace that DOOR-OPENING,
       PANEL-WIDTH and STRINGER-QUANTITY
       contributed to MAXIMUM-CAR-JAMB-RETURN.

       Leave a declarative representation of
       the details of the precondition and
       calculation and its justification.
```

The third rule type generated uses knowledge in the PROPOSE-A-FIX role. This rule uses a collection of pieces of fix knowledge like the next one.

```
Knowledge Piece 3:

1 Violated constraint: MAXIMUM-CAR-JAMB-RETURN
2 Value to change:     STRINGER-QUANTITY
3 Change type:         INCREASE
4 Step type:           BY-STEP
5 Step size:           1
6 Preference rating:   4
7 Reason for
     preference:       Changes minor equipment
                       sizing
```

For every constraint that can be violated, a rule is generated that suggests all of the potential fixes to the problem-solver.

```
Rule 3:

IF    there has been a violation of
      MAXIMUM-CAR-JAMB-RETURN,

THEN  Try an INCREASE of STRINGER-QUANTITY
      BY-STEPs of 1.  This costs 4 because it
      CHANGES MINOR EQUIPMENT SIZING.

      Try a SUBSTITUTION of SIDE for
      DOOR-OPENING. This costs 8 because it
      CHANGES MAJOR EQUIPMENT SIZING.

      Try a DECREASE of PLATFORM-WIDTH
      BY-STEPs of 2 in.  This costs 10
      because it CHANGES MAJOR CONTRACT
      SPECIFICATIONS.
```

The final three rule types are used to explore the success of a proposed fix or fix combination in a lookahead context before extending the proposed design on the basis of the proposed revision. In order to do this, the problem-solver uses PROPOSE-A-DESIGN-EXTENSION knowledge to draw out the implications of the change suggested by the fix and IDENTIFY-A-CONSTRAINT knowledge to re-evaluate the value of the constraint under the change. In operation, the lookahead contexts function like the possible worlds in KEE [IntelliCorp 87]. What is significant is that a SALT analysis of the knowledge base is used to compile instructions that set up the entry conditions of the possible world and limit exploration within it.

The fourth rule type directs the problem-solver to propagate the change to just those values that contribute to either the violated constraint or its constrained value.   SALT conducts a search through the dependency network in order to generate the actions in these rules. The list of values to "FIND" essentially limits the lookahead by the generated expert system to the immediate constraint violation under repair.

> **Rule 4:**
>
> IF   MAXIMUM-CAR-JAMB-RETURN has been
> violated, and
>
>   the problem-solver has decided on which
> changes to try,
>
> THEN   FIND-CAR-JAMB-RETURN and
>
>   FIND-MAXIMUM-CAR-JAMB-RETURN.

This rule directs control to a set of lookahead rules that take the proposed fix changes and propagate the values through the relevant PROPOSE-A-DESIGN-EXTENSION and IDENTIFY-A-CONSTRAINT procedures. Rules used for propagating lookahead changes differ from the first two constructive groups with respect to the circumstances under which they fire. No additional kinds of knowledge need be collected from the user beyond the ones described so far.   SALT will generate Rule 5 using Knowledge Piece 1 and Rule 6 using Knowledge Piece 2.

> **Rule 5:**
>
> IF   the active command is to FIND-CAR-JAMB-
> RETURN, and
>
>   any of DOOR-OPENING, PLATFORM-WIDTH or
> OPENING-WIDTH has been revised, and
>
>   the most recently derived value (mrdv)
> of DOOR-OPENING is CENTER, and
>
>   there is no revised value for
> CAR-JAMB-RETURN,

THEN   Calculate the formula [mrdv of
        PLATFORM-WIDTH - mrdv of OPENING-WIDTH]
        / 2.

        Assign the result of this calculation as
        the value of CAR-JAMB-RETURN.

        Mark this value as revised.

Rule 6:

IF   the active command is to
        FIND-MAXIMUM-CAR-JAMB-RETURN, and

        any of DOOR-OPENING, PANEL-WIDTH or
        STRINGER-QUANTITY has been revised, and

        the mrdv of DOOR-OPENING is SIDE, and

        there is no revised value for
        MAXIMUM-CAR-JAMB-RETURN,

THEN   Calculate the result of the formula mrdv
        of PANEL-WIDTH * mrdv of STRINGER-
        QUANTITY.

        Assign the result of this calculation as
        the value of MAXIMUM-CAR-JAMB-RETURN.

        Identify this value as a constraint of
        type MAXIMUM on CAR-JAMB-RETURN.

        Mark this value as revised.

When asked to compile the knowledge base, SALT proceduralizes the
knowledge pieces into these six rule types. Roughly, for every piece of
PROPOSE-A-DESIGN-EXTENSION knowledge and every piece of
IDENTIFY-A-CONSTRAINT knowledge, SALT generates one constructive rule
and one lookahead rule. For each constraint, a rule for directing the
lookahead is generated if its fixes propose direct changes to values other
than the constraint or its constrained value. In that case, the change needs to
be propagated through intermediate values in order to re-evaluate

compliance with the constraint. The rule is generated also if the constraint is a member of an antagonistic set.

It is probably clear from this description of SALT's generation capability that the compiler allows the problem-solver to use the knowledge base in a form fairly directly reflecting that in which it was acquired from the domain expert. This has advantages in explaining the expert system's line of reasoning and supporting interactive problem solving with the user of the expert system. SALT-generated systems are similar in architecture to EL [Stallman 77], an expert system that performs analysis of electrical circuits, and to CONSTRAINTS [Sussman 80], a related shell. Both show similar advantages, but there are some important differences. CONSTRAINTS allows the user to direct backtracking in a way similar to SALT-generated systems when run in interactive mode or performing what-if explanation (see section 4.5). CONSTRAINTS, however, does not use domain knowledge of fix preferences to automatically revise decisions. EL's decision of where to backtrack to is based solely on the dependency network's record of what guesses contributed to the conflicting constraints. Furthermore, EL is committed to a search that will try all possible combinations of all guesses, although it prevents thrashing by keeping track of combinations already tried and not repeating them.

Even though there is a fairly close correspondence between acquired knowledge and compiled knowledge, the SALT compiler does process the knowledge to improve the efficiency of the problem-solver. For example, SALT identifies the relevant sphere of influence of a revision in addressing a particular constraint violation and contains the problem-solver in that sphere until quiescence is reached. SALT also identifies in advance where thrashing could take place and narrows its try-all-possible-combinations approach to just those areas where thrashing is likely to occur. Substantial work has been done to develop domain-independent algorithms for efficiently ordering value assignments in a class of constraint-satisfaction problems [Freuder 82, Dechter 85, Dechter 87]. In these problems, generation of any solution that satisfies all constraints constitutes success. This is generally not true in domains for which SALT is intended. In domains like VT's, domain-specific considerations such as cost and customer satisfaction affect preference for solutions. These domain-specific considerations directly affect the decision ordering compiled by SALT;

SALT-generated systems will try for plausible, preferred solutions first. However, the control derived from domain-specific constraints and preferences is sometimes under-determined; multiple decision orderings may be possible. Other shells and problem-solving systems that perform tasks like the ones SALT is intended to acquire employ efficiency strategies in ordering decisions to propose design extensions. These strategies are hand-coded by the designers of systems such as MPA [Herman 86] written in DSPL [Brown 87], OPIS [Smith 86] and PRIDE [Mittal 86]. There is a potential for SALT either to generate similar goal structures in compiling the knowledge base or to support a user in describing top-level strategies by supplying useful proposals and analyses [Marcus 88b].

4.5. Explaining Problem-Solving Decisions

A SALT-generated expert system explains its decisions using records of the problem-solver's use of the domain knowledge pieces. The dependency network built up for the truth-maintenance system can provide the foundation for a very useful explanation facility [Doyle 79, Sussman 80]. The network is augmented by the details of the contribution relation; for example, a description of an algebraic formula or the relation between values required by a precondition. In addition, the problem-solver records constraint violations encountered in developing a design and adjustments to the proposed design that it makes. Explanation pieces these individual actions together to describe the problem-solver's line of reasoning.

The explanation facility offers the user a choice among a small number of query types. The **how** query supplies a trace facility and can be thought of as asking the question "How did you determine the value of x?" Explanation looks for the node in the dependency network that recorded the problem-solver's assignment of a value to x. The dependency network provides pointers to the actual values that were used in determining the value in question.

If the user were to ask the expert system how the machine groove pressure was determined, it would respond with a message such as:

```
The MACHINE-GROOVE-PRESSURE (90.0307) =
SUSPENDED-LOAD (6752.3042) /
[ [ MACHINE-SHEAVE-DIAMETER (30) * 0.5 ] *
HOIST-CABLE-QUANTITY (5) ]
```

The machine groove pressure was determined by a calculation, which is displayed in terms of names of system values with the values assigned to them given in parentheses.

A **why** query would produce the justification for the procedure:

```
THIS PROCEDURE IS TAKEN FROM STANDARDS MANUAL
II, P. 13.
```

The **how** query also finds possible reasons why a design parameter or constraint in the system might have a value that the expert believes to be unexpected. A value changed in response to a constraint violation can look unusual to a user, particularly if the value changed was an input or if a low-preference fix was required. An example is shown below:

```
Explain:  how hoist cable quantity

The HOIST-CABLE-QUANTITY (4) was determined by
a fix:

The MAXIMUM-MACHINE-GROOVE-PRESSURE constraint
was violated. The MACHINE-GROOVE-PRESSURE was
149.5444, but had to be <= 119. The gap of
30.544 was eliminated by the following
action(s):
        Increasing HOIST-CABLE-QUANTITY from 3 to 4
```

Of course, it is a simplification of the process of extending a design to say that a value is determined by its direct contributors or "unusual" decisions that directly change its value. Everything upstream in the dependency network contributes to the proposed value. Explanation allows the user to step back through the network by repeated questioning and provides default queries after each answer to aid in this. Explanation also searches the upstream network on its own, and in answering any **how** query also reports any unusual decisions made about upstream contributors. In searching for reasons why x may be unusual, explanation will examine all of the items that contributed directly to x, as well as the items used in evaluating any preconditions on x's method. This examination is recursive, in that each of these contributors is also examined similarly, and so on until explanation "grounds out" on either inputs or constants.

The following is an example of an unusual explanation:

```
Explain: how supported load

The SUPPORTED-LOAD (1796.574) =
 MAX [
   SUPPORTED-LOAD-CAR-TOP-FULL (1759.741)
   SUPPORTED-LOAD-CAR-BOTTOM-FULL (1796.574)
   SUPPORTED-LOAD-CAR-TOP-EMPTY (1742.178)
   SUPPORTED-LOAD-CAR-BOTTOM-EMPTY (1696.701) ]

The value for SUPPORTED-LOAD may be unusual
because:
   The MACHINE-MODEL was changed due to a
   CHOICE-SET constraint on the HOIST-CABLE-
   DIAMETER.   (Depth = 3)
```

"Depth" indicates how far upstream the contributor is.

The explanation facility does more than examine past decisions; it also performs hypothetical reasoning to demonstrate the effects of alternative decisions the user suggests. The generated system offers two hypothetical queries: The user may ask why the value of a variable was not the one the user expected (**why not**). The user may also ask what would happen if the value of a variable were changed to something else (**what if**). For **why not** explanations, the system will report any changes to contributors to the variable that would have to be made in order to have the value come out to be the one expected. For **what if** explanations, the system displays how output values would differ from those for the original run.

Hypothetical explanations are relatively simple to generate, given SALT's knowledge-representation scheme. What the system must do in order to answer hypothetical queries is closely related to how it resolves constraint violations. The expected or desired value becomes a kind of dynamic constraint and the system applies "fixes" that would allow the currently proposed value to be the one the user proposes. SALT collects this explain-fix knowledge with a format like that used for regular problem-solving fixes. It then generates domain-specific rules similar to the two types of fix rules described earlier; the explanation facility uses many of the domain-independent fix control and truth-maintenance rules used for problem solving.

Two examples of **why not** responses to the query, "why not safety model B4?" are shown next.

```
The SAFETY-MODEL (currently B1) could be B4,
but that is less desirable because it has a
larger HEIGHT.  A SAFETY-MODEL of B1 was
selected because it met the following
constraints:

  Its MAX-SPEED (500) was at least as much as
    the SPEED (250).
  Its MAX-PLATFORM-WIDTH (93) was not less than
    the PLATFORM-WIDTH (70).
  Its MIN-PLATFORM-WIDTH (54) was not more than
    the PLATFORM-WIDTH (70).
```

In this case the user's expectation is possible, but not preferred. Here explanation locates and reports all constraints in the system that constrained the safety-model; this includes implicit constraints in database calls.

The following is the opposite case; the suggested value would be preferred, but is not possible, except perhaps by changing values upstream (for example, introducing nonpreferred values elsewhere).

```
A SAFETY-MODEL of B4 would have been used
  (instead of B6) if:
    The PLATFORM-WIDTH were 82 instead of 84.
```

What if can be thought of as asking the question "What would happen if I changed *x* to be a particular value?" In response to this query, the user is shown the effect the change would make on the design parameters.

```
Explain: what if safety model B4

The SAFETY-MODEL is currently B1.
If it were B4, the following changes would
occur:
```

```
NAME:                             ACTUAL: PROPOSED:

MACHINE-GROOVE-PRESSURE           114.118   155.563
TRACTION-RATIO                    1.80679   1.76682
CWT-OVERTRAVEL                    49.835    52.835
CAR-BUFFER-REACTION              26709.4   27652.4
CWT-STACK-PERCENT                84.1122   88.148
CWT-BUFFER-REACTION              19684     20627.0
CWT-PLATE-QUANTITY               90        94.3184
CWT-WEIGHT                       4921.0    5156.76
CAR-BUFFER-LOAD                  6677.35   6913.11
CAR-WEIGHT                       3677.35   3913.11
DEFLECTOR-SHEAVE-DIAMETER        25        20
CAR-BUFFER-BLOCKING-HEIGHT       18        17.125
HOIST-CABLE-MODEL                (4)-0.5   (3)-0.5
CAR-RUNBY                        6.125     6
SAFETY-MODEL                     B1        B4
```

Would you like to implement this [NO]:

As indicated in the last line of this example, **what if** explanation allows the user to change decisions that the system made after a run is completed. The generated system also allows users to affect decisions during a run when set in interactive mode. Whenever a revision is made, the system will pause after lookahead and provide an explanation like the one below:

The MAXIMUM-TRACTION-RATIO constraint has been violated. The TRACTION-RATIO is 1.806591, but must be <= 1.783873. The gap of 0.2272000E-01 can be eliminated by the following action(s):
Decreasing CWT-TO-PLATFORM-FRONT from 4.75 to 2.25
Upgrading COMP-CABLE-UNIT-WEIGHT from 0 to 0.5

Should this be implemented [YES]:

If the user does not wish to implement the fix, the system will accept suggestions from the user to use other fixes that it knows about or to use new fixes. These suggestions are accepted in the same structured language that SALT uses to acquire pieces of fix knowledge. The problem-solver will then attempt the fix and report the results for user acceptance before continuing.

SALT-generated expert systems automatically log records of user-overrides. The system maintainers can then read the log file and decide whether the knowledge base should be changed to reflect new priorities on old fixes or to add new fix knowledge. If the knowledge base should be changed, they can enter the appropriate knowledge through SALT. This provides SALT-generated systems with a kind of debug/apprentice function with a human "programmer" in the loop. As with true learning apprentice systems, such as LEAP [Mitchell 85] and LAS [Smith 85], the system's ability to provide this communication link is based on an explicit model of how domain knowledge is used by the problem-solver.

4.6. Evaluating Test Case Coverage

For tasks that require constructive problem-solving methods, it is not practical to enumerate all of the possible solutions. It is also not possible to collect a suite of test cases that will produce all possible solutions. Still, testing is required to help judge the validity of an expert system. Understanding the ways in which knowledge could be used by the problem-solver can help in analyzing a set of test cases to see whether important features of the system's problem-solving behavior are being exercised in that set.

For any expert system, the most important behavior to test is that which is hardest to predict based on the building blocks from which the system was created. It is the interaction of individual pieces that is hardest to understand. In SALT-generated systems, the most derivative behavior, the behavior that is furthest from the step-by-step procedures given by the expert, is what the system does when a constraint violation is detected. For this reason, any validity test should observe a violation of each constraint that the system knows about and should observe the implementation of every suggested kind of revision for each constraint violation. Since individual pieces of fix knowledge are collected with a local focus on a single constraint violation, an even bigger concern is seeing how revisions for different constraint violations interact. Therefore, a validity test should also observe every potential fix interaction.

SALT sifts through the knowledge base to generate a list of all constraints and a list of all suggested fixes for these constraints. SALT also uses the analysis described in section 3.3, on convergence, to generate a list of sets of potentially interacting fixes. These generated lists are used by a module of the domain-independent control shell to screen a set of test cases. As test cases are run, the module uses these lists to check off what has been tested. This module aims to make sure that within the test case set, each constraint is violated and each fix for each constraint violation is tried in at least one of the test cases. In addition, for each chain of interacting fixes, the test case checker notes whether within some single test case, all of the constraints on the chain are violated. The test-coverage evaluator can be used to identify test cases that don't check additional features off the list and can be used to describe particular features not covered by the test suite.

4.7. Understanding SALT's Scope

Understanding the roles that knowledge can play in problem solving helps map a task's problem-solving demands onto a problem-solving system. Creating knowledge-acquisition tools that are explicit about how knowledge is used in the systems they generate and testing their applicability to different problem-solving domains is a way to begin to understand how to make this mapping. To date, we have only two data points for SALT: custom designing elevator systems and flow-shop scheduling. SALT was developed in building VT, the expert elevator designer whose task was described briefly in section 2. All of the examples described so far have been based on the generation, maintenance and running of VT. SALT's second use was its extension to develop a prototype for a flow-shop scheduler [Stout 88]. The Scheduler's task is to route an order for an escalator or elevator system through departments for engineering, manufacturing and delivering it.

The keystone to the SALT approach is the knowledge role definition that SALT assumes in order to create its internal representation of the knowledge base. Based on our interviews with the domain expert, the scheduling domain knowledge does fit these roles. The initial schedule for an order is determined by PROPOSE-A-DESIGN-EXTENSION procedures that set up preferred (that is, routine) handling of an order. Knowledge that can IDENTIFY-A-CONSTRAINT includes such considerations as the limited order-handling capacity of each department and promised completion dates for various events for particular orders. In response to a constraint violation, such as a schedule's exceeding a department's capacity, the expert has PROPOSE-A-FIX knowledge that may recommend revising schedules of particular orders in ways that will repair the constraint violated.

The ability to identify a correspondence between SALT-assumed knowledge roles and the domain knowledge for the Scheduler meant that the knowledge could be represented using SALT's primitives: nodes representing value assignments connected by relations of contribution, constraint and revision. This representation is used by the functions described in this chapter. In order to provide some of these functions for the scheduling domain, SALT had to be extended. Analyses of how the knowledge pieces fit together, explanation, and evaluation of test case coverage remained pretty much intact. Areas where the original, VT version of SALT became cumbersome and/or inappropriate were in the details of the language used to acquire the knowledge pieces and the operation of the compiled system.

4.7.1. Acquiring Relevant Knowledge Pieces
Although the knowledge roles used to identify relevant knowledge pieces are appropriate for the Scheduler, a user interface based on these pieces for a scheduling application can be rather cumbersome. Some of the awkwardness has to do with how legal responses are defined for some of the prompts associated with each knowledge piece. For example, for VT all preconditions were easily expressed in terms of comparisons of values using >, >=, <, <=, =, <> (greater-than, greater-than-or-equal-to, less-than, less-than-or-equal-to, equal-to and not-equal-to). Giving SALT an understanding of ways of describing time relations would have made the system easier to use for scheduling. In order to state that a PROCEDURE should be used only if event A occurred before event B, the user would have to say something like "the value of the date at event A must be < the value of the date at event B." We made a brief exploration into providing a kind of editor to allow the user to define domain terms like "before" and "after" that could be used as shorthand for the longer expression. Even this doesn't go quite far enough. For example, it would have been even better if the expert could convey knowledge about the routine schedule by laying out a critical-path diagram with associated durations, which SALT could then translate into PROCEDUREs to extend a proposed design. An interface such as this would have been more in the spirit of OPAL [Musen 87] or KNACK (see

[Klinker 87b] or chapter 5 of this book). Creation of such customized interfaces is not necessary, but would definitely improve SALT's ease of use for the scheduling domain.

Aside from the awkwardness, there was a critical lack in the means for expressing preference in a piece of fix knowledge. For VT, the expert could supply a ranked list of negative effects that revisions could have on a proposed design that applied to virtually any design VT was likely to encounter. For the Scheduler, the expert could identify in advance of any run some properties of the value that might be revised. However, the identification of the exact value could only be made at run time on the basis of what orders were input and their effect on the overall schedule. For example, suppose a constraint on the capacity of the electrical engineering department was exceeded by assignment of an order to that department in week 29. A potential revision would be to reschedule one of the orders currently in EE in week 29 to be processed there in week 30 instead. Selection of which order to reschedule should be based on priority associated with the job and any contract deadlines it has to meet. SALT was extended to allow the expert to supply evaluation functions as part of a piece of fix knowledge. These functions would then be evaluated during run time to select the order to reschedule with minimal job priority and maximal slack time till deadline.

4.7.2. Compiling the Knowledge Base
Just as the knowledge that the problem-solver should use in handling revisions differed between the two domains, how the problem-solver performed revisions also differed somewhat. There were two major changes in going from VT to the Scheduler -- both affect the precompiled control shell and one required changes in the routines for compiling the knowledge base.

In order to make use of evaluation functions like the one described in section 4.7.1, the problem-solver should wait until it completes a proposed schedule for all orders it knows about before it responds to constraint violations. Completing a rough schedule gives it the information it needs to evaluate where best to reschedule. This contrasts with VT, which responds to constraint violations as soon as they are detected; that is, as soon as a constraint is identified and the constrained value is proposed.   This immediate attention helps prevent costly elaboration based on what might be a bad guess.

For the same reason, VT performs a limited lookahead. This helps identify a locally good guess before elaborating on it. The Scheduler completes a reschedule after every revision. This is because if the reschedule fails, information gained in completing the reschedule will be used in the evaluation to select another revision.

The added expressive capability that allows users to supply evaluation functions for indicating what value to revise created a version of SALT that is useful for both VT and the Scheduler. Where there are mutually exclusive variations in SALT's assumed problem-solving shell and compiler, such as when to do constraint checking, we are currently maintaining a unified SALT by offering a user-operated switch. What we hope to do is develop SALT's knowledge of when to apply or recommend such switches.

4.8. Conclusion

SALT has proved quite useful in generating and maintaining VT. VT's first SALT-acquired knowledge base was entered by an elevator engineer with moderate exposure to AI. VT was handed over to the organization that now uses it in April, 1985, with 1,300 SALT-generated rules. Since then, SALT has been used regularly by elevator-engineering personnel to debug, refine and add to the knowledge base. By summer of 1986, VT had 3,062 total rules; 2,130 of these were generated by SALT. SALT essentially rides herd on the system development. This makes the approach we took in developing SALT a very useful methodology for large knowledge-based systems.

SALT makes a strong commitment to the problem-solving strategy that will be used for the task it will acquire. This allows SALT to represent domain-specific knowledge according to the role it will play in finding a solution for any task that can use this basic strategy. This commitment gives it considerable power in identifying relevant domain knowledge, in detecting weaknesses in the knowledge base in order to guide its interrogation of the domain expert, in generating an expert system that performs the task and explains its line of reasoning, and in analyzing test case coverage. An exploration into understanding SALT's applicability highlighted a number of areas in which SALT could be strengthened.

SALT is weak in its ability to elicit knowledge to handle tradeoffs among alternatives; this is true both for selecting an original value to extend a proposed design and for selecting a revision to the proposal. Currently a user can enter such knowledge. For example, some design tasks may require selection of parts involving tradeoffs among attributes of the parts. A user of the current SALT could enter a procedure for proposing candidates, a procedure for calculating a function for evaluating how well each fits the design requirements, and yet another procedure for using the evaluation function to make the selection. However, entering this knowledge requires quite a bit of AI sophistication. We need to improve SALT's ability to acquire tradeoff knowledge.

For any SALT-stored knowledge base, represented appropriately for propose-and-revise, there are some options in how to use the knowledge. Although SALT has created a useful expert system, SALT might better exploit the representation to improve the efficiency of the systems it creates. For example, efficiency can become a factor in deciding what part of the dependency network the problem-solver should work on first or when it should do constraint-checking. In using SALT in different domains, we hope to understand how to automate compilation strategies that can respond to such efficiency issues using its analysis of this knowledge representation framework.

Acknowledgements

John McDermott and Jeff Stout were particularly important contributors to the work reported here. I would like to thank Gilbert Caplain, Michael Gillanov, Charles Pepe, Emile Servan-Schreiber, Paul Sitruk, Junpu Wang, and Tianran Wang who also contributed to the SALT project. I am indebted to Robert Roche, first domain expert for VT and first user of SALT, for feedback and suggestions that were incorporated into the SALT design. Many of the ideas contained in this paper were presented in a discussion group attended by Larry Eshelman, Gary Kahn, Tom Mitchell, and Allen Newell, and I am very grateful for their input. I am also indebted to B. Chandrasekaran, Georg Klinker, Steve Smoliar and Bill Swartout for their very useful comments on an earlier draft of this paper. I would like to thank Linda Green for her comments on the paper and her preparation of the figures.

5. KNACK: Sample-Driven Knowledge Acquisition for Reporting Systems

Georg Klinker

Abstract

KNACK is a specialized knowledge-acquisition tool that generates expert systems for reporting tasks. The tool derives its power from exploiting the presupposed acquire-and-present problem-solving method used by the expert systems it generates. The method incrementally acquires relevant information and produces a report. It can also be combined with other problem-solving methods. An important goal in the development of KNACK is to create a tool that elicits knowledge from domain experts without requiring knowledge-engineering skills on their part. To reach that goal, KNACK's approach to knowledge acquisition uses existing AI techniques to derive a general description of how to acquire and present information from a specific sample description.

5.1. Introduction

Existing expert systems have proved that AI techniques can be used to solve a variety of knowledge-intensive problems. But expert systems are time-consuming to develop and difficult to maintain. A key issue in developing any expert system is how to update its large and growing knowledge base. It has been shown that a large knowledge base can be kept maintainable by organizing it according to the roles that knowledge plays [Chandrasekaran 83, Clancey 83, Neches 84]. Based on this realization, a variety of knowledge-acquisition tools have been produced during the past years to overcome development and maintenance problems.

Existing knowledge-acquisition tools focus on different aspects of the knowledge-engineering task. For example, KREME [Abrett 87] provides an environment for editing large knowledge bases. SEAR [van de Brug 86], AQUINAS [Boose 87], KRITON [Diederich 87], and TDE [Kahn 87d] are examples of systems that integrate a variety of methodologies and tools for the development of expert systems into a workbench for a knowledge engineer. Other knowledge-acquisition tools try to automate the knowledge-acquisition process. An automated knowledge-acquisition tool typically interacts with domain experts directly. No knowledge engineer is necessary to translate the expert's knowledge into production rules. An automated knowledge-acquisition tool further organizes the knowledge it acquires and generates an expert system. The domain expert can also use the tool to test and maintain the program it generates. The critical feature of such a tool is that a domain expert can use it without having to know about programming in general and AI techniques in specific.

One approach to automated knowledge acquisition is general tools. CYC [Lenat 86] and SOAR [Laird 87] are two examples that advocate general problem-solving methods. In contrast to this approach are specialized tools. Specialized tools derive their power by presupposing the problem-solving method of the expert systems they generate [McDermott 86, Gruber 87a]. A problem-solving method establishes and controls the sequences of actions required to perform a task. This control knowledge dynamically defines the order in which subtasks have to be solved to perform the overall task. It also defines the kind of domain-specific knowledge that is applicable within each step, thereby making explicit the different roles knowledge plays. The granularity of the problem-solving method is determined by the requirement that the knowledge represented by a knowledge role be applied without further control knowledge; that is, the time at which that knowledge will be brought to bear is determined by its role. Thus, the problem-solving method helps to identify and classify the domain knowledge. It makes the different roles knowledge plays in a task explicit and suggests ways to organize the knowledge base according to the knowledge roles. It further defines the way knowledge interacts during problem solving.

A useful distinction between automated, specialized knowledge-acquisition tools is whether they help to create expert systems that select or that construct a solution [Clancey 84]. TEIRESIAS [Davis 82], ETS [Boose 84], MORE [Kahn 85b], and MOLE [Eshelman 87a] generate expert systems that select a solution from a pre-enumerated set of candidates. SALT [Marcus 87] is an example of a knowledge-acquisition tool for systems that construct a solution compatible with a set of constraints. MOLE and SALT are described in chapters 3 and 4. Each program that MOLE creates uses the cover-and-differentiate problem-solving method for selection tasks. SALT presupposes the propose-and-revise method for constructive tasks.

This chapter describes KNACK [Klinker 87b], an automated, specialized knowledge-acquisition tool that can be used by domain experts to create expert systems that assist with reporting tasks. Reporting tasks involve collecting data and presenting them in the form of a document to communicate facts, ideas, and decisions. Writing proposals and progress reports, documenting design decisions, and defining requirements for a product are only a few examples. Producing a good report is a difficult task. Some of the problems involved are gathering the right data efficiently and presenting the information intelligently. Examples of KNACK-generated reporting systems are expert systems to produce technical documents for the design of electromechanical systems; an expert system to report on the requirements for a planned software system, including an executive summary; and expert systems to document the progress of a project, including a proposal writer and a progress report writer.

A KNACK-generated expert system uses the acquire-and-present problem-solving method. The expert system identifies relevant pieces of information for writing a report. It determines procedures that can be used to gather the relevant information and selects one piece of information to acquire next, together with an appropriate strategy. The expert system applies the selected strategy and integrates the acquired information with the existing information. This acquisition process goes on until the user quits or no additional information is needed. The system produces a report to document the acquired information.

A variety of tasks other than report generation per se require a considerable amount of information gathering. Improving the design of an electromechanical system to meet some external requirements and assisting with the definition of requirements for a planned software system are two examples. The simple acquire-and-present problem-solving method can be used to gather information for those tasks and provide it to other problem-solving methods. For example, the information can be viewed as complementary to SALT's propose-and-revise systems. The acquire-and-present problem-solving method serves as a front end to acquire information and as a back end to present results. Combining KNACK's and SALT's methods broadens the scope of propose-and-revise systems to include constructive tasks that need a considerable amount of information to start with or require a report to be produced.

When KNACK generates an expert system, it presupposes and exploits the associated problem-solving method. Explicit knowledge about an assumed problem-solving method and its associated knowledge roles defines what kinds of knowledge the expert must provide and when and how to apply the provided knowledge. This understanding of method and knowledge roles can be used during knowledge acquisition to guide a domain expert in defining, analyzing, and testing a knowledge base.

However, using only the framework provided by the problem-solving method, the expert may be required to enter knowledge in a structured format that is unfamiliar to him. This imposes a learning burden on the expert. An important goal in the development of KNACK is to acquire knowledge from domain experts without requiring knowledge-engineering skills on their part. To achieve that goal, KNACK exploits a domain model and takes a sample-driven approach to acquiring knowledge.

Like OPAL [Musen 87] and STUDENT [Gale 87], KNACK exploits a domain model during knowledge acquisition. The domain model contains a structural and functional definition of a particular domain. It describes the concepts experts use and their interdependencies. KNACK uses the domain model to elicit knowledge in a format familiar to the expert and to develop expectations about the knowledge the expert might provide. KNACK differs from OPAL and STUDENT in that the domain model can be customized for a particular domain and no knowledge-engineering expertise is required to build a domain model.

KNACK uses a sample-driven approach to acquiring knowledge. It expects the expert to communicate a portion of his knowledge as a sample report and a domain model. The sample report is a document that exemplifies the report a KNACK-generated expert system is expected to produce. The domain model describes the concepts and the terms used in the sample report. During knowledge acquisition, KNACK divides the sample report into small fragments and integrates each fragment with the domain model; that is, KNACK replaces specific terms in a fragment with the concepts they represent. To instantiate the identified variables for different applications, KNACK asks the expert for sample strategies and generalizes them. It displays several different instantiations of the generalized fragments and strategies, and the expert edits any of these that need editing. The corrections motivate and guide KNACK in refining the knowledge base. This process of abstraction and completion results in a knowledge base containing a large collection of generalized report fragments and strategies more broadly applicable than the sample report and sample strategies. Finally, KNACK examines the acquired knowledge for incompleteness and inconsistency.

Figure 5-1 presents an overview of the interdependencies between KNACK and its generated expert systems adapted from Dietterich's simple model of learning systems [Dietterich 82].   A domain expert uses KNACK to generate or update a knowledge base.   The presupposed problem-solving method operates on the knowledge base, acquires additional information from a user, and produces a report. The knowledge base plus the problem-solving method form an expert system.   The performance of the expert system provides feedback to the domain expert.

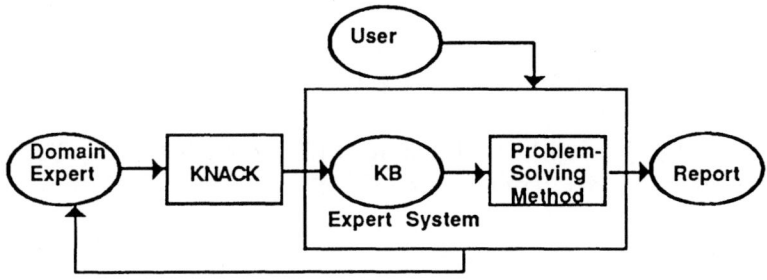

Figure 5-1: Overview

The following sections describe this process in detail.   Section 5.2 introduces the KNACK-generated expert systems and explains their problem-solving method and the knowledge roles KNACK assumes. Section 5.3 discusses the approach KNACK takes to acquiring knowledge and presents a sample interaction with KNACK.   Section 5.4 shows how KNACK detects cues that its knowledge base might be incomplete or inconsistent.   The knowledge base KNACK generates as a result of a knowledge-acquisition session is described in section 5.5.   Section 5.6 focuses on how KNACK's method can be combined with other problem-solving methods. Section 5.7 introduces the systems built with KNACK so far. A summary and a discussion of limitations in section 5.8 concludes this paper.

5.2. The Presupposed Problem-Solving Method and Its Knowledge Roles

Each of the reporting systems produced by KNACK is called a WRINGER. A WRINGER operates on a KNACK-generated knowledge base using the acquire-and-present problem-solving method. The method starts out by identifying pieces of information that are relevant to the task at hand. To determine the appropriate information, a WRINGER selects necessary information in a data-driven manner; the decision to gather a particular piece of information is based on previously gathered information. But it is often the case that more than one piece of information can be gathered at any time. Therefore, the order in which the pieces of information are acquired may be important; the user might feel more natural providing information in a certain order. In deciding which piece of information to gather next, the WRINGER tries to reduce the burden placed on the user in providing information. It follows the outline of the report it is expected to produce. That skeletal report organizes the relevant information around related topics. In following the outline of the report, the WRINGER collects related information in a coherent manner.

After determining which piece of information to acquire, the WRINGER's problem-solving method selects and applies a strategy to gather that piece of information. To take into account the different sources of information available, the WRINGER has several ways to elicit information from the user or to infer it. For example, it elicits information from the user by asking a question; interpreting a graphical design description (for example, a drawing of a system's components); asking the user to fill in the slots of a table, diagram, or form; or asking the user to choose among the items in a menu. The WRINGER infers additional information based on previously gathered information. For example, it fills in gaps by directly applying domain-specific knowledge, computing numeric values, or referring to a database. Often more than one way exists to gather a piece of information. When this is the case, the WRINGER selects a strategy for gathering it. It prefers inference strategies that avoid asking the user unnecessary questions. Once a strategy is selected, the WRINGER applies the strategy, checks the provided pieces of information for synonyms, and updates the design description.

After that, the WRINGER identifies the next piece of information to gather. This iterative process ends when all of the required information is available or the user quits. The WRINGER now presents the gathered information in the form of a report. It uses the report outline to determine the report structure, selects report fragments that can be instantiated with the acquired information into the skeletal report, instantiates the selected report fragments with the acquired information, and generates the report.

For the rest of this chapter, the Design Parameters Report WRINGER (DPR WRINGER) will be used as an example to illustrate the WRINGERs and KNACK. The DPR WRINGER is a member of the Data Item Description WRINGER family. Its domain is nuclear hardening. Nuclear hardening requires the use of specific engineering-design practices to increase the resistance of an electromechanical system to the environmental effects generated by the detonation of a nuclear weapon. Designers of electromechanical systems usually have little or no knowledge about the specialized analytical methods and engineering practices of the hardening domain. The purpose of the DPR WRINGER is to assist a designer in presenting a given design of an electromechanical system in such a way that hardening experts have readily available the information they need to evaluate the system from a hardening perspective.

The WRINGER first gathers information about the ElectroMagnetic Pulse (EMP) environment, such as rise time and electrical field. It then asks for the geometry and a description of the major components of the system, such as cables, equipment, and protective measures. Values for system and environment properties are determined through analyses that differ depending on the level of description of the system; for example, whether it is described at the level of normal operating environment, screen analysis, or resistor analysis. The poorer the description is, the more conservative are underlying assumptions. The level of description can be refined to the level of individual semiconductors in order to carry out a more precise analysis and compute more accurate values, such as the bulk resistance of a diode or the transfer impedance of a cable. The WRINGER's output is a report about the design of the system.

The acquire-and-present problem-solving method operates on a KNACK-generated knowledge base. The knowledge base is organized according to the roles knowledge can play in the reporting task:

- IDENTIFY-RELEVANT-INFORMATION.

- DEFINE-A-STRATEGY to acquire information.

- INTEGRATE-INFORMATION with existing information.

- DEFINE-THE-SKELETAL-REPORT to determine the report structure.

- DEFINE-A-FRAGMENT to present the information.

The remainder of this section describes how the different kinds of knowledge are seen by a WRINGER user. Examples of the actual knowledge pieces are shown in section 5.5.

IDENTIFY-RELEVANT-INFORMATION knowledge is used to identify pieces of information relevant to each part of the report. This role organizes the required information around related topics and is used by the WRINGER to select the piece of information to gather next. For example, the DPR WRINGER acquires a general system description before asking about details of every system component.

The DEFINE-A-STRATEGY role describes the different ways to gather a piece of information. Relying on previously elicited information and other predefined knowledge, it further defines the circumstances in which these techniques can be applied. One strategy available to a WRINGER is the question strategy. The following example gives a flavor of the kind of questions the DPR WRINGER asks.[10]

> **What enclosures are part of the COMMUNICATIONS UNIT system?** : <u>**S-280C, Metal Box**</u>
>
> **Please list the apertures of the S-280C enclosure.** : <u>**window, cable entry panel**</u>

---

[10]In this and the following examples, the WRINGER's and KNACK's prompts and messages appear in boldface, the user's responses in underlined boldface. A word in brackets at the end of a WRINGER's or KNACK's prompts is the default response. The user may reply with the default by hitting return: <u><cr></u>.

DEFINE-A-STRATEGY knowledge further includes information about the validity of newly gathered information. This includes finding out whether input provided by the user is obviously wrong or merely implausible. In the first case, an answer might be outside of a predefined numeric range or it might not be a member of a predefined complete set of possible answers. In the second case, an answer might be flagged as questionable because it is not a member of a predefined incomplete set of possible answers. For example:

```
Please list the cables of the COMMUNICATIONS
UNIT system? : audio cable, power cable

I am not familiar with the term AUDIO CABLE.
Some of the following terms are expected
answers:
    SIGNAL CABLE,
    POWER CABLE
Please confirm or revise your answer.
[ AUDIO CABLE ]: signal cable
```

INTEGRATE-INFORMATION knowledge includes instructions about what to do with the elicited information. The user's answer in the above example will be stored in a slot representing the name of a cable.

The DEFINE-THE-SKELETAL-REPORT role includes knowledge about which chapters, sections, and subsections are part of the report the WRINGER is expected to produce; their order; and how to appropriately place report fragments within the report. Using this information, the WRINGER determines the appropriate chapters, sections, and subsections; selects the fragments describing the particular application; inserts them into the skeleton; and assembles the report. The example below shows a part of the table of contents for the DPR WRINGER.

```
1. Evaluation of EMP Hardness
    1.1. Summary of the System Description
    1.2. Shielding Requirements for the
         Enclosures
         1.2.1. Diffusion through the Skin of
                the Enclosure
         1.2.2. EMP Leakage through the
                Apertures
    . . .
```

DEFINE-A-FRAGMENT knowledge describes a small possible piece of an actual report. This includes the text to be printed in a report and the variables containing the information specific to the particular application that is the subject of the WRINGER report. It also incorporates the gathered information into the report. A report part produced by the DPR WRINGER is shown in section 5.3.1.

5.3. Acquiring Knowledge

An important goal in the development of KNACK is to create a tool that acquires knowledge from domain experts without requiring knowledge-engineering skills on their part. To reach that goal, KNACK's approach to knowledge acquisition uses existing AI techniques to derive a general description of how to acquire and present information from a specific sample description. It uses a process of abstraction and extension. Figure 5-2 summarizes KNACK's approach to knowledge acquisition.

KNACK requires a sample report as an initial input. The sample report is a document that exemplifies the report a WRINGER is expected to produce. KNACK also asks the expert to provide a preliminary model of a particular reporting domain and uses general knowledge about reporting tasks to elicit the model. That knowledge is incorporated into KNACK. During knowledge acquisition, KNACK refines the preliminary domain model into a detailed structural and functional model of the domain. The domain model describes the concepts, their interdependencies, and the vocabulary the expert uses in the sample report.

Once the sample report is entered and an initial domain model is defined, KNACK divides the sample report into small fragments and substitutes variables for constants in each fragment by integrating it with the domain model in successive interactions with the expert. It replaces specific terms in a fragment with the concepts they represent. This integration process generalizes the sample report, making it applicable to different tasks. To demonstrate its understanding of the sample report and to predict and exemplify the performance an expert can expect from the WRINGER, KNACK instantiates the generalized report with known concept representatives taken from the domain model. It displays several differently instantiated examples for each generalized report fragment. The expert edits

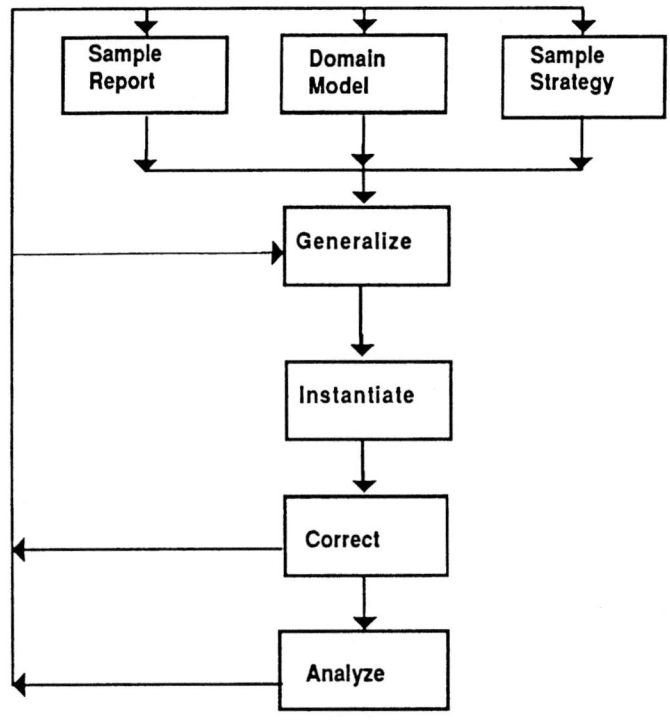

Figure 5-2: KNACK's Approach

any examples that make implausible statements. KNACK uses this feedback as additional knowledge to correct its generalizations and refine the domain model.

Once the expert accepts KNACK's understanding of the sample report, KNACK elicits knowledge about how to customize the generalized sample report for a particular application. The expert defines strategies that a WRINGER will use to acquire values instantiating the concepts in the generalized fragments. Experts define strategies in the same way that report fragments are defined -- by typing in samples. Strategies can be questions, formulas, inferences, and other forms. KNACK generalizes the strategies and displays some example instantiations of them for review and correction by the expert.

KNACK's knowledge-acquisition approach results in a knowledge base the generated WRINGER can use for a range of applications. However, the sample report covers only one simple document and almost certainly lacks some important concepts needed for a broader range of tasks. For this reason, KNACK searches the knowledge base for report fragments or strategies that indicate gaps or conflicts with its domain model. If a possible flaw is found, KNACK asks the expert to correct the report, the strategies, or the domain model.

The following detailed description of KNACK's knowledge-acquisition approach is organized around an example of an actual KNACK case, the creation of the DPR WRINGER. It leads through the process of typing in a small part of a sample report, acquiring a partial domain model, generalizing the part of the sample report, and defining strategies. The analysis of the acquired knowledge is demonstrated in section 5.4. In the interest of brevity, the excerpts used as examples are only a small fraction of the full KNACK case.

KNACK starts out by displaying the top-level menu.[11]

```
model                 : acquire domain model
report                : acquire report
generalize-report     : generalize report
strategy              : acquire strategies
generalize-strategy   : generalize strategies
analyze               : analyze knowledge base
exit                  : exit KNACK
```

KNACK's sample-driven approach to acquiring knowledge determines the expert's choices on the top level: define or update the domain model, enter a sample report or generalize it, enter strategies or generalize them, or analyze the knowledge base for incompleteness or inconsistency. Once the sample report is typed in and an initial domain model is defined, the expert can choose any of these functions. Our sample interaction starts with typing in the sample report.

---

[11]Menu selections are made with a mouse and are indicated in the examples by underlining.

5.3.1. Acquiring the Sample Report

KNACK requires a sample report as an initial input. The sample report exemplifies the document the expert intends the WRINGER to produce. It may be written specially for this purpose by a domain expert or group of experts, or selected from existing reports. It is a familiar and convenient medium for the expert to express his knowledge in.

The selection of the REPORT option in the top-level menu leads to the report menu shown below.

```
next      : display next fragment
previous  : display previous fragment
edit      : edit current fragment
insert    : insert fragments
delete    : delete current fragment
quit      : quit sample report editor
```

The selection determines the top-level features of a simple text editor that can be used to define, update, or leaf through the sample report. The INSERT function allows any person familiar with text editors to input the sample report.

```
1. Evaluation of EMP Hardness

1.1. Summary of the System Description

The system Communications Unit is designed to
resist to EMP threat.  It consists of a
Computer, a Modem, a Radio, and a Motor
Generator.  Power is supplied from the Motor
Generator to the Computer, Modem, and Radio by
the Power Cable.

The Computer, Modem, and Radio are protected
by a S-280C enclosure.  The Motor Generator is
protected by a Metal Box enclosure.

The S-280C enclosure has the following
apertures: Window and Cable Entry Panel.  The
Metal Box enclosure has the following
apertures: Cable Entry Panel.

1.2. Shielding Requirements for the S-280C
       Enclosure

1.2.1. Diffusion through the Skin of the
       Enclosure
```

> The S-280C enclosure is made of aluminum and
> is 30 mils thick. Aluminum has a
> relative-conductivity of 0.15 mhos/m. A plate
> of aluminum must be at least 20 mils thick to
> reduce the diffusion factor to an negligible
> level. Therefore, the diffusion factor can be
> neglected.

KNACK divides the report into fragments corresponding to paragraphs. The above example represents eight report fragments.

5.3.2. Acquiring the Domain Model

The sample report describes a particular application in the terms familiar to the expert. To generalize the sample report, making it applicable to other applications, KNACK needs a model of the particular domain. The domain model contains a detailed structural and functional description of the task at hand. The structural part of the domain model describes a taxonomy of the concepts, vocabulary, and terms the expert uses in the sample report and the interdependencies between concepts. The functional part of the domain model describes procedures for determining and propagating relevant parameters. Thus, the model customizes KNACK for a particular domain.

In addition to generalizing the sample report, KNACK uses the concepts and terms described in the domain model to acquire knowledge in a format familiar to the expert. The model further represents a preview of the knowledge base the expert wants to create. KNACK uses it to develop expectations about the knowledge the expert might provide. Based on these expectations, KNACK checks the expert's input, generates knowledge pieces, and analyzes the resulting knowledge base. The expert then refines KNACK's expectations (as described in sections 5.3.4, 5.3.5, and 5.4) and, thus, refines the domain model.

To define a preliminary domain model, the expert uses a graphical interface. That domain-model editor allows the user to define concepts, their interdependencies, concept characteristics, and concept representatives. KNACK provides a predefined set of concept classes (for example, top-level concept, component, connection) and interrelations (for example, comprises, connected with) to choose from. This represents KNACK's incorporated, general understanding of the reporting task. That understanding describes the knowledge common to a range of reporting domains on a high level of abstraction.

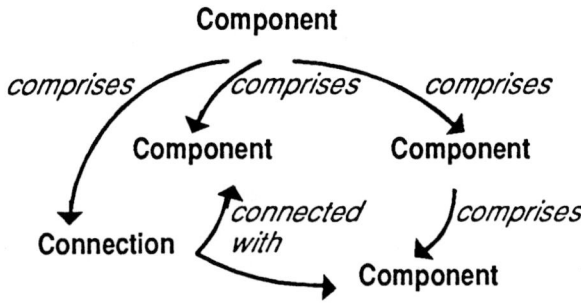

Figure 5-3: Abstract Domain Model

The example in figure 5-3 gives a flavor of the knowledge applicable to a range of reporting tasks. The nodes are concepts, and the links between the nodes encode structural knowledge. For example, a component comprises a set of components interrelated by connections. To define a familiar vocabulary, the expert chooses among the predefined concepts and interrelations and labels them. This customizes KNACK's abstract knowledge into a preliminary model of a particular domain. The example in figure 5-4 defines a part of the preliminary model needed to generalize the sample report above.

Once the concepts are known, the expert defines characteristics and representatives for each concept. KNACK elicits this knowledge by asking the expert to fill in the slots of a table. Table 5-1 defines the characteristics and the representatives of the concept ENCLOSURE.

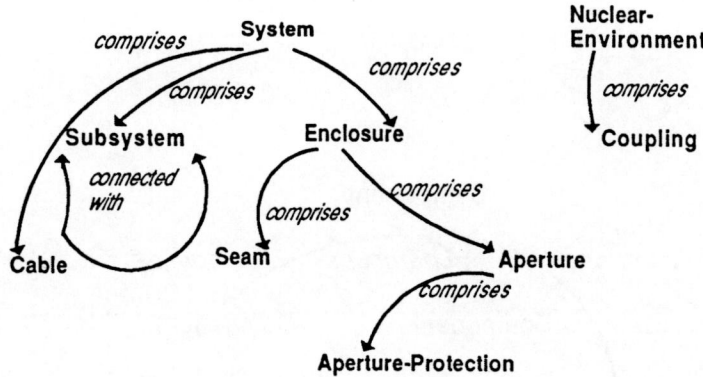

Figure 5-4: Preliminary Domain Model -- Concepts

ENCLOSURE concept	
Characteristic	Representative(s)
Name	S-280C, Metal Box
Material	Aluminum
Thickness	number
Relative-Conductivity	number
Minimum Thickness	number

Table 5-1: Enclosure Concept

This process results in a preliminary model of a particular domain. An example is shown in figure 5-5 (see [Klinker 87c] for additional examples).

The preliminary domain model is not sufficient for a successful generalization process. It represents a structural description -- that is, the vocabulary and the terms experts use -- but does not contain any functional

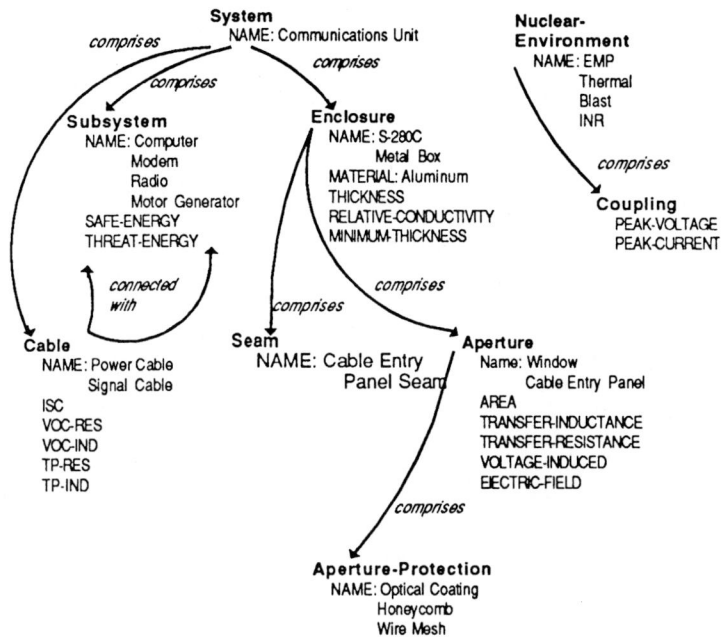

Figure 5-5: Domain Model -- Structural Knowledge

knowledge -- that is, knowledge of how experts obtain and propagate parameters. Figure 5-6 demonstrates a portion of the domain model representing functional knowledge. The nodes describe procedures for obtaining parameters. The links, indicated by dotted lines, define the way values are propagated through the network. Section 5.3.5 describes the process of deriving that functional knowledge.

The example in figure 5-6 states that a question strategy can be used to determine the kinds of ENCLOSUREs incorporated in a SYSTEM. It shows further that a formula strategy uses values of the ISC, VOC-RES, VOC-IND, TP-RES, and TP-IND characteristics of CABLE to determine the value for the THREAT ENERGY.

It is likely that the initial structural model is incomplete and not detailed enough. During knowledge acquisition, KNACK augments the initial domain model to include the functional aspects of the domain and to obtain

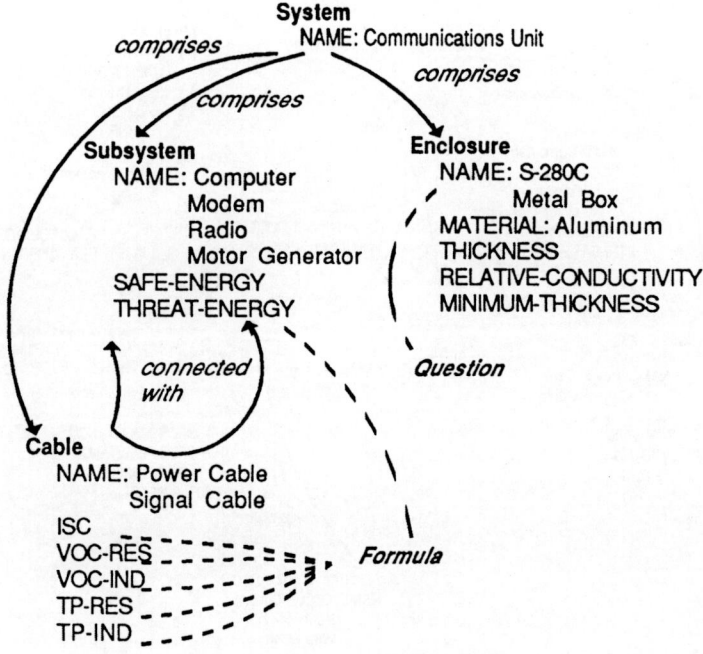

Figure 5-6: Domain Model -- Functional Knowledge

a more detailed structural model. It gradually customizes the domain model to represent the expert's understanding of a particular reporting task. This process is described in section 5.3.4.

5.3.3. Generalizing the Sample Report
Once the sample report is typed in and an initial domain model is defined, KNACK interacts with a domain expert to generalize the sample report, fragment by fragment. KNACK integrates the specific sample report with the domain model in successive interactions with the expert. It replaces specific terms in a fragment with the concepts they represent. Deriving the generalized report involves extracting the report's basic structure and integrating the domain model with the report fragments. The technique employs simple heuristics to infer the concepts each fragment mentions. The heuristics are based on keywords, representatives of concepts in the

fragment, and knowledge of relations between candidate concepts contained in the domain model.

In the first stage of this process KNACK looks for keywords (for example, "chapter," "section," "subsection," "heading," "itemize," "enumerate," "bold," "underline"), instances of keywords (for example, "2." for chapter, "2.3.2." for subsection, "(1)" for enumerate), and the form of the input (for example, only a few words in a line separated from the remaining text by blank lines to indicate a heading). From this analysis, KNACK generates a skeletal report defining the form of the sample report. It includes the outline and special formats (for example, table of contents, itemizations, enumerations, filled or unfilled environments) encoded as commands for a document-formatting system.

In the second phase of the process KNACK converts fixed report text into generalizations representing the concepts detected in the fragment. Cues to locate and identify concepts in a report fragment are numbers representing the value of quantitative parameters and nonnumeric symbols denoting tokens of known concepts in the domain model.

The following examples give an impression of the heuristics KNACK uses to integrate the domain model with the sample report. These generalizations are internal constructs for KNACK's use; the expert sees only instantiated generalizations. The examples show generalizations of some of the fragments in the sample report. The relevant sample fragments are repeated here.

The first fragment of the sample report shows a chapter heading. Numbers at the beginning of a line followed by a dot indicate chapter, section, or subsection headings. For example, "1." is assumed to be a chapter heading. Representatives of known concepts can be generalized by replacing them with a variable representing that concept. For example, EMP is inferred to be a NAME of a NUCLEAR ENVIRONMENT due to a unique match with the domain model. In this and the following generalizations, the angle brackets enclose concepts detected in a fragment. Asterisks enclose commands denoting the report structure. Unmarked text indicates fixed text strings to be printed exactly as formulated by the expert.

Sample report fragment:

1. Evaluation of EMP Hardness

Generalization:

```
*CHAPTER* Evaluation of
<NUCLEAR-ENVIRONMENT.NAME> Hardness
```

In the next example, "Communications Unit" is recognized as a representative of the NAME of a SYSTEM and "Power Cable" the NAME of a CABLE. KNACK replaces the representatives with variables. A list of representatives for a concept is replaced with text that contains a variable for that concept surrounded by a LOOP structure. For example, "a Computer, a Modem, a Radio, and a Motor Generator" is assumed to be a list of NAMEs of SUBSYSTEMs. The LOOP structure identifies the beginning and end of the text to be repeated and gives the name of the variable the WRINGER should loop over. In a WRINGER report, the text outside a LOOP structure will be printed once, whereas the text within the structure will be repeated for each instantiation of the variable that the WRINGER user supplies.

Sample report fragment:

> **The system Communications Unit is designed to resist to EMP threat. It consists of a Computer, a Modem, a Radio, and a Motor Generator. Power is supplied from the Motor Generator to the Computer, Modem, and Radio by the Power Cable.**

Generalization:

```
The system <SYSTEM.NAME> is designed to resist
to <NUCLEAR-ENVIRONMENT.NAME> threat.  It
consists of *LOOPOVER* <SUBSYSTEM.NAME> a
<SUBSYSTEM.NAME> ,*ENDLOOP*.  Power is
supplied from the <SUBSYSTEM.NAME> to the
*LOOPOVER* <SUBSYSTEM.NAME> <SUBSYSTEM.NAME>,
*ENDLOOP* by the <CABLE.NAME>.
```

If the generalizations of parts of a report fragments are the same, these parts can both be represented by the same generalization. For example, the generalization of the two sentences in the sample fragment below results in the single generalization shown.

Sample report fragment:

```
The Computer, Modem, and Radio are protected
by a S-280C enclosure.  The Motor Generator is
protected by a Metal Box enclosure.
```

Generalization:

```
The *LOOPOVER* <SUBSYSTEM.NAME>
<SUBSYSTEM.NAME>, *ENDLOOP* is protected by
a <ENCLOSURE.NAME> enclosure.
```

A number is assumed to be a representative of some numerical characteristic of a concept. If the text adjacent to a number refers to a known concept and one of its characteristics, the number is replaced with the corresponding variable. Below, "0.15" is assumed to be the RELATIVE-CONDUCTIVITY of an ENCLOSURE because ALUMINUM is known to be an example of an ENCLOSURE MATERIAL and the term "relative conductivity" was encountered in the text of the fragment.

Sample report fragment:

```
The S-280C enclosure is made of aluminum and
is 30 mils thick.  Aluminum has a
relative-conductivity of 0.15 mhos/m.  A plate
of aluminum must be at least 20 mils thick to
reduce the diffusion factor to an negligible
level.  Therefore, the diffusion factor can be
neglected.
```

Generalization:

```
The <ENCLOSURE.NAME> enclosure is made of
<ENCLOSURE.MATERIAL> and is
<ENCLOSURE.MINIMUM-THICKNESS> mils  thick.
<ENCLOSURE.MATERIAL> has a relative
conductivity of
<ENCLOSURE.RELATIVE-CONDUCTIVITY> mhos/m.  A
plate of <ENCLOSURE.MATERIAL> must be at least
<ENCLOSURE.THICKNESS> mils thick to reduce the
diffusion factor to an negligible level.
Therefore, the diffusion factor can be
neglected.
```

When helpful clues are not present in adjacent text, KNACK simply guesses the concept from the ambiguous set of matches. Its guesses are based on the concepts recognized in the fragment. These guesses can be wrong, and KNACK corrects them when the expert critiques instantiations of the generalized fragments as described below.

5.3.4. Demonstrating Understanding of the Sample Report

KNACK predicts and exemplifies the performance an expert can expect from the WRINGER he is working to create. It instantiates the concepts of the generalized fragments with known concept representatives taken from the domain model and displays several differently instantiated examples of each generalized report fragment. The expert edits any examples that make implausible statements about the domain. KNACK treats such events as incorrect use of the knowledge base and interprets the corrections as new knowledge to update the generalization and improve the domain model. For example, if the expert indicates that values from the domain model combine too loosely, KNACK adds a constraint to the model, restricting possible combinations. A correction can also imply that KNACK's guess about the identity of a concept is wrong, leading to its retraction and the introduction of a new, initially less probable guess. Applying the new knowledge, the generalization is instantiated again, and display of several examples gives the expert immediate feedback on the effects of the knowledge base modification.

KNACK extends the domain model whenever the editing adds variability between examples that it cannot parse. Extensions can be new concepts, new characteristics for known concepts, and restrictions on existing relations between representatives of two concepts. The model serves as a collection of examples suggesting guesses for KNACK as to the form of the extension. The following examples illustrate the editing process with some of the generalized report fragments shown above.[12]

---

[12]The expert uses the mouse and menus in order to change displayed examples. It is beyond the scope of this paper to present this part of the interaction exactly as it proceeds on the terminal screen. Thus, in the following examples the expert's actions are described in short, underlined sentences.

```
1. Evaluation of EMP Hardness

2. Evaluation of Thermal Hardness

Corrections? [ NONE ]: delete example 2
```

KNACK assumes that this fragment represents a chapter heading and that there will be a chapter about the different environments defined in the domain model: EMP, THERMAL, BLAST, and INR. Therefore, it displays examples of possible chapter headings. The expert deletes the second example. KNACK guesses that only the value EMP is relevant for the fragment. It further constrains the remaining fragments of the chapter to the EMP environment, assuming that the topic will not change within a chapter.

```
The system Communications Unit is designed to
resist to EMP threat. It consists of a
Computer, a Modem, a Radio, and a Motor
Generator. Power is supplied from the Motor
Generator to the Computer, Modem, Radio, and
Motor Generator by the Power Cable.

The system Communications Unit is designed to
resist to EMP threat. It consists of a
Computer, a Modem, a Radio, and a Motor
Generator. Power is supplied from the
Computer to the Computer, Modem, Radio, and
Motor Generator by the Signal Cable.

Corrections? [ NONE ]: delete the second
occurrence of TO in example 1, delete the 2nd
occurrence of MOTOR GENERATOR in example 1,
change the 2nd occurrence of COMPUTER in
example 2 to MOTOR GENERATOR, change SIGNAL
CABLE in example 2 to POWER CABLE
```

The expert first makes a minor change to the fixed text of the fragment, deleting the word "to." The next user commands indicate that KNACK's domain model is inadequate. KNACK made the default assumption that the report fragment was valid for all possible SUBSYSTEMs. However, a MOTOR GENERATOR SUBSYSTEM does not supply power to another MOTOR GENERATOR SUBSYSTEM, a COMPUTER SUBSYSTEM does not supply power to any other SUBSYSTEM, and power is not supplied by a SIGNAL CABLE. The expert's corrections are now used to refine the model. The original model stated that a CABLE relates a SUBSYSTEM to another SUBSYSTEM. KNACK now adds the restriction that only a POWER CABLE relates a MOTOR GENERATOR SUBSYSTEM to another SUBSYSTEM and that the latter cannot include a MOTOR GENERATOR. This restriction is based on the user corrections shown. If more than one relation connects concepts in a report fragment, KNACK guesses which relation to restrict until it is corrected. KNACK then revises its earlier decision and restricts another relation.

```
1.2. Shielding Requirements for the S-280C
Enclosure

1.3. Shielding Requirements for the Metal Box
Enclosure

Corrections? [ NONE ]: <cr>
```

KNACK displays two examples corresponding to the representatives of ENCLOSUREs in its domain model. In a WRINGER report, the section will be repeated for each particular ENCLOSURE the WRINGER user mentions. Any NAME of ENCLOSURE within the report fragments of a section will automatically be instantiated with the ENCLOSURE NAME given in the section heading. Also, fragments specific to a particular ENCLOSURE will be included only in a section with the relevant heading.

5.3.5. Defining, Generalizing, and Correcting Strategies
Concepts in the generalized fragments must be instantiated with values describing a particular application when a WRINGER acquires information and writes its report. Once the sample report is generalized, KNACK asks the expert to define strategies for a WRINGER to acquire or produce the instantiation values. Experts define strategies in the same way that report fragments are defined, by typing in samples. Each strategy describes a way to determine a representative of a concept and includes instructions about valid possible values. Relying on previously elicited information and other prior knowledge, KNACK defines the circumstances in which these methods can be applied. The strategies are also used to refine the domain model; they describe the procedures for obtaining and propagating parameters.

KNACK asks the expert to define at least one strategy for each concept in the report fragments. A strategy can be interactive; that is, it can call for acquiring concept representatives by asking questions; interpreting a graphical design description; asking the user to fill in the slots of a table, diagram, or form; or asking the user to choose from the items in a menu. Other strategies are autonomous: a strategy can infer concept representatives by directly applying domain-specific knowledge, computing numeric values using formulas, or referring to a database. The following example demonstrates how the expert defines a question strategy for the ENCLOSUREs of a SYSTEM.

```
Which strategy can be used to determine the
ENCLOSUREs of a SYSTEM?

[question, inference, table, menu, graphics,
formula, database, postpone, quit]
[ QUESTION ]: <cr>

question text....: Please list the enclosures

possible answers.. [ INCOMPLETE-SET, S-280C,
                     METAL BOX ] <cr>
default answer.... [ S-280C ]: unknown
status........... [ NOT-MANDATORY ]: <cr>
```

The expert defines the question "Please list the enclosures." KNACK suggests defaults for the expert's input. These are taken from report fragments or the domain model. For example, KNACK knows that S-280C and METAL BOX are examples for an ENCLOSURE and suggests these as possible answers. INCOMPLETE-SET indicates that other responses may also be valid.

KNACK now parses the text of the question in an attempt to generalize it by replacing concept representatives with variables denoting the concepts. KNACK also uses heuristics to focus a question strategy. For example, since the domain model states that a SYSTEM comprises ENCLOSUREs, KNACK generalizes the text of the above question to:

```
Please list the enclosures of the
<SYSTEM.NAME> system
```

KNACK then displays several different examples for confirmation or correction by the expert. Since the domain model only lists one representative for the NAME of a SYSTEM, the above example results in one instantiation.

```
Please list the enclosures of the
Communications Unit system?

Corrections? [ NONE ]: <cr>
```

KNACK adds the acquired knowledge to the domain model.

The interaction continues with an example of an autonomous formula strategy to determine the THREAT ENERGY for a SUBSYSTEM.

```
Which strategy can be used to determine the
THREAT ENERGY of a SUBSYSTEM?

[question, inference, table, menu, graphics,
formula, database, postpone, quit]
[ QUESTION ]: formula

THREAT ENERGY = Isc * ( ( Voc-res * Tp-res ) +
( Voc-ind * Tp-ind ) )
```

KNACK parses the formula to generalize it. Since all the terms in the formula are characteristics of the CABLE concept, KNACK introduces variables to produce the following formula:

```
<CABLE.ISC> * ( ( <CABLE.VOC-RES> *
<CABLE.TP-RES> ) + ( <CABLE.VOC-IND> *
<CABLE.TP-IND> ) )
```

To confirm its generalization, KNACK displays the following instantiations:

```
THREAT ENERGY = Isc * ( ( Voc-res * Tp-res ) +
( Voc-ind * Tp-ind ) )
with Isc     = Isc of CABLE
     Voc-res = Voc-res of CABLE
     Tp-res  = Tp-res of CABLE
     Voc-ind = Voc-ind of CABLE
     Tp-ind  = Tp-ind of CABLE

Corrections? [ NONE ]: <cr>
```

Again, KNACK updates its domain model with the knowledge of how to obtain the THREAT ENERGY parameter using the defined formula strategy.

A final example demonstrates an autonomous inference strategy to determine the APERTURE PROTECTIONs for an APERTURE. This strategy describes a procedure for inferring values by directly applying domain-specific knowledge.

```
Which strategy can be used to determine the
APERTURE PROTECTIONs of an APERTURE?

[question, inference, table, menu, graphics,
formula, database, postpone, quit]
[ QUESTION ]: inference
```

KNACK now asks the expert to choose the value to be inferred from the list of representatives for an APERTURE PROTECTION in its domain model.

```
Which value will be inferred?
[OPTICAL COATING, HONEYCOMB, WIRE MESH,
variable, quit] [ OPTICAL COATING ]: wire mesh
```

KNACK uses this knowledge to generate a general rule for inferring a value from some previously gathered information.

```
if   some APERTURE exists,
then add a WIRE MESH APERTURE PROTECTION, and
     relate it to the APERTURE
```

Again, KNACK instantiates the rules with specific examples taken from the domain model, displays several differently instantiated examples, and uses the expert's corrections to refine the domain model.

```
if   a WINDOW APERTURE exists,
then add a WIRE MESH APERTURE PROTECTION, and
     relate it to the APERTURE

if   a CABLE ENTRY PANEL APERTURE exists,
then add a WIRE MESH APERTURE PROTECTION, and
     relate it to the APERTURE

Corrections? [ NONE ]: delete example 2
```

Since the expert deletes the second example, KNACK adds the restriction to the domain model that a WIRE MESH APERTURE PROTECTION cannot be used for a CABLE ENTRY PANEL APERTURE.

The definition, generalization, and correction of strategies such as the ones shown here complete the initial interaction between KNACK and the domain expert. This results in a declarative knowledge base of domain facts that KNACK can analyze for completeness and consistency.

5.4. Analyzing the Knowledge Base

The knowledge KNACK acquires during its interaction with an expert, or group of experts, is transformed into an internal representation and stored in a knowledge base. The knowledge base is organized according to the roles knowledge plays. The domain model, implemented as a semantic network, serves as the kernel of the knowledge base. Each node represents a domain concept. Each concept can have several characteristics, each of which represents a variable whose value must be acquired or inferred by the generated WRINGER. The interdependencies between concepts and variables are defined by the links in the domain model, which encode structural and functional knowledge. Structural links define a taxonomy of concepts; they include COMPRISES and CONNECTED-WITH relationships. Functional links relate strategies for acquiring values to variables. They define which variables are input to a strategy, which variable contains the result of a strategy, and how the inputs are used to obtain a value for the result variable.

The domain model is also the kernel of a second knowledge structure that represents the document a WRINGER produces. That knowledge is defined by the REPORT FRAGMENT, INFORMATION IDENTIFICATION, and SKELETAL REPORT roles. REPORT FRAGMENT knowledge represents a possible paragraph of the actual report. The variables in the domain model are linked to each REPORT FRAGMENT that uses them. The order of the fragments and the structure of the report (chapter, section, subsection) are defined by SKELETAL REPORT knowledge. INFORMATION IDENTIFICATION knowledge identifies the variables relevant to different report parts (chapter, section, subsection).

Since KNACK initiates knowledge acquisition using only a single sample report, it is likely that the knowledge base is incomplete. KNACK exploits the explicit organization of its knowledge base to search for gaps in the report structure or strategies or conflicts with the domain model. The user can select the ANALYZE function at any time, but it is most efficient to conduct the review of the knowledge base at the end of the acquisition process; an apparent gap might be filled in by the user in the course of adding to and correcting the knowledge base through the other functions.

Some of the heuristics KNACK uses to identify incompleteness and inconsistency in its knowledge base are:

- Each concept characteristic in the domain model must have at least one strategy associated with it to instantiate the concept.

- Each concept or concept representative should be either mentioned in the sample report or used by a strategy.

- The expert should be given additional opportunities to define concepts, concept characteristics, or concept representatives where they are likely to be needed.

When a conflict is detected or a gap is found, KNACK asks the expert to correct either the fragment, the strategy, or the domain model. In cases where the domain model is changed, KNACK reviews all fragments or strategies that use the changed concept or relation to propagate the change through the knowledge base automatically, making guesses when ambiguities arise. When the expert adds or changes report fragments or strategies, KNACK processes them through integration of the domain model, display of examples, strategy definition, and further checking. The remaining part of this section explains the heuristics in more detail.

A WRINGER must have available at least one strategy to instantiate each concept characteristic in the domain model. KNACK looks for concept characteristics in the generalized report fragments and strategies that do not have a corresponding strategy:

```
The characteristic MATERIAL of the concept
ENCLOSURE was mentioned in the sample report.
No strategy exists to acquire that
information.  Do you want to define one now?
[ YES ]: no
```

The expert can define the missing strategy using the normal procedure for adding a strategy or postpone the process. KNACK allows the expert to go on with the interview but will remind the expert of the insufficiency, if it still exists, the next time the ANALYZE function is selected.

A flaw in the knowledge base is indicated if a concept or a representative of a concept was introduced into the model but never used:

```
The representatives THERMAL, BLAST, and INR
for the concept NUCLEAR ENVIRONMENT are known
but never used.  Do you want to add a
fragment? [ YES ]: no
```

Again, the expert postpones work on the potential problem. The answer YES will activate the sample report editor, allowing the expert to add additional fragments or change existing ones. KNACK will generalize the changed or added fragment and display instantiations for confirmation by the expert as described earlier.

The knowledge base might be incomplete or inconsistent because the expert forgot to mention concepts, characteristics, or representative values. An indication of this problem is generalized fragments that do not contain any variables. KNACK looks for those fragments, displays them to the expert, and asks for concepts that should have been discovered by the generalization process. The expert then can add concepts, concept characteristics, or concept representatives to the domain model.

KNACK also tries to extend its domain model by examining its existing model. For each concept and characteristic figuring in relations with several others and for the representative values of each concept and characteristic, KNACK asks for possible extensions to the set.

```
A system comprises the following concepts:
SUBSYSTEM, ENCLOSURE.  Do you want to
consider any other component comprised in a
SYSTEM? [ NO ]: antenna
```

This introduces a new concept: ANTENNA. KNACK integrates new concepts into the model using the same process it used to acquire the original domain model. The concept definition is shown in table 5-2.

ANTENNA concept	
Characteristic	Representative(s)
Name	**Wip Antenna**, **Dish Antenna**
Length	**number**
Diameter	**number**
Min Operating Frequency	**number**
Max Operating Frequency	**number**

Table 5-2: Antenna Concept

KNACK then examines the sample report to find fragments mentioning the ANTENNA concept. As the domain model previously did not include knowledge about ANTENNAs, any occurrences in the sample report fragments were treated as fixed text. KNACK now introduces variables for the new concept in those fragments and displays instantiated examples. The example of the sample report does not mention the concept ANTENNA. If there are no fragments mentioning the new concept, KNACK looks for related concepts in the domain model; that is, for the concepts figuring in the same relations as the new concept. It then integrates the new concept with fragments dealing with the related concepts and displays instantiations for confirmation by the expert. Using the domain model from the previous examples, KNACK finds that a SYSTEM also comprises SUBSYSTEMs and ENCLOSUREs. It integrates ANTENNA with the first fragment mentioning the SUBSYSTEM concept and displays an instantiation for review by the expert:

```
The system Communications Unit is designed to
resist EMP threat. It consists of a Computer,
a Modem, a Radio, a Motor Generator, a Wip
Antenna, and a Dish Antenna. Power is
supplied from the Motor Generator to the
Computer, Modem, Radio, Wip Antenna, and Dish
Antenna by the Power Cable.
```

```
Corrections? [ NONE ]: delete the 2nd
occurrence of WIP ANTENNA, delete the 2nd
occurrence of DISH ANTENNA, insert  "Signals
are received by the Wip Antenna and
transmitted to the  Radio via the Signal
Cable." after the example
```

KNACK adds the restriction to the model that a POWER CABLE does not interrelate a MOTOR GENERATOR SUBSYSTEM with ANTENNAs. The expert's corrections also introduce a new fragment dealing with the special case of ANTENNAs.   KNACK generalizes the newly defined fragment and displays instantiations for confirmation or correction by the expert.   It then continues to integrate the ANTENNA concept with fragments mentioning SUBSYSTEM or CABLE concepts.

5.5. Rule Generation

KNACK stores the domain-dependent knowledge it acquires from the expert in declarative form in its knowledge base. To create an expert system, this knowledge is proceduralized into OPS5 production rules [Forgy 81] using a simple parser written in Lisp. These rules are then combined with domain-independent rules.   The domain-independent knowledge embodies the problem-solving method.   It establishes and controls the sequences of actions required to perform the reporting task and defines the knowledge roles applicable within each step.

The domain-dependent knowledge is organized in units according to the role that knowledge plays. Rule generation for each knowledge role is described below.

IDENTIFY-RELEVANT-INFORMATION Rules

A WRINGER collects related information in a coherent manner by following the outline of its report. KNACK generates a rule for each chapter, section, or subsection identifying the information relevant to that report part. The following example gives an English version of part of the IDENTIFY-RELEVANT-INFORMATION rule for the section "Shielding Requirements for the Enclosures."

```
If   the goal is to determine information, and
     the current report part is chapter 1,
        section 2,
then create the subgoal to determine the NAME
        of a NUCLEAR ENVIRONMENT, and
     create the subgoal to determine the NAME
        of an ENCLOSURE, and
     create the subgoal to determine the NAME
        of an APERTURE, and
     create the subgoal to determine the
        MATERIAL of an ENCLOSURE, and
     create the subgoal to determine the
        THICKNESS of an ENCLOSURE ...
```

DEFINE-A-STRATEGY Rules

A WRINGER uses strategies to instantiate generalized concept characteristics with values describing a particular application. The kind of rules generated will depend on the strategy. For example, KNACK translates a question strategy into two OPS5 rules. Rule 1 verifies that a question strategy can be used to gather a specific piece of information and asks the question. Rule 2 checks whether the result of applying a strategy is valid. Rules for applying a question strategy to determine ENCLOSUREs of a SYSTEM are shown below:

```
Rule 1:

If   the goal is to identify strategies, and
     the subgoal is to determine the NAME of
        an ENCLOSURE, and
     a SYSTEM with some NAME is known,
then create a request to determine the NAME of
        an ENCLOSURE using a QUESTION
        strategy, and
     create the question "Please list the
        enclosures of the <SYSTEM.NAME>
        system," and
     classify the answer as NOT-MANDATORY.
```

```
Rule 2:

If    the goal is to validate a strategy
          result, and
      the NAME of an ENCLOSURE was determined,
          and
      it is not S-280C or METAL BOX,
    then mark the result as POSSIBLY INCORRECT.
```

Rule 2 flags a strategy result as questionable if it is not a member of a predefined, incomplete set of possible answers. The WRINGER asks the user for confirmation of the result.

INTEGRATE-INFORMATION Rules

Once a WRINGER accepts the result of a strategy, it must integrate that result with the already existing information. The expert's input to define a strategy is also used to determine this knowledge.

```
If    the goal is to integrate a strategy
          result, and
      the result is a value for the NAME of an
          ENCLOSURE, and
      a SYSTEM with some NAME is known,
    then create a concept ENCLOSURE with a NAME
          characteristic, and
      instantiate it with that value, and
      create a link that the SYSTEM COMPRISES
          the ENCLOSURE.
```

The rule creates the concept ENCLOSURE with a NAME characteristic and instantiates the concept characteristic with the strategy result. It further creates a relation linking the ENCLOSURE to the existing SYSTEM concept.

DEFINE-THE-SKELETAL-REPORT Rules

DEFINE-THE-SKELETAL-REPORT report rules represent the outline of the report a WRINGER produces. As indicated in the sample interaction, KNACK will insert a new chapter, section, or subsection whenever it discovers a keyword, such as "chapter," "section," or "subsection," in a report fragment. An OPS5 rule representing a part of the skeletal report is created for each chapter, section, and subsection heading. The skeletal report rule for a section heading is shown below:

```
If    the goal is to create the skeletal
            report,
then create section 2 of chapter 1
      with the heading "Shielding Requirements
            for the Enclosures," and
      establish that fragment 9 can be
            selected, and
      establish that fragment 10 can be
            selected, and
      establish that fragment 11 can be
            selected, and ...
```

The rule defines the section heading as it appears in the table of contents of the report the WRINGER is trying to produce. It also specifies the fragments that can be included in the section and determines the order of the fragments.

DEFINE-A-FRAGMENT Rules

DEFINE-A-FRAGMENT rules represent the content of a WRINGER's report.

```
If    the goal is to print the report, and
      report fragment 9 can be selected, and
      a NUCLEAR-ENVIRONMENT with NAME EMP is
            known, and
      an ENCLOSURE with some NAME is known,
then print "*LOOPOVER* <ENCLOSURE.NAME>
            @SECTION [ Shielding Requirements for
            the <ENCLOSURE.NAME> ENCLOSURE ]."
```

To present the report in an appealing format (include headings, tables, and so forth) the output of a WRINGER is formatted by a text formatting program. For that reason, the print action of the rule contains commands for the text formatting program, in our example @SECTION.

The term "*LOOPOVER* <ENCLOSURE.NAME>" in the above example is a command for the Lisp parser to create control rules. Control rules are necessary whenever a single report fragment is proceduralized by multiple OPS5 rules. Fragments that were generalized to contain a list of representatives for the same concept need additional control to realize the intended repetitions of parts of the fragment. Multiple OPS5 rules are necessary to control the repetitions: one rule to identify the variable denoting the list of representatives, one to print the text preceding the repetition once, one to print the repetition for each instantiation of the variable, and one to print the text succeeding the repetition once. The same principle applies to chapter, section, and subsection headings that contain variables. Rules are added to control the repetition of an entire chapter, section, or subsection for each instantiation of the variable. KNACK inserts a corresponding "*LOOPEND*" as the last word of the chapter, section, or subsection.

5.6. Combining Problem-Solving Methods

The previous sections described how KNACK can be used to generate expert systems that assist with reporting tasks. Reporting tasks can be part of other problems. For example, a variety of selective and constructive tasks need a considerable amount of information to begin with or require results to be documented. Existing expert systems and the associated knowledge-acquisition tools concentrate their effort on the problem-solving process. They are not focused as much on obtaining preliminary information and presenting results. KNACK's simple acquire-and-present problem-solving method can be viewed as complementary to other problem-solving methods. For example, KNACK's method can be viewed as complementary to SALT's propose-and-revise systems. The acquire-and-present problem-solving method serves as a front end to acquire information and as a back end to present results. Combining KNACK's and SALT's methods broadens the scope of propose-and-revise systems to include constructive tasks that need a large amount of information to start with or require that a document be produced.

The remainder of this section describes work to combine KNACK's and SALT's methods, resulting in evaluative and constructive systems. First, the combined method and the associated additional kinds of knowledge are introduced. The section continues with a brief discussion of how KNACK acquires the knowledge organized in the new knowledge roles and concludes with examples of rules for the additional knowledge roles.

5.6.1. The Combined Method

SALT's propose-and-revise method proposes an extension to a partial plan or design and then checks for constraint violations. If a constraint is violated, the method finds the least costly fix that will eliminate the violation and applies it. This process continues until no more additions can be made to the plan or design or no constraints are violated.

The method that combines KNACK's and SALT's methods first uses appropriate interactive or autonomous strategies to gather necessary preliminary information representing an existing but partial plan or design. It then uses autonomous strategies to extend the partial plan or design; for example, it infers values using domain-specific knowledge, formulas, or database lookups. For each plan or design extension, the method checks for constraint violations. If a constraint is violated, the combined method finds the least costly fix that will eliminate the violation and applies it. This process continues until no more additions can be made to the plan or design or no constraints are violated. Finally, the method produces a report that documents the plan or design.

Depending on the kinds of knowledge provided by the expert, KNACK generates WRINGERs that dynamically decide which steps of the combined problem-solving method to use. This results in different problem-solving behavior by the generated expert systems creating, for example, design systems, evaluative systems, and reporting systems.

Design systems require all of the steps just described. Examples of KNACK-generated design systems are expert systems to improve the design of electromechanical systems that may be suboptimal from a hardening perspective, an expert system to improve a proposal for an investment opportunity, and an expert system to design computer networks.

Evaluation tasks require knowledge of constraints but no knowledge of remedies for violated constraints. The purpose of an evaluation system is to decide whether to reject or accept a proposal. It identifies possible flaws in a plan or design but suggests no fixes. A WRINGER assisting with evaluation tasks will not use the steps of the combined method that propose fixes for identified constraints. Examples of KNACK-generated evaluation systems are expert systems to evaluate designs of electromechanical systems from a hardening perspective, an expert system to identify problems with the requirements for a planned software system, and expert systems to evaluate the progress of a project from a management perspective.

The DPR WRINGER, which so far has been described as a reporting system, has been extended to be a design system. Its purpose is to assist a designer in improving designs of electromechanical systems that may be suboptimal from a hardening perspective. The WRINGER acquires information describing an initial design and assumes that the initial design describes a technically functional system. It evaluates the design from a hardening perspective and suggests improvements if constraint violations are found. The suggested improvements are either extensions to the design or recommendations for using different design components. The WRINGER presents the design in the form of a technical document that meets government requirements.

In addition to the knowledge roles identified in section 5.2, the combined problem-solving method defines the following roles knowledge can play:[13]

- DEFINE-A-CONSTRAINT on acquired information.

- PROPOSE-A-FIX for a constraint violation.

DEFINE-A-CONSTRAINT knowledge defines how contradictory information is to be uncovered. For example, the DPR WRINGER makes sure that a cable carrying power is not connected to a cable carrying a signal. DEFINE-A-CONSTRAINT knowledge further describes how to detect that information provided by the user is incomplete. For example, the DPR WRINGER checks whether a power source is specified for the system and whether a defined antenna is connected to the rest of the system. Finally, DEFINE-A-CONSTRAINT knowledge describes how to identify problem cues associated with possible flaws. For example, the DPR WRINGER might give the following message:

```
The SAFE ENERGY (3.6e-04) for the D4 DIODE is
less than the THREAT ENERGY (8.29e-03) for the
D4 DIODE.
```

---

[13]KNACK's DEFINE-A-CONSTRAINT and PROPOSE-A-FIX knowledge roles are roughly equivalent to SALT's IDENTIFY-A-CONSTRAINT and PROPOSE-A-FIX roles, respectively.

This example identifies a problem with an interface circuit; the threat energy produced by the given EMP environment and coupled with the circuit would damage diode D4.

PROPOSE-A-FIX knowledge suggests remedies for violated constraints and identifies the variables to be updated as a consequence of the remedy. For example, if the energy coupled with an interface circuit through a cable exceeds an upper limit, the semiconductor devices of the interface circuit will be damaged. The DPR WRINGER will suggest using a terminal protection device to limit that energy to an acceptable level:

> The 15KP280 TPD will reduce the threat energy
> for the D4 DIODE sufficiently.

5.6.2. Acquiring Additional Knowledge

To generate evaluative or design systems, KNACK needs to acquire the knowledge organized in the DEFINE-A-CONSTRAINT and PROPOSE-A-FIX roles.   KNACK acquires the knowledge in the same way it acquires knowledge about concepts for the domain: it asks the expert to fill in additional slots in the table used to define concept characteristics and concept representatives.   Table 5-3 illustrates a filled-in table for the SUBSYSTEM concept.

SUBSYSTEM concept			
Characteristic	Representative(s)	Constraint(s)	Fix(es)
Name	**Computer, Modem, Radio, Motor Generator**		
Threat Energy	**number**		
Safe Energy	**number**	**<= Threat Energy**	**TPD**

Table 5-3: Subsystem Concept

Constraints are defined via keywords. For example, "range," "<," "<=," and "=," indicate numerical constraints. Keywords such as "enumerated set," "incomplete set," or "excluding set" are used to test set membership. A fix may introduce a new strategy for changing the constrained value. A fix may also introduce a new concept for extending the partial plan or design. If the fix introduces a concept, the expert must define additional strategies for instantiating the concept and determining the effect of the fix on the constrained value. In the above example, the fix is a concept.

KNACK stores the acquired DEFINE-A-CONSTRAINT and PROPOSE-A-FIX knowledge in its knowledge base. When analyzing the knowledge base, KNACK uses additional heuristics, in addition to the ones introduced in section 5.4, to identify incompleteness and inconsistency:

- Each concept characteristic might have a constraint associated with it.

- Each constrained concept characteristic should have a fix associated with it.

The knowledge base might be incomplete or inconsistent because constraints are missing. KNACK looks for concept characteristics that have no associated constraint.

```
No constraints are known for the THREAT ENERGY
characteristic of the SUBSYSTEM concept.  Do
you want to add one now? [ YES ]: no
```

The knowledge base might be incomplete or inconsistent because fixes are missing. KNACK assumes that fixes exist whenever a constraint is violated. If KNACK detects that a constraint has no associated fix, it indicates that to the expert.

5.6.3. Generating Additional Rules
This section describes examples of the rules organized by the DEFINE-A-CONSTRAINT and PROPOSE-A-FIX roles.

DEFINE-A-CONSTRAINT Rules
DEFINE-A-CONSTRAINT rules define the restrictions for values of variables. For example, the rule below determines that the value for SAFE ENERGY must be less than or equal to the value for THREAT ENERGY:

```
If   the goal is to identify constraints, and
     a SUBSYSTEM with some SAFE ENERGY, and
          some THREAT ENERGY is known,
then create the constraint that the SAFE
          ENERGY must be less than or equal to
          the THREAT ENERGY
```

PROPOSE-A-FIX Rules

KNACK ensures that at least one fix exists for every constraint that can be violated. It generates one rule for every potential fix.

```
If   the goal is to suggest a fix, and
     a SUBSYSTEM with some SAFE ENERGY and
          some THREAT ENERGY is known, and
     the constraint exists that the SAFE
          ENERGY must be less or equal to the
          THREAT ENERGY, and
     the constraint is violated,
then suggest a 15KP280 TPD as a fix, and
     create the request to update the SAFE
     ENERGY using the FORMULA strategy.
```

This rule suggests a 15KP280 TPD as one possible fix for the violated constraint. The WRINGER determines which of the possible fixes will satisfy the constraint, gathering additional information if required. It then suggests the fix, integrates the TPD with the existing model of the system, and updates any affected parameters.

5.7. KNACK's Scope

KNACK is a specialized, automated knowledge-acquisition tool; that is, a tool that derives its power by exploiting a presupposed problem-solving method and the associated knowledge roles. A problem-solving method must be specific enough to guide a domain expert in defining, analyzing, and testing a knowledge base. On the other hand, a specific method limits the scope of an expert system that uses it. To get a better understanding of the kinds of tasks KNACK's assumed method can solve, KNACK has been and is being used by knowledge engineers to create a series of expert systems. This section introduces these systems and provides some data on KNACK's performance and scope.

5.7.1. KNACK Tasks

KNACK was used to generate an initial knowledge base for a number of expert systems. The knowledge bases were then manually enhanced to accommodate the specific demands of a particular task. The enhancements uncovered deficiencies and shortcomings in KNACK's approach to acquiring knowledge, assumed problem-solving method, and associated knowledge roles. KNACK has been improved to address the encountered problems and is now being used to regenerate the initial systems. The application systems described below are being created with KNACK.

The Data Item Description WRINGER Family. The DPR WRINGER is a member of the Data Item Description WRINGER family. Three WRINGERs assist with different stages in the design of electromechanical systems for the nuclear-hardening domain. The WRINGERs assist a designer in improving designs of electromechanical systems that may be suboptimal from a hardening perspective. The WRINGERs assume that the given design describes a technically functional system and are not required to know all of the constraints the design has to satisfy. They therefore suggest improvements only from a hardening perspective and ask the designer to select one of the proposed fixes. The suggested improvements are either extensions to the design or recommendations for using different design components. The WRINGERs present the design, together with the results of the evaluation, in the form of a technical document that meets government requirements.

The first WRINGER, the Program Plan writer, produces the primary top-level report covering all phases of the design project. It took 7 person-days to create this WRINGER with KNACK. Its knowledge base contains 742 OPS5 rules. The second expert system, the Design Parameters Report writer, improves and presents a detailed description of an electromechanical system ranging from the level of major components to the level of individual semiconductors. It took 21 person-days to create this WRINGER with KNACK, and its knowledge base contains 1244 OPS5 rules. The last WRINGER, the Test Plan writer, presents a plan for confirming the hardness of a design. This includes a list of the design components to be tested, a description of the tests to be performed, and the expected test results. It took 8 person-days to create this WRINGER with KNACK; its knowledge base consists of 228 rules.

These WRINGERs were created with an earlier implementation of KNACK [Klinker 87a] and are now being tested by the organization that will use them. The earlier implementation required the expert to manually define the generalized report and strategies. The experience gained with this task led to the introduction of the domain model and the automation of the generalization process.

The NAC WRINGER. A WRINGER is being developed to assist a salesperson with the design and configuration of computer networks. In general, a salesperson has a good understanding of customer requirements involving cost, compatibility, and extendability when he is designing a network, but usually he has little or no knowledge about the detailed technical aspects of such a network. The WRINGER takes as input whatever the salesperson can provide, ranging from an incomplete list of high-level components (for example, a VAX-11/780 host, a VT100 terminal) to a completely specified network. The WRINGER then revises and completes that description as a technically functional computer network. The corrections and additions are either extensions to the design or interconnections between design components. The WRINGER's output is a list of generic network components and their interconnections, which serve as input for a program that will select the specific parts.

This WRINGER is in the very early stages of development, and data that describe KNACK's performance are not yet available. However, the experience gained with this task led to a refinement of the PROPOSE-A-FIX knowledge role. While acquiring PROPOSE-A-FIX knowledge, KNACK requires the domain expert to specify whether a WRINGER should automatically apply that knowledge or wait for confirmation. The NAC WRINGER assumes complete knowledge about the constraints involved in configuring a computer network. It therefore does not need to ask a user to confirm a fix, as is the case for the DPR WRINGER.

The Software Requirements WRINGER. A WRINGER is being developed to assist a systems analyst with the definition of requirements for software. Defining requirements for new software is a very complex process. The WRINGER assumes that the user will describe the new software on a high level of abstraction. It supports the systems analyst in functionally decomposing that description into basic modules and defining the data requirements for the modules. The WRINGER checks for consistency (for example, internal input data for one module must be produced by another module) and compatibility (for example, the planned software must be integrated with the existing software environment). It suggests refinements to the requirements in case a flaw is found (for example, it may suggest defining a module that will produce required input data). The WRINGER produces a technical document that describes the requirements for the software system and contains an executive summary with an opinion about whether the new software will be a valuable enhancement of the existing software. It took 18 person-days to create this WRINGER with KNACK. Its knowledge base consists of 338 rules.

Experience gained from this task led to the introduction of two new strategies for acquiring information: simple graphics and forms. Simple graphics allow requirements for software and data to be represented as nodes and the data flow as directed links between nodes. Forms are used to add further information to the nodes.

The Project Progress Report WRINGER Family. WRINGER expert systems are being developed to assist a project leader with the assessment of a project's progress. They include the Proposal Writer and the Progress Report Writer. The Proposal Writer acquires information about a planned project (for example, objectives, schedule, resources, tasks, project plan), points out inconsistencies (for example, objectives that cannot be achieved by the planned tasks, budget constraints), and produces a proposal. It took 4 person-days to create the Proposal Writer with KNACK. Its knowledge base consists of 332 rules. The Progress Report Writer periodically acquires information about the project status (for example, budget, schedule, resources), compares the status to the actual project plan, and generates a progress report. The progress reports emphasize deviations from the project plan. It took 13 person-days to create the Progress Report Writer with KNACK. Its knowledge base consists of 347 rules.

The experience gained from this task led to an extension of KNACK's representation of the domain model: interdependencies between concepts are now represented by a network structure. For the Data Item Description WRINGER family of expert systems, a tree structure was sufficient.

The Business Plan WRINGER. A WRINGER is being developed to assist an entrepreneur in the preparation of business plans. The first step in creating a business is to seek investment capital. For this purpose, entrepreneurs generate business plans. A business plan contains information about the planned business, such as the industry, the product, the market and marketing plan, production, personnel, and financial projections. An entrepreneur usually has little knowledge about how to create a business plan. The purpose of the WRINGER is to support an entrepreneur in developing a marketing plan for the planned business. The WRINGER assumes that the entrepreneur can provide a description of the product and the goals of the proposed business. It then advises the entrepreneur in creating the marketing plan. Its output is a document containing the necessary details and justifications to recommend the proposed business to an investor.

This WRINGER is in the very early stages of development. Data that describe KNACK's performance are not yet available.

5.7.2. Some Performance Data

This section discusses KNACK's performance in creating the Program Plan WRINGER (PP) Design Parameters Report WRINGER (DPR), Test Plan WRINGER (TP), Software Requirements WRINGER (SR), Project Proposal Writer (PP1), and Project Progress Report Writer (PP2). The data of table 5-4 describe the complexity of the domains, table 5-5 contains some data about the complexity of the generated knowledge bases, and table 5-6 summarizes the effort involved in creating the expert systems with KNACK.

Table 5-4 gives an impression of the complexity of the domains for the six WRINGERs. It describes the input the experts had to provide in terms of the sample report, the domain model, and the sample strategies. Interactive strategies include questions, graphical design descriptions, menus, forms, and tables. Autonomous strategies include inferences, database lookups, and formulas.

Table 5-5 describes the knowledge bases generated for the six WRINGERs. The size of a knowledge base is determined by the number of OPS5 rules it contains. The conditionality of a rule is described by the number of its condition elements. Each condition element can be instantiated by a

	PP	DPR	TP	SR	PP1	PP2
Number of fragments in the sample report	237	455	88	203	73	97
Average size of each fragment in words	9.5	14.7	14.3	10.2	6.3	5.9
Number of concepts	43	92	28	55	32	40
Average number of characteristics for each concept	2.3	3.7	2.5	3.6	4.7	6.3
Number of interactive strategies	72	152	35	21	82	31
Number of autonomous strategies	22	159	4	32	--	23

Table 5-4: Complexity of the Domain

concept. The complexity of a condition element is defined by the number of characteristics that describe a concept. The action part of a rule is described by the number of actions the rule performs. An action either creates a new concept or modifies an existing concept characteristic.

	PP	DPR	TP	SR	PP1	PP2
Number of rules	742	1244	228	338	332	347
Average number of condition elements per rule	3.7	4.6	3.0	4.2	5.4	13.1
Number of characteristics per condition element	2.9	3.3	2.8	3.3	4.1	5.2
Number of actions per rule	5.7	6.3	5.3	7.3	3.9	4.1

Table 5-5: The Knowledge Base

Finally, table 5-6 shows the time spent by knowledge engineers to generate a WRINGER using KNACK. Creating WRINGERs is an iterative process. Whenever a WRINGER reveals inadequacies, KNACK is used to improve it. Table 5-6 shows the time spent to generate the initial knowledge bases for the WRINGERs. This includes the effort for the initial input (sample report, domain model, and sample strategies), the generalization process (sample report and sample strategies), and the review of the knowledge base. The effort required to produce the generalizations includes the expert's corrections to the sample instantiations of the generalized fragments and strategies.

Since the PP WRINGER, DPR WRINGER, and TP WRINGER were created with an earlier implementation of KNACK, no detailed data are available and only the total time is given. The actual numbers are based on estimates and have to be taken with a grain of salt. They reflect the approximate time each of KNACK's functions was used by the knowledge engineer. Since creating a WRINGER with KNACK is not a sequential process (that is, problems discovered during the generalization process require updates to the domain model, sample report, or sample strategies), the effort shown for the generalization process includes some of the effort needed to define the sample fragments and strategies. Also, the use of KNACK requires a well structured sample report and an understanding of the concepts used, their interdependencies, and associated strategies. The numbers do not reflect the time required at the beginning to manually design the initial sample report, strategies, and domain model. On the other hand, the numbers do include the effort of refining those inputs through iterative use of KNACK.

5.8. Conclusion
KNACK is a knowledge-acquisition tool that generates expert systems to assist with reporting tasks. The purpose of reporting systems is to acquire data efficiently and present information intelligently. Combining KNACK's acquire-and-present problem-solving method with SALT's propose-and-revise method broadens the scope of the latter method to include design tasks for which a large amount of information must be collected or that require a document to be produced.

KNACK is a specialized, automated knowledge-acquisition tool; that is, a tool that derives its power by exploiting a presupposed problem-solving method and the associated knowledge roles. A problem-solving method

	PP	DPR	TP	SR	PP1	PP2
Number of days to create the sample report	--	--	--	2	1	5
Number of days to create the preliminary domain model	--	--	--	4	1	3
Number of days to create the sample strategies	--	--	--	3	0.5	1
Number of days to generalize the sample report	--	--	--	4	0.25	0.5
Number of days to generalize the sample strategies	--	--	--	4	0.25	0.5
Number of days to review the knowledge base	--	--	--	1	1	3
Total	7	21	8	18	4	13

Table 5-6: Effort

must be specific enough to guide a domain expert in defining, analyzing, and testing a knowledge base. On the other hand, a specific method limits the scope of an expert system that uses it. It fails irreparably when confronted with problems that are outside its scope. The development of cooperating problem-solving methods has been suggested to broaden the scope of expert systems without sacrificing power [McDermott 86].

Like OPAL and STUDENT, KNACK exploits a domain model during knowledge acquisition. KNACK uses the domain model to elicit knowledge in a format familiar to the expert and develop expectations about the knowledge the expert might provide. KNACK differs from OPAL and STUDENT in that the domain model can be customized for a particular domain and no knowledge-engineering expertise is required to build a domain model. Also, KNACK does not assume that its domain model is complete and consistent. It expects that the expert can provide a preliminary model and gradually augments that preliminary model during knowledge acquisition so that it becomes a domain model describing the design and the evaluation process.

An important characteristic of KNACK is its sample-driven approach. The generalization process is critical for KNACK's performance. A successful generalization requires that the concepts and concept representatives used in the domain model correspond closely to the terms used in the sample report. Moreover, the domain model must contain a detailed structural and functional description of the domain. This assumption reveals a weakness in KNACK's current capabilities. KNACK does not provide guidance to the expert in defining a domain model that corresponds closely to the sample report. Furthermore, although our experience shows that creating the sample report constitutes a significant part of the expert's task, KNACK does not support the expert in defining the sample report. Future work will concentrate on providing this aid.

KNACK's different applications give some insight into its scope. At a first glance, those applications seem to be quite different. But a closer look reveals that although the domain-dependent knowledge is quite different, the applications all use a common problem-solving method. This method defines the scope of the KNACK-generated expert systems and imposes requirements on the expert: the expert must be able to provide an initial model of the domain, he must be able to express some of his knowledge in the form of a sample report, and he must be able to define strategies that a WRINGER can use to instantiate concepts with values describing a particular application.

The different applications also had some implications for the development of the KNACK tool. They define the dimensions along which KNACK should be improved. The goal is to create a tool that a domain expert can use to generate the knowledge bases for the WRINGERs described in this chapter without requiring knowledge-engineering skills on their part. While KNACK's approach as described in this paper is an important step towards that goal, it is only a short way along the path.

Acknowledgements

This research was sponsored by the Defense Nuclear Agency (DNA) and the Harry Diamond Laboratories (HDL) under contract DNA001-85-C-0027, the Bares Foundation, Boeing Computer Services (BCS), and Digital Equipment Corporation (DEC). The views and conclusions contained in this document are those of the author and should not be interpreted as representing the official policies, either expressed or implied, of DNA, HDL, the Bares Foundation, BCS, or DEC.

Many people made significant contributions to the KNACK project. John McDermott helped shape the direction of the project from the beginning. Joel Bentolilia, Casey Boyd, Gilbert Caplain, David Dong, Serge Genetet, Michael Grimes, Don Kosy, Jon Maiman, Beatrice Paoli-Julliat, Bob Schnelbach, and Martin Stacey were or still are members of the group. William Rodi (S-Cubed) also made important contributions. Thomas Flory and Roland Polimadei of Harry Diamond Laboratories (HDL), Rodney Perala of Electro Magnetic Applications (EMA), Bob Redinger, Don Vincent of Booz-Allen&Hamilton, and Richard Young served as our domain experts. I would also like to thank Andrej Bevec (HDL), John Northrop (S-Cubed), William Proffer (S-Cubed), and Alex Stewart (HDL) for their support. Randy Brost, Sandy Marcus, and Tom Mitchell provided very helpful comments on an earlier draft of this paper.

6. SIZZLE: A Knowledge-Acquisition Tool Specialized for the Sizing Task

Daniel Offutt

Abstract

SIZZLE is a prototype knowledge-acquisition tool for building sizers: expert systems that solve sizing problems. SIZZLE uses an extrapolate-from-a-similar-case problem-solving method. Using this strategy, a sizer produces a solution by first becoming reminded of a *source* sizing case similar to a *target* sizing problem to be solved, and then adjusting the solution of the source case to account for the differences between the source and the target. The problem-solving strategy assumed by SIZZLE makes strong assumptions about the problem domain. SIZZLE assumes that knowledge about sizing can be organized as a collection of validated cases (each case is a problem-description/solution pair) and that similarities among problem descriptions imply similarities among solutions.

6.1. Introduction

Like the other tools described so far in this book, SIZZLE is a knowledge-acquisition tool that makes a strong assumption about the problem-solving method that will be used by any expert system that it creates. SIZZLE builds expert systems that reason quantitatively and use a case-based reasoning method. SIZZLE is targeted for sizing problems. Sizing is a problem class that both requires quantitative reasoning and lends itself to case-based reasoning.

The inputs (resource demands) and outputs (capacity recommendations) of a sizer are quantities. The major problem in solving complex sizing problems such as computer-system sizing is approximating the functions relating these quantities. Although increases in the inputs to these functions generally imply corresponding increases in the outputs, the relation of the inputs to the outputs is not easily approximated as an arithmetic function. Also, such functions cannot be accurately approximated with a linear surface: There are significant interactions between resource demands in their effect upon capacity recommendations. For example, physical computer memory is shared. Consequently it is not appropriate to compute a memory capacity recommendation as a linear function of quantities of computer users.

Nevertheless, it may be useful to approximate the nonlinear capacity-recommendation function as a piecewise linear surface over resource-demand space. This is the approach we have taken. (For a discussion of problem-solving techniques applicable to such quantitative reasoning tasks see [Omohundro 87].) In the computer-system sizing domain, for example, the resource-demand space is a space of vectors of quantities of different types of computer users: AI programmers, managers, accountants, engineers, and so forth. Each such vector represents factors that affect resource demand. The capacity-recommendation space is a space of vectors of quantities of different computing resources including disk space, physical memory, and CPU capacity. Each such vector gives capacities of resources that might address some demand. A sizing function in this domain maps a vector of quantities of computer-system users into a vector of equipment capacities.

A given mapping from a point in resource-demand space to a point in capacity-recommendation space is a *sizing case*; that is, a sizing case is a problem-solution pair. Such a mapping consists of one function for each type of equipment capacity (for example, one function for disk space, one for physical memory, one for CPU capacity). Each function relates all of the resource-demand factors (for example, quantity of AI programmers, managers, accountants and engineers) to each type of equipment capacity. The sizing method SIZZLE assumes approximates each such function as a finite collection of linear surfaces over resource-demand space. Each such surface passes through a point representing an example supplied by a sizing expert.

The remaining degrees of freedom of each linear surface are constrained by a collection of *user demand models* also supplied by a sizing expert. A user demand model specifies how each capacity recommendation must change with changes in each resource demand. For example, a user demand model for an AI programmer might contain the information that for each additional AI programmer, an additional 50 megabytes of disk, 2 megabytes of physical memory, and 5 pages per minute of printer capacity are required. In short, sizing cases give the exact value of the sizing function at a few expert-validated points, and the user demand models indicate how to extrapolate from those few validated points.

The piecewise linear approximation of the capacity-recommendation surface is always defined everywhere. This means that the surface may be used to propose solutions to novel sizing problems. If there were only one sizing case in a sizer, then the capacity-recommendation surface would be approximated as a single plane determined by applying the user demand models to the single sizing case. That plane would give capacity recommendations for all possible resource-demand descriptions. But if there are two sizing cases in the sizer's knowledge base, then there are two planes, both of which are defined everywhere. If the two planes are different (that is, make different capacity recommendations for the same resource demand), then which plane should be used?

Our approach is to use the plane whose sizing case is nearest to the resource-demand description of a sizing task we wish to solve. A consequence is that each sizing case is associated with a region in the resource-demand space representing the area within which it would be selected as the source sizing case. These regions collectively partition and completely cover the entire resource-demand space. Adding a new sizing case to a sizer effectively introduces a new region and causes the regions of one or more nearby cases to shrink appropriately. Deleting a case from a sizer results in the takeover of the region vacated by the next-nearest sizing case to that region. These characteristics of the knowledge representation are quite useful in making knowledge acquisition tractable.

By exploiting these characteristics of a sizer's knowledge representation SIZZLE makes rapid but controlled evolution of a sizing knowledge base possible. Manufacturers are continually finding new and better ways to make machines more efficient and less expensive. As a result, their structure changes over time. In some industries, the rate of change is so high that machines manufactured only a few years ago are already obsolete. Consequently, a sales representative who sells such machinery must continually relearn the company's changing product line. If the machinery sold is customized for each customer, then the sales community confronts the additional problem of relearning good ways of sizing equipment capacities for given types of customers. These observations suggest that an automatic sizer must change over time, often quite rapidly, as a function of changing equipment capacities and costs. The sizing knowledge-acquisition task is closely analogous to the relearning tasks described above. SIZZLE is well adapted for continually relearning a rapidly changing body of sizing knowledge.

SIZZLE is a tool that builds sizers that use a case-based reasoning method [Carbonell 85], [Schank 82], [Schank 86]. SIZZLE drops units of knowledge gleaned from experts into steps of a rigidly-structured sizing method so that no search control knowledge needs to be added to the sizing knowledge base. The two types of knowledge units are: sizing cases and user demand models. The case-based sizing method permits the retraction of obsolete sizing cases and user demand models, and the introduction of new ones without introducing global changes to the behavior of the sizing system. The introduction of a new sizing case changes the behavior of the system only for those sizing problems similar to the introduced sizing case. The removal of a case simply introduces a gap that is immediately filled by the next most similar sizing case in the knowledge base. In short, the sizing method permits the independent addition or deletion of cases, producing well behaved and localized changes to the capacity-recommendation surface. This ability to introduce localized changes to the knowledge base makes relearning efficient.

Sizing involves two types of reasoning, which may be termed *qualitative* and *quantitative*. An important part of computer-system sizing, for instance, is the selection of applications programs to be run on the chosen hardware. This selection task is strongly qualitative in two senses. First, software packages cannot be obtained in increments in the same way that disk space or CPU capacity can. A FORTRAN compiler may not be obtained in increments; it is either present or absent. Second, the ingredients that go into the decision to recommend a software package are primarily qualitative, depending much more on types of users that will use the computing system and the tasks in which they will be engaged, than their quantities. The MOLE knowledge-acquisition system described in chapter 3 may be well suited to the sort of qualitative reasoning required to select software packages. SIZZLE, by contrast, has been developed to efficiently acquire and operationalize a very different sort of knowledge: quantitative sizing knowledge.

SIZZLE builds sizers that reason quantitatively. In the computer-system sizing domain, quantitative characteristics of an organization might include the fact that it contains four accountants, two analysts and one manager. The number of megabytes of disk space, number of megabytes of physical memory, and the number of disk drives of a computing system are examples of quantitative characteristics of a computer system. Knowledge of the form of the capacity-recommendation function relating quantitative organizational characteristics to computing system characteristics is quantitative knowledge. The problems of representing and acquiring this type of knowledge are somewhat different from those of representing and acquiring more qualitative knowledge.

The most important difference is the much larger size of the resource-demand space underlying the capacity-recommendation functions to be acquired. Qualitative reasoning systems, such as those built by MOLE, reason from few-valued symptoms to few-valued hypotheses. A quantitative reasoner must reason from many-valued resource demands (any non-negative number of AI programmers, and any non-negative number of accountants, and...) to many-valued capacity recommendations (a wide range of disk, printer and cpu capacities). The approximation of a quantitative capacity-recommendation function consequently requires careful attention to the matter of generalization. In a large space, poor generalization can mean a knowledge base that is almost everywhere invalid. The need for good (or acceptable) generalization is closely related to the problem of fitting a spline curve to a collection of data points. Such numerical analysis techniques are not practical for sizing due to the very high dimensionality of the resource-demand spaces and the consequent need for many more data points than could possibly be acquired from a sizing expert. The piecewise linear surface approximation method outlined above seems to be a good compromise among all of the competing constraints on a tool for acquiring and using sizing knowledge. The system described in this chapter tackles the problems of representing, acquiring, and applying knowledge needed to make reasonable and justifiable recommendations for quantitative system characteristics.

Since SIZZLE is a special-purpose knowledge-acquisition tool, we will begin by discussing the specialized nature of the task that SIZZLE's target system is intended to solve: the sizing task. Examples of sizing tasks include: electric-motor sizing, copier sizing, and computer-system sizing. This paper will discuss knowledge acquisition primarily in the context of computer-system sizing.

The sizing task is that of finding the minimum acceptable capacities some system must have, given information about the uses to which that system will be put. In sizing motors, horsepower and maximum motor torque may be the capacities for which minimum acceptable values are required. These values may be constrained by such factors as the friction forces involved and the mass of the mechanical system the motor will be driving.

Computer-system sizing is the task of developing an abstract description of a computing system that is well suited for a given collection of users and system applications, specifying such quantities as minimum total disk space required, minimum total physical memory, and minimum lines per minute of printing capacity. An important type of data available from a prospective customer and used by SIZZLE-built sizers is the number of each type of expected user of the system to be sized such as the number of managers, the number of programmers, and the number of accountants. The most important products of the sizing process are quantities of various classes of computing resources, such as megabytes of disk space, megabytes of physical memory, peak lines per minute of printing capacity.

Section 6.2 discusses some of the sizing methods that have been explored and concludes with a detailed discussion of the method SIZZLE-built systems use. Section 6.3 shows how SIZZLE is used. Section 6.4 discusses how knowledge is represented in SIZZLE-built systems and describes the knowledge operationalization that SIZZLE performs. Section 6.5 discusses the potential for applying SIZZLE to problem domains other than computer-system sizing. The conclusion, section 6.6, compares SIZZLE to knowledge-acquisition tools for heuristic classification.

6.2. Problem-Solving Strategies for Sizing

This section introduces some of the issues that have shaped SIZZLE. Four sizing methods and explorations using each are described. Each method placed constraints upon the shape of co-adapted knowledge-acquisition facilities. The knowledge-acquisition facilities associated with each problem-solving method are described in light of these imposed constraints.

The nature of the sizing-domain expertise available has played an important role in the selection of a sizing knowledge representation, sizing problem-solving methods, and sizing knowledge-acquisition methods. The nature of this expertise is discussed here. This section concludes with a description of the extrapolate-from-a-similar-case method that SIZZLE's sizers use.

6.2.1. Sizing Knowledge

In the computer-sizing domain, the experts are experienced computer sales representatives. In general, sales representatives report that they size computers by becoming reminded of an old sizing problem similar to the new one, but which has already been solved, and using the old problem and its solution as the basis for construction of a plausible solution to the new problem. Confronted with an unusual sizing problem, a sizing expert will telephone other sizing experts, searching for someone who has sized a system for a situation similar to the current problem. Publications for the sales community tend to describe whole sizing solutions for specific situations, rather than provide rules of thumb from which solutions may be constructed. When asked to solve a particular sizing problem, sizing experts volunteer anecdotes about computing systems they have sized in the past for similar situations. Clearly, many sales representatives size systems according to their similarity to sizing problems that have already been solved. Insofar as the sizing knowledge-acquisition tool is coordinated with this way of thinking about the sizing task, sizing experts may find the tool easier to use in building a base of sizing knowledge.

Sizing knowledge possessed by computer-sizing experts has a high obsolescence rate, due to the rapid pace at which hardware and software advances occur in the computer industry. Today, an appropriate quantity of disk space to assign to a timesharing user such as an accountant might be ten megabytes. In two years, falling costs of disk space and new software could render the ten megabyte figure too low. Sizing experts continually revise their methods for solving the "same" sizing problem, tracking such changes in hardware, software, and especially cost, *as they arise*. A sizing knowledge-acquisition tool will be more useful if it is well adapted to this rapid change. This does not mean that the tool has to predict change. Rather, the tool will be more useful if it permits obsolete knowledge to be easily retracted and replaced as needed.

Sizing experts attempt to do what traditionally works: what maximizes income, produces repeat business, minimizes customer complaints, and minimizes lost orders. Sales representatives do not display more than a superficial understanding of *why* the systems they size work in the environments for which they are sized. Analogously, doctors do not always have a complete understanding of how a particular medication works in curing a human ailment. Nor is this necessary for their prescriptions to have value. Doctors are experts at prescribing the right medicine; sales representatives are experts at prescribing the right computer hardware and software. Neither expert fully understands *why* his prescription works. Sizing knowledge and medical treatment knowledge originates empirically, with the informal experience of many people. Therefore, a computer-sizing knowledge-acquisition tool will be more useful insofar as it attempts to capture the experience of these many sizing experts.

6.2.2. Methods for Computer Sizing and Knowledge Acquisition

Devising a sizing method and a coordinated knowledge-acquisition method have not been two completely separable research tasks; each has constrained the other. This point will be elaborated by describing four successive stages in the development and discovery of the case-based sizing method. The implications of each stage for knowledge acquisition will be emphasized. During the successive stages we investigated these problem-solving methods:

1. Sizing by formula

2. Linear combination of user demand models

3. Nonlinear combination of user demand models by simulation

4. Extrapolation from a similar case

Sizing by Formula.

An early system sized computing systems by computing several dozen algebraic formulas obtained from an instructional manual on computer sizing. This system obtained needed input values by questioning the customer and evaluating the formulas. This sizing system had no knowledge of the computing resource demands posed by different types of users. Knowledge acquisition was embodied in a formula translator that generated production rules for computing each formula and for requesting the necessary formula input values.

This approach had two important characteristics. Although sales representatives are initially taught similar formulas, they do not generally use them in practise, in part because customers are unable to supply the inputs these formulas require. Customers would be confronted with questions such as, "How many records of what size will be required for your database applications?" Given answers to such detailed questions, the sizing formula method easily produced correct solutions to sizing problems using arithmetic formulas. However, customers could rarely supply those answers.

Difficulties with this approach arise when one attempts to extend such a system to infer the answers to these detailed questions from answers to more abstract questions that customers can actually answer. Customers are comfortable with such questions as, "How many accountants will use the computing system you wish to purchase?" However, the mapping from such abstract facts to capacity recommendations is not available from sizing experts in the form of formulas. Inducing such arithmetic formulas from detailed examples of correct sizer behavior is also beyond the state of the art in AI today, the main difficulty being that a simple arithmetic formula cannot usually be modified to accommodate an exceptional situation without changing its behavior in many other situations.

Linear Combination of User Demand Models.

We first directly modified the sizing-by-formula method to work from the more abstract initial data available from customers, primarily user quantities. This method produced estimates of computing resource quantities required by a collection of user groups constituting the timesharing users of the to-be-sized system. Each group of users of a given type was assumed to have an independent effect on the demand for each type of resource. Users were represented by instantiating *user demand models*. A user demand model might specify that an accountant requires ten megabytes of disk space and two megabytes of physical memory. A group of five accountants would thus contribute 50 megabytes to total disk space needed, and ten megabytes to total physical memory required. Groups of managers, programmers, or engineers would also contribute independently based upon their respective quantities and the contents of their respective user models. Sizing knowledge was acquired for this system by an interactive program that maintained a large collection of user demand models and permitted retrieval, modification, and indexing of these models. The program generated production rules that embodied these user demand models, as well as rules for driving customer questioning.

The assumption that user groups have an independent effect on capacity recommendations did not produce satisfactory sizing behavior. Timesharing users pose resource demands that do not contribute independently to total system resource requirements. For instance, on a centralized computing system, the physical memory of a timesharing system is serially shared; twice the users do not require twice the memory. We investigated two methods for capturing this nonlinearity, described next.

Nonlinear Combination of User Demand Models by Simulation.

This sizing method took into account the nonlinear interactions between different groups of users in their effects upon total resource requirements. The system did a stochastic simulation of a "typical" day of computer use by designated users. User demand models were augmented to include detailed information about the temporal distribution of demand expected from a given type of interactive user. The recommended sizing solution was constructed from the results of the simulation in such a way that the solution would fail to meet posed resource demands no more than a small percentage of the time during the day. Knowledge-acquisition capabilities were embodied in an extension of the program described above. The generated rules included additional information characterizing temporal variation in demand for each resource type for each user type.

Although computer-system sales representatives do have a feeling for how and when various types of users pose various sorts of resource demand, the information they are able to provide is not sufficiently detailed to support a valid simulation. (More recently, other sources for this detailed information have become available, and the simulation approach is again being investigated.) We learned from this experiment that a different kind of knowledge would have to be collected if the expertise of sales representatives was to be exploited.

Extrapolation from a Similar Case.

This method takes into account nonlinear interactions between user groups without doing a simulation. Cases are expert-validated problem-solution pairs. User demand models do not require detailed information about temporal distribution of resource demand. Rather, user demand models specify how to modify the solution associated with a case as a function of differences between that case and a new case for which a solution is not yet known. This method is fundamentally a form of localized linear extrapolation. The cases are the points from which extrapolation takes place. User demand models carry the information needed to transform a known-to-be-correct solution into a plausible solution to a new sizing task. The means of identifying a similar sizing case from which to extrapolate is embodied in case indexing knowledge in the form of a discrimination tree and a general similarity metric for comparing a new sizing problem to old sizing problems.

This problem-solving method makes knowledge acquisition tractable. It permits SIZZLE to make localized and well behaved modifications to the sizing knowledge base. The method is also easily understood by our domain experts; it is somewhat similar to a common sizing method they use. A sizing case corresponds to a sales representative's notion of a sizing anecdote or a description of an adequately-sized system and its organizational environment. This means that the sizing tool we have devised using this problem-solving method works with knowledge structures easily understood by those from whom the knowledge must be acquired. The remainder of this chapter will be devoted to a description of our approach to the knowledge-acquisition techniques we have found appropriate to this case-based method of automatic sizing.

6.2.3. The Choice: Extrapolation from a Similar Case

Extrapolate-from-a-similar-case sizing involves maintaining a collection of sizing problems and their associated expert-validated solutions (the case knowledge base) and knowledge about how to vary a solution in an appropriate manner as a function of variation of the corresponding problem (user demand models). When a new sizing problem is to be solved, a sizer searches for, and identifies one or more similar cases in the case knowledge base and uses their solutions as the starting points for construction of one or more candidate solutions to the new problem. Each solution retrieved from the case knowledge base is called a *source* solution because it will be modified to produce a plausible solution to the new *target* sizing problem.

A discrimination tree allows the customer or sales representative to identify a collection of useful candidate source sizing cases. The choice of one or more *source* sizing cases is made from this collection using a built-in similarity metric to rate the similarity of each case in the collection to the new sizing problem to be solved.

Generalization from a case is to a region surrounding the case. This method of generalizing is reasonable when a sizer has a lot of knowledge since the covered volume around each case can become arbitrarily small as feedback from customers indicates where extrapolation was inappropriate (exceptions). Cases are modular and preserve information about interactions of case features in a way that highly decomposed rules of thumb do not. Changes to the case knowledge base do not result in catastrophic global damage to system behavior.

It is possible to solve the same sizing problem using several different source cases. This method assumes that the problem similarity metric orders the set of cases used according to the similarity of their *solutions* to the correct solution. As problem similarity increases, so should solution similarity. Similar cases should lead to similar solutions.

Case-based sizing allows available feedback about incorrect behavior to be exploited to improve the sizing knowledge base. A sizer's function may be corrected in a single step by adding a new case to the knowledge base, without doing any computationally expensive data fitting.

6.3. Using SIZZLE

SIZZLE is a tool for interactively acquiring sizing knowledge from a domain expert. A sizing expert poses sizing tasks to an existing automatic sizer and evaluates the sizer's proposed solution. If the sizer performs appropriately, then nothing need be done. If the sizer performs inappropriately, then the sizing expert has the option of invoking SIZZLE and correcting the behavior of the sizer, thereby adding knowledge to the sizer's knowledge base.

This section shows how SIZZLE acquires knowledge when the sizer it is developing performs incorrectly. In the two following sample runs, the expert is shown menus and is expected to select items from the menus that accurately describe an organization within which the to-be-sized computer system is to function. Some of the menus require the specification of quantities of expected users. Menu selections and user responses are underlined.

```
Do you want to (s)ize or (g)enerate rules?
  size

INDUSTRIES
  BANKING
  INSURANCE

BANKING
  BANKING LOAN DEPARTMENT
  BANKING COLLECTION DEPARTMENT

BANKING LOAN DEPARTMENT
  ACCOUNTANTS
  ANALYSTS
  MANAGERS

HOW MANY ACCOUNTANTS ARE THERE?   [ 0 ]: 4

BANKING LOAN DEPARTMENT
  ACCOUNTANTS
  ANALYSTS
  MANAGERS

HOW MANY ANALYSTS ARE THERE?   [ 0 ]: 2

BANKING LOAN DEPARTMENT
  ACCOUNTANTS
  ANALYSTS
  MANAGERS

HOW MANY MANAGERS ARE THERE?   [ 0 ]: 1
```

At this point, the sizer has established that the computer system to be sized will function within the loan department of a bank, and that the computer system will be used by four accountants, two analysts, and one manager. This information will be used in two ways during sizing. First, the information is used to locate a small set of similar sizing problems in the case knowledge base (the Valley Bank and United Bank cases in what follows). Each member of this set has an associated expert-validated solution. Each of these problem-solution pairs is a source sizing case. The criteria for selecting source cases include matching or partially matching industry, department, user types and user quantities. Second, the information collected will be used in the computation of differences between the source and target sizing problems. These differences will, in turn, be used to guide adjustment of the solution to the source case. For example, if the source case involves one accountant and the target case involves four accountants, then these quantitative differences indicate that the resource recommendations of the source solution must be increased to account for the three additional accountants.

> Your sizing task reminds me of the Valley
>   Bank case.
>
> Your sizing task also reminds me of the
>   United Bank case.
>
> I'm not very sure that my solution to your
> sizing problem is reasonable in this case,
> since I sized your posed problem in two
> different ways (that is, from two
> different source sizing cases) and the
> solutions from the two sources did not
> agree with each other very well.
>
> The source sizing problem:
>
>   secretaries   1
>   managers   1
>   accountants   1
>
> Source solution:
>
>   vax 11/780 equivalents   0.9
>   megabytes of physical memory   5
>   disk spindles   1
>   megabytes of disk space for users   10
>   megabytes of system disk space   60
>   megabytes backed up to tape per day 0.3
>   pages per minute of printing   5

```
Your posed sizing problem:

    managers                                     1
    analysts                                     2
    accountants                                  4

Solution to your sizing problem:

    vax 11/780 equivalents                     1.7
    megabytes of physical memory                12
    disk spindles                                2
    megabytes of disk space for users           80
    megabytes of system disk space              60
    megabytes backed up to tape per day        1.0
    pages per minute of printing                12
```

At this point, the posed sizing task has been solved in two independent ways using two different source sizing cases, the Valley Bank and United Bank cases. The sizer was reminded first of the Valley Bank case because it is the most similar to the new sizing task. The sizing solutions derived from the two source cases differs enough to cause the sizer to report some uncertainty about the validity of the solution. The sizer has displayed the more similar of the two source cases, and the solution to the target problem derived from that source case via the extrapolate-from-a-similar-case sizing method. The solution from the other source case is discarded unless requested by the user.

Next, the sizing expert is given an opportunity to invoke SIZZLE to criticize and correct the proposed solution. Note that SIZZLE is always invoked in the context of the solution of a specific a sizing task. This means that it has access to all of the intermediate ingredients in the calculation of the solution to the target problem. Moreover, requiring that knowledge acquisition happen in the context of the solution of a specific sizing task is likely to increase the validity of the knowledge acquired from the sizing expert because he will have a concrete problem in mind when he adds knowledge to the sizer.

```
Do you want an explanation? [ YES ]: no

Do you want to correct my proposed solution?
[ YES ]: <cr>
```

```
Please correct my proposed solution:

What is a better value for megabytes of system
    disk space? [ 60.0 ]: 100
What is a better value for pages per minute of
    printing? [ 12.0 ]: 20
What is a better value for megabytes backed up
    to tape per day? [ 1.0 ]: 2
What is a better value for megabytes of disk
    space for users? [ 80.0 ]: 100
What is a better value for disk spindles?
    [ 2.0 ]: <cr>
What is a better value for megabytes of
    physical memory? [ 12.0 ]: 20
What is a better value for vax 11/780
    equivalents? [ 1.7 ]: 2.3

Please give me a unique name for this case
    [ 1 ]: Morgan Bank

I will remember your sizing problem and
its solution.  If I encounter the same or a
similar problem, I will use your sizing case
as a source analogue.
```

At this point the sizing expert has invoked SIZZLE, presumably because he
does not consider the proposed sizing solution to be reasonable. SIZZLE
displays the parts of the proposed solution to the expert, and requests better
solution values. For example, SIZZLE shows the expert that the sizer
recommended 12 megabytes of physical memory for the to-be-sized system.
The expert indicates that 20 megabytes of physical memory would be a
more appropriate recommendation. Once a corrected solution is obtained
from the expert, SIZZLE prepares a new sizing case for addition to the case
knowledge base. It does this by linking the originally-posed sizing task with
the just-collected validated solution and attaching a name supplied by the
expert to the new case. In this illustration, the new case is named the
"Morgan Bank" case. This case is added to the case knowledge base and
may be used as a source case for solving some sizing task it is similar to, as
illustrated in the following.

Next, the sizing expert is again given an opportunity to pose a sizing task to
the sizer. This example illustrates that SIZZLE has introduced the sizing

case just manufactured (the Morgan Bank case) into the case knowledge base in such a way that the new knowledge is immediately exploitable. Notice here that the expert poses a problem that is similar to the Morgan Bank sizing problem, differing in that there are now one additional analyst and one additional manager.

```
Do you want to (s)ize or (g)enerate rules?
size

INDUSTRIES
  BANKING
  INSURANCE

BANKING
  BANKING LOAN DEPARTMENT
  BANKING COLLECTION DEPARTMENT

BANKING LOAN DEPARTMENT
  ACCOUNTANTS
  ANALYSTS
  MANAGERS

HOW MANY ACCOUNTANTS ARE THERE?   [ 0 ]: 4

BANKING LOAN DEPARTMENT
  ACCOUNTANTS
  ANALYSTS
  MANAGERS

HOW MANY ANALYSTS ARE THERE?   [ 0 ]: 3

BANKING LOAN DEPARTMENT
  ACCOUNTANTS
  ANALYSTS
  MANAGERS

HOW MANY MANAGERS ARE THERE?   [ 0 ]: 2
```

Note below that the Morgan Bank case is chosen as most similar to the new sizing task. Note also that the second-most similar sizing case retrieved is the case originally determined to be most similar to the Morgan Bank case.

Your sizing task reminds me of the Morgan Bank case.

Your sizing task also reminds me of the Valley Bank case.

The source sizing problem:

managers	1
analysts	2
accountants	4

Source solution:

vax 11/780 equivalents	2.3
megabytes of physical memory	20
disk spindles	2
megabytes of disk space for users	100
megabytes of system disk space	100
megabytes backed up to tape per day	2.0
pages per minute of printing	20

Your posed sizing problem:

managers	2
analysts	3
accountants	4

Solution to your sizing problem:

vax 11/780 equivalents	2.6
megabytes of physical memory	23
disk spindles	3
megabytes of disk space for users	130
megabytes of system disk space	100
megabytes backed up to tape per day	2.3
pages per minute of printing	23

Do you want an explanation? [YES]: no

Do you want to correct my proposed solution? [YES]: no

The source and target solutions in this example are quite similar to each other. Since the target problem involved more users than the source problem, the target solution values are all at least as large as the source solution values.

Interactive development of the knowledge base, like that just shown, means that the expert from whom knowledge is extracted is always thinking of a concrete sizing task, rather than of generalized rules of thumb for solving sizing tasks. The illustration shows that acquired knowledge is immediately available for use and that the knowledge is represented in a way that permits it to be of use in solving sizing tasks that do not perfectly match any case in the knowledge base. SIZZLE also compiles user demand models and the associated indexing knowledge into rules. This is an important noninteractive feature not illustrated in this section.

6.4. Knowledge Representation and Proceduralization
SIZZLE represents sizing knowledge gathered from the sizing expert in the case knowledge base as production rules. The case knowledge base contains knowledge about sizing cases and knowledge of how to modify the solutions to these cases when confronted with a novel sizing problem. All of this knowledge is indexed in a discrimination tree, permitting efficient retrieval when a new sizing task is to be solved.

SIZZLE supplies the extrapolate-from-a-similar-case sizing inference engine used by a sizer. The two most important steps in a sizer's problem-solving method are (1) the selection of a similar case, and (2) the adjustment of the solution of the selected case. SIZZLE drops cases into the former step and drops user demand models into the latter step.

SIZZLE adds cases to a sizer's knowledge base by building rules that suggest when a sizing case is likely to be an appropriate source case for solving a given target sizing task. The origin of the sizing cases is described in the previous section. Sizing cases may also be added to the case knowledge base of a sizer by specifying their working memory representation manually. This includes everything after the arrow in the propose-case rule shown below. The user then invokes SIZZLE to generate permanent rules from this schema-like specification. The following rule proposes a case that could have originated when a sizing expert attempted to size a system for an organization called "United Bank."

```
(p propose.cases:1002
;   ================
;   If the BANKING LOAN DEPARTMENT has been
;   selected, then propose case 1002.
;
    (gc ^status current ^name propose.cases
      ^sizing.run <sizing.run>
      ^case.class BANKING.LOAN.DEPARTMENT )
   -(sizing.case
      ^case.class BANKING.LOAN.DEPARTMENT
      ^id 1002 )

-->

    (make sizing.case
      ^case.class BANKING.LOAN.DEPARTMENT
      ^id 1002
      ^target.or.candidate.or.source candidate
      ^sizing.run <sizing.run>
      ^sizing.path nil
      ^organization.name
          |United Bank|
      ^main.application.of.computer
          |Business & Office|
      ^subapplication.of.computer
          |Multifunction Office Systems|

      ^accountants                   3.0
      ^analysts                      0.0
      ^cs.graduate.students          0.0
      ^cs.undergraduate.students     0.0
      ^data.entry.clerks             5.0
      ^librarians                    0.0
      ^managers                      2.0
      ^non-cs.undergraduate.students 0.0
      ^programmers                   0.0
      ^sales.representatives         3.0
      ^secretaries                   2.0
      ^total                         15.0

      ^vax.11/780.equivalents              1.6
      ^megabytes.of.physical.memory       10.0
      ^disk.spindles                       2.0
      ^megabytes.of.disk.space.for.users 200.0
      ^megabytes.of.system.disk.space     80.0
      ^megabytes.backed.up.to.tape.per.day 1.2
      ^pages.per.minute.of.printing        9.0
))
```

Knowledge of how to correct chosen source sizing cases is contained in *user demand models*. A user demand model contains a variety of facts about a particular user type. The most important facts are *adjustment rates*, which encode the rates at which various requirements for resources change with a change in the quantity of the type of user. An adjustment rate represents the demand of a certain type of user for some specific computing resource. For example, in the context of a particular case, each additional accountant may imply a need for an additional 10 megabytes of user disk space. The adjustment rates are used to compute *corrections* to solution values obtained from a source sizing problem. User demand models are added to a sizer by specifying a filled-in schema similar to the working memory representation shown for cases above, and invoking SIZZLE to generate permanent rules from this specification.

SIZZLE generates a variety of types of rules. Discrimination tree rules make and drive the menus that collect information from the customer. For example, a rule generated for the sizer might narrow consideration of source sizing cases to those that are 'banking loan departments' on the basis of information supplied by the customer. Yet other rules implement terminal nodes in the discrimination tree and are responsible for requesting quantities of users. SIZZLE generates rules that activate appropriate user demand models, once a terminal node has been reached in the discrimination tree. For example, the following rule activates the user demand model for the type of accountant that would be found in a banking loan department.

```
(p retrieve.model:BANKING.LOAN.DEPT:accountant
;   ==========================================
;   If the target case involves any accountants
;   then drop the user demand model for that
;   user type into working memory.
;
    (gc ^status current
      ^name retrieve.user.demand.models
      ^sizing.run <sizing.run>
      ^case.class <> nil)
    (sizing.case
      ^target.or.candidate.or.source target
      ^case.class BANKING.LOAN.DEPARTMENT
      ^ACCOUNTANTS > 0.0)
   -(user.demand.model
      ^case.class BANKING.LOAN.DEPARTMENT
      ^user.type ACCOUNTANTS )
```

```
-->
        (make user.demand.model
          ^id (genum)
          ^case.class BANKING.LOAN.DEPARTMENT
          ^sizing.run <sizing.run>
          ^sizing.path nil
          ^user.demand.model.set (genum)

          ^case.class      BANKING.LOAN.DEPARTMENT
          ^user.type       ACCOUNTANTS
          ^determiner      an
          ^singular.name   accountant
          ^plural.name     accountants

          ^vax.11/780.equivalents             0.1
          ^megabytes.of.physical.memory       1.0
          ^disk.spindles                      0.1
          ^megabytes.of.disk.space.for.users 10.0
          ^megabytes.of.system.disk.space     0.0
          ^megabytes.backed.up.to.tape.per.day 0.1
          ^pages.per.minute.of.printing       1.0
    ))
```

6.5. The Scope of the Knowledge-Acquisition Tool

SIZZLE has been used to develop only one system -- a computer-system sizer. However, it is likely that there is a wide variety of tasks that SIZZLE-built systems would be able to perform. In this section, three other sizing tasks are briefly examined. Their similarity to the computer-system sizing task is hypothesized.

The task in computer-system sizing is to map a description of a customer environment into an abstract description of a minimal collection of computing hardware needed to satisfy the customer. In this domain, cases are recorded that describe organizations that have purchased a computing system found to be satisfactory. Frequently, each case indicates the numbers of workers of various types in the organization and the capacity, along various dimensions, of the computer system in that organization. Each case also includes an abstract description of the hardware configuration found to be satisfactory. The three similar tasks we will examine here are: (1) electric-motor sizing, (2) legal-claim sizing, and (3) copier sizing.

Electric-motor sizing: This task involves choosing a motor of optimal horsepower to drive a system of rotating components. In principle this can be done by precisely calculating the polar moment of inertia of each of the rotating components. In practice, such calculations are much too time-consuming. Consequently, a mechanical engineer will allow for the effect of the rotating components by comparing their size and shape to the sizes and shapes of other objects with known polar moments of inertia. Knowledge of these objects of known size, shape and inertia may be interpreted as a knowledge base of cases. The reasoning method just described is fairly similar to the reasoning method of a SIZZLE-built sizer. The methods differ primarily in that the engineer will seek to "trap" the polar moment of inertia (and hence the needed horsepower) between the known inertias of two objects, while a SIZZLE-built sizer would extrapolate upwards or downwards from the inertia of a single object.

Sizing the amount of money to seek in a malpractice suit: Here the task is to decide the damages to claim in a lawsuit. (For comparison, see [Waterman 85].) In this domain, documented cases exist that consist of descriptions of malpractice suits that succeeded; each case would indicate, along various dimensions, the type and magnitude of injury suffered by the party bringing suit and the size of the compensatory amount that was awarded by the court. In this domain, the size of largest claim that can reasonably be requested without losing the legal case depends on many unknown variables interacting in a very complex process (involving, for example, the moral judgments of jurors). The legal community copes with this complexity by maintaining a collection of cases, in much the same way that a computer-system sales community copes with the complexity of organizational niches for computers: Both communities keep track of cases and their associated success or failure, and use these cases in future problem solving.

Sizing an automatic copier: Here the task is to determine the minimum amount of copier capacities of various sorts a given customer will require to meet stated needs. In this domain, the knowledge base would consist of descriptions of organizations with appropriate copiers; each case would indicate the number of workers of various types in the organization and the capacity, along various dimensions, of the copier in that organization.

Each of these sizing tasks has the features that SIZZLE presupposes:

- Solutions are expressed primarily in quantitative terms, whether megabytes of physical memory, horsepower, dollar compensation to seek, or copies per minute.

- A large collection of validated cases is available. There are thousands of sites at which computer systems have been sized where the customer is satisfied. Likewise for motors, and copiers. Similarly, a record is kept of legal cases and their details.

- Experts have a notion of *overall* degree of similarity between different problems.

- Experts can note specific, gradated differences between sizing problems. In the computer- and copier-sizing tasks, differences in quantities of users are relevant. And, legal cases can be discriminated on the basis of magnitude of various sorts of injury.

- Knowledge exists of how to change a solution to a sizing problem appropriately for changes to the associated problem, at least when such changes are not too large. More legal damages means you can demand greater compensation, and lawyers may be able to attach dollar amounts to such increments in damage. More computer users means more disk space, and sizing experts can say how *much* more, per user in a given context.

- The precise nature of the process is not very well understood. The organizations into which copiers and computers are placed are complex, as is the behavior of juries that decide the outcome of lawsuits. Put another way, concise and accurate laws governing the degree of customer satisfaction resulting from the introduction of a particular collection of hardware into the customer's environment are not available, due to the complexity of computers, customer environments, and of the interaction between the two.

6.6. Conclusion

SIZZLE's develpment included explorations into selecting a problem-solving method both appropriate for sizing tasks and capable of supporting effective knowledge-elicitation strategies. SIZZLE assumes an extrapolate-from-similar-case problem-solving method. Each sizer it builds collects a description of factors affecting resource demand and selects the expert-validated sizing case most similar to this description. It then modifies the solution according to the differences between the validated case and the case to be sized by applying user demand models.

The problem-solving method makes knowledge acquisition tractable. It allows SIZZLE to make localized and well behaved modifications to the knowledge base. The method is easily understood by sizing experts since it is similar to a common method they use. The knowledge-elicitation strategy allows experts to add to the knowledge base while solving a concrete problem. Poor behavior can be corrected immediately.

SIZZLE was developed to build quantitative sizers and has been used to create an expert computer-system sizer. It is similar to tools that build heuristic classifiers. Given a new sizing problem, the process of identifying a good source sizing case is equivalent to classifying the new sizing case. However, SIZZLE also differs from tools that build heuristic classifiers. First, the "classes" into which SIZZLE-built sizers classify new sizing problems are actually specific sizing cases. Second, a SIZZLE-built sizer is not finsihed once it has identified a source sizing case; the source serves only as a starting point for corrections that produce a final sizing solution.

For example, like the MOLE knowledge-acquisition system described in chapter 3, SIZZLE presupposes a problem-solving method that chooses one best alternative (the source sizing case) from a pre-enumerated set of alternatives (the sizing cases in the case knowledge base). It differs from MOLE in that it acquires knowledge used in the adjustment or correction of the chosen alternative. User demand models have no counterpart in MOLE, but they are needed in order to generalize from the best-matching source sizing case, which is rarely a perfect or even close match.

Acknowledgements

John McDermott provided substantial assistance with the research described in this chapter. He also supplied valuable feedback on drafts of the chapter. David Marques and Sandy Marcus also provided helpful comments. David Sweetman was helpful in a variety of ways, especially in the important task of putting me in contact with people who do computer-system sizing for a living. Stephen Judd, James Pompano, James Delahouse and many other sizing experts volunteered many hours of their valuable time to help me understand how computer-system sizing is done. Michael Offutt explained electric-motor sizing to me. The first version of the sizer was primarily implemented by John McDermott and Kim Smith. In addition to myself, a number of others, including Karen Kukich, Bob Schnelbach, Tianran Wang, George Wood, and Sandy Marcus, also contributed to the early work described in section 6.2.2. I had especially helpful discussions about sizing knowledge acquisition and sizing methods with John McDermott, Georg Klinker, George Wood, Karen Kukich, Sandy Marcus, Larry Eshelman, and Mike Hannon.

7. RIME: Preliminary Work Toward a Knowledge-Acquisition Tool

Judith Bachant

Abstract

When analyzing a task for potential use of a knowledge-acquisition tool, it may not be clear whether to use an existing tool or build a new one. If the latter is indicated, it is even less apparent how to proceed. XCON[14] (also known as R1) [McDermott 82, Bachant 84], an expert system application that configures DEC computer systems, has evolved over time and expanded in scope. At one level, its task is understood, as the program is used extensively on a daily basis and performs well. However, this understanding appears incomplete when considering a knowledge-acquisition tool for XCON's task. Additional groundwork needs to be covered and foundations set before it will be feasible to design such a tool. RIME is an attempt to establish some of that foundation. It is a programming methodology that takes a step toward understanding the nature of a potential automated tool and, in so doing, helps human knowledge engineers design and develop an expert system.

7.1. Introduction

The problem-solving methods and representations used by knowledge-acquisition tools, as presented in this book and elsewhere, may now appear obvious. Each provides a logical and reasonable way to perform an associated task that is amenable to automation. However, the methods were created after a great deal of careful analysis of one or more tasks and, frequently, after examining less regular and structured approaches to the problem (see, for example, [Clancey 86]). The analysis included scrutinizing applications for potential regularities and structure that could be consistently imposed, and then exploited, by an automated tool.

---

[14]The following are trademarks of Digital Equipment Corporation: XCON, RIME, and DEC.

The work described here is at this stage. XCON is a production-level expert system whose programming effort was examined for automation potential. XCON was then reimplemented using RIME, a methodology that structures, formalizes, and organizes programming practices. The reimplemented XCON is in a form that allows the creation of automated tools to aid its further development. It may be a long time before the level of automation is comparable to that of a knowledge-acquisition tool; however, progressing to even this stage has proven beneficial.

Section 7.2 presents issues that must be addressed by a knowledge-acquisition tool in the context of XCON's task and then highlights those that were, at least in a preliminary way, considered by RIME. RIME itself will be described in section 7.3. Section 7.4 outlines its current scope of applicability, and section 7.5 presents some future directions.

7.2. A Knowledge-Acquisition Tool for XCON?
The concept of a knowledge-acquisition tool includes two very different, but interrelated, functions. One involves the elicitation of information from an expert by asking a minimum number of questions and checking for inconsistencies or gaps. The other entails the generation or extension of an expert system application from that knowledge. These functions are performed today by human knowledge engineers as the core of their job. It is hoped that by automating this work, an expert in a particular domain could then create an application himself, without artificial intelligence and software-engineering expertise. To progress toward this automation, it is critical to examine the work performed and the issues faced by the knowledge engineers.

7.2.1. Acquiring Knowledge
Some of the most difficult issues faced by XCON's knowledge engineers when eliciting knowledge from experts are obtaining the knowledge unobtrusively, handling the sheer quantity of information, and dealing with the diversity of sources. XCON's experts do not provide domain information in a format that maps directly onto XCON's representation. The ratio of irrelevant to relevant knowledge is very high, especially since many of the source documents are written for other purposes. Sometimes it is difficult to assess the relevance of a piece of knowledge because the

boundaries of the task are not constant. XCON receives knowledge from a large number of diverse sources distributed worldwide. There are hundreds of experts and thousands of users. Any given option[15] (for example, a particular disk), typically involves about four experts at any point in time. Different experts become involved as the option progresses through its life cycle. There are approximately a dozen different categories of human users, as well as expert systems and other applications that receive input from XCON. These users provide input to the development of the application in the form of business requirements. The logistics of coordinating sources and the concerns of ownership and responsibility for the knowledge are difficult issues under these circumstances.

XCON developers attempt to minimize the time and effort required of the experts. They analyze available documentation and extract potentially relevent knowledge. The actual artifacts, in this case computer hardware, are examined. Only after a significant amount of preliminary work is a human expert interviewed in depth. Many inferences and assumptions have already been made based on the preliminary investigations, extensive knowledge of the domain itself, and how it is characterized in the application. Thus, a particular expert needs only to affirm or disaffirm those assumptions and describe aspects that are totally new or confusing. The questions then have the character of exception handling, primarily focusing on the unique aspects of the new information.

There are many promising research efforts that attempt to deal with these issues through automation. The efforts include explorations in analogy, learning from examples, program simulation, use of graphics, vision, and distributed systems. These capabilities would, most likely, need to be combined in a knowledge-acquisition tool that used a variety of techniques to gather large quantities of information from diverse sources in order to satisfy XCON's knowledge-acquisition requirements.

---

[15]XCON currently handles over 30,000 options.

7.2.2. Generating an Application

The automated generation of an application like XCON presents another set of problems. The predominant problem is dealing with pervasive, unpredictable change. XCON's domain is dynamic; its scope of functionality has expanded and mutated throughout its history. It is difficult to identify any aspect that has remained static. XCON's rule base has changed at the rate of 40 to 50% per year. This dynamism, coupled with the sheer size and complexity of the system, make its automatic generation particularly challenging. As an expert system that is embedded in business processes and depended upon by its users, it is sensitive to the limitations imposed by time, cost, people, and many other types of resources. Therefore, XCON's knowledge engineers constantly make tradeoffs based on efficiency, language and tool limitations, hardware availability, and cost to the users; the tradeoffs can compromise an ideal solution to a coding problem. In addition, some solutions change with time because better ways are discovered to solve the problems. These issues imply a need for a high degree of flexibility that must be balanced with a knowledge-acquisition tool's requirements for structure and consistency.

7.2.3. Issues addressed by RIME

The concerns in generating an application are the ones that were considered in the development of RIME. There was no attempt to deal with issues involving the actual elicitation of knowledge from an expert. The focus centered on creating a programming methodology that would effectively facilitate change while maintaining stability. Although the RIME project involved the definition of structure, organization, and regularities in general, this was done with the consideration that these are subject to change.

7.3. What is RIME?

Providing groundwork for a knowledge-acquisition tool was one motivation for the RIME project. It was also hoped that by applying the experience gained in years of developing XCON and by examining related research efforts, the programming of XCON could be enhanced, with or without an actual tool. The initial problems that needed to be addressed to prepare for automation were also ones that caused difficulties for humans in developing XCON code. The problematic features of the code included implicit control and functionality, decentralization of knowledge, inconsistency, and idiosyncracy. Because of these, it was sometimes difficult to implement changes or comprehend unfamiliar sections of the code.

The acronym "RIME" stands for "R1's Implicit Made Explicit." The theme of explicitness is pervasive throughout the methodology, and gives it coherence. Making things explicit implies bringing them out in the open and exposing them to scrutiny. This was seen as the only way to deal with the overriding dynamism and complexity of the task. The greater the ability to identify, access, and manipulate only the relevant entities involved in any change, the greater the assurance of stability for the rest of the system, eliminating unexpected effects and uncertainty as much as possible. Identifying and stating commonalities and differences, naming and defining entities, defining boundaries, and separating compound functions were some of the techniques used toward the realization of this goal.

An overview of the RIME methodology follows. The details describe the concrete ways in which RIME attempts to make explicit the various aspects of XCON's software-engineering enterprise. Some aspects deal with low-level, code-related activities in an attempt to realize general software-engineering principles. Others relate to what are sometimes referred to as "knowledge-level" concepts. These concepts are used in the distinction "between the knowledge required to solve a problem and the processing required to bring that knowledge to bear in real time and real space" [Newell 81]. An ideal knowledge-acquisition tool would deal with an expert only at the knowledge level and would automate the processing of the knowledge acquired. Explicit differentiation of the levels, at least conceptually, is needed to deal with each accordingly.

RIME addresses four major areas: control, focus of attention, organizational structures, and programming conventions. Each is described by presenting samples of the guidelines involved and mechanisms to realize them. An inherent difficulty in defining an entity that assumes pervasive change is that the definition itself is subject to change. The RIME methodology has, in fact, assumed various forms. The guidelines and mechanisms described are particular to its implementation in XCON, although many can be applied more generally. An example is also presented in each area. This is not a complete description, but it should provide a sense of the project.

Figure 7-1 ties together the elements described in the rest of the section. The RIME methodology assumes that each program is composed of problem spaces, the basic functional unit recognizable at the task level. Each problem space employs a single problem-solving method that defines what knowledge should be brought to bear when. Each problem-solving method consists of a sequence of steps, where each step specifies when a group of rules can become active. The sequence of steps may be repeated within a problem space; a given rule can only activate in one step within its problem space. Rule type is an organizational structure that classifies a rule according to its role within a step. Subgroup is an organizational structure within rule type that relates the function of a rule to the explicit function and organization of the task. In the RIME methodology, each rule represents a unit of knowledge that has singular functionality.

7.3.1. Control
Control deals with formalities introduced to realize the flow of program execution, primarily in sequencing events. It includes techniques that guide the activities of a program itself rather than concentrating on the functionality that is produced by a program.

Guidelines/Principles.

The following state control guidelines or principles:

- Any type of control should be realized by explicit means. This requires consciousness of the types of control exercised in program execution and standard mechanisms to realize each type. This conforms to the trend of striving to separate the knowledge from the inferencing.

- The features provided by a language for conflict resolution may encourage implicit rather than explicit control. If this is true, mechanisms to encourage explicit control must be defined. XCON is written in OPS5 [Forgy 81], which evaluates the recency of matched data and specificity of rules in order to decide which rule to apply to what data. These conflict resolution techniques are applied generally and act at too low a level to relate to the task itself. Using them has not promoted clarity of program control.

- It is important to realize appropriate means of control, striking a balance between the tendencies to over-control and under-

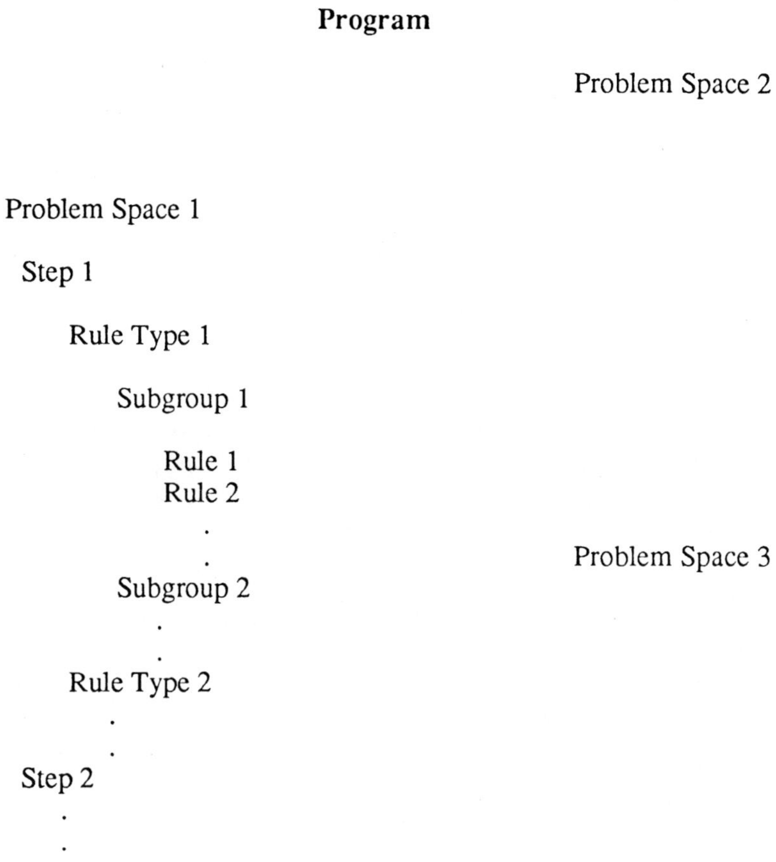

Program

Problem Space 2

Problem Space 1

Step 1

Rule Type 1

Subgroup 1

Rule 1
Rule 2

.

. Problem Space 3

Subgroup 2

.

.

Rule Type 2

.

.

Step 2

.

.

Figure 7-1: RIME Overview Diagram

control sequences of actions. Sequential programming tends to over-control by sequencing each line of code regardless of the task. Data-driven programming tends toward under-control, until it becomes painfully obvious that control is needed and temporal issues cannot be ignored. Then, because of typically inadequate control mechanisms, over-control can become the tendency.

Mechanisms.

The following mechanisms are used to realize control:

- Problem-solving methods are used for algorithmic control whenever a series of steps needs to be performed in a prespecifiable sequence. One method will be presented in the example; others are detailed in other chapters of this book. Currently, the RIME version of XCON uses six methods. RIME places no restrictions on the potential generality of a method. A method may be tightly coupled to a specific domain or applicable in a wide variety of tasks.

- Situational control is realized by proposing alternative actions and choosing among them using domain-specific knowledge. Part of XCON's task knowledge includes conditional orderings of activities. The content of the configuration input determines some of the steps that should occur and has an impact on sequencing.

- Pattern-matching on relevant conditions is used when data-driven control is appropriate. The rules themselves do not include implicit mechanisms to realize the order of their execution in relation to other rules.

EXAMPLE: The Propose-Apply Method.

XCON uses a variety of problem-solving methods in its problem spaces, the major subtasks into which it is partitioned. Instead of the entire application utilizing one method, XCON is divided into many problem spaces with each one using a single method. Movement between the problem spaces is determined using domain considerations. Currently, the RIME version of XCON includes 32 problem spaces. The term "problem space" and the method described here were adapted from the SOAR research [Laird 83]. SOAR-built systems also partition their tasks into problem spaces, the difference being that the same method is used in each problem space.

This example details a version of the *propose-apply* problem-solving method that is most frequently used in XCON. It is similar in nature to the other problem-solving methods presented in this book. In general, the propose-apply method formalizes the decision-making process. It is used to choose from alternatives that represent either action plans or objects. It is particularly useful for allowing domain considerations in the arbitration process of decisions related to program execution, in contrast to the standard pattern-matching view of taking immediate action upon satisfaction of all the conditions and resolving conflicts using general principles. Propose-apply can be used to decide explicitly which course of action to take when more than one is possible. In some cases, this is like splitting apart the conditions and actions of a rule to delay the action. The action is carried out only after relevant plans have been proposed and evaluated and a single plan has been chosen. This method is useful when it is difficult to express the exact situation under which one plan should be carried out rather than another, or when a particular object should be chosen before all others. On the other hand, it is tedious and cumbersome to represent an algorithm whose steps are clearly defined and must occur in a specified order using this method. It also does not add value to the solving of problems that do not involve complex decisions or that can be handled in a more straightforward way.

The steps of propose-apply follow.

1. **INITIALIZE-GOAL**: This step prepares for the   cycle through a problem space. It creates a control element that includes the list of steps appropriate for the method. It also removes obsolete elements.

2. **PROPOSE-OPERATOR**:   This step proposes plausible courses of action or appropriate objects represented by "operators." An operator is an element that represents one alternative in the decision-making process. It also rejects the operators that are disqualified for some immediately apparent reason.

3. **PRUNE-OPERATOR**: This step is used to remove obvious losers. Operators with lower preference classes[16] will be removed, as well as rejected operators, if there are nonrejected operators contending.

4. **ELIMINATE-OPERATOR**: This step eliminates operators using domain-specific considerations. Each rule looks at two operators and favors one. This step is used strictly for pairwise comparison. A variation of the propose-apply method includes a step for voting, similar to the voting concept in an early version of SOAR [Laird 83]. It is only used in cases where the evidence is truly cumulative.

---

[16]There are three classes -- better, acceptable, worse -- with most preferences being acceptable. Within the acceptable class, domain considerations are used to choose among the alternatives. Better and worse are used only for cases in which the preference is nonconditional.

5. **SELECT-ONE-OPERATOR:** This step examines the results of the evaluation and chooses one operator. If there is a tie, it chooses one at random. A possible extension includes the use of an evaluation function in the event of a tie.
6. **APPLY-OPERATOR:** This step realizes the configuration functionality. Actions are taken to further the configuration or other problem spaces are entered to implement a more complex plan.
7. **EVALUATE-GOAL:** This step evaluates the goal at the end of a cycle in order to recognize success or failure. If there is success or failure, the problem space is exited and control returns to the parent problem space. If no rules in this step fire, another iteration through the problem space occurs.

Two propose rules and one eliminate rule that mediates between them are presented to illustrate the organization imposed by the propose-apply method. These are examples of OPS5 code. Comments are preceded by semicolons. Each condition or action element is delimited by parentheses, and condition elements are separated from action elements by an arrow. Within an element, the first word denotes the element class; the attributes are indicated by "^," with the value following each attribute. Variables are indicated by angle brackets (for example, <variable-name>). Same-named variables must match exactly within a rule, but not across rules. A condition element preceded by not ("-") indicates that there must be no element that matches the condition.

The following is a reasonably general rule to find an appropriate space in a cabinet for a rack-mountable device. The spaces are numbered to indicate, in general, in what order the spaces are to be filled. This rule looks for the lowest-numbered drive slot.

```
(p select-drive-space:propose:110f:lowest-drive-slot
; Justification: Rack-mountable devices must be mounted in cabinets so
;                propose the lowest numbered unused drive-slot in the
;                current cabinet.
; Specificities: A box-space set-attribute can be used for a device when
;                the ^drive-slot attribute has a number assigned to it. It
;                is unused when it is ^state unused.
; Loop Inhibitor: Refraction
; Subgroups: 1. select-drive-space
;            2. primary-task
;
  (gc ^activity-phase current ^step propose-operator ^instance <instance>
       ^problem-space select-drive-space ^parent-space <parent-space>)
  (device ^activity-phase current ^floor-category rack-mountable)
  (container ^class cabinet ^capacity-phase current ^token <token>)
  (capacity-template ^class cabinet ^token <token> ^box-space <box-space>)
  (set-attribute ^parent-attribute box-space ^pointer <box-space>
                 ^state unused ^drive-slot { <drive-slot> <=> 0 }
                 ^token { <token1> <> nil })
  -(set-attribute ^parent-attribute box-space ^pointer <box-space>
                 ^state unused ^drive-slot { <=> 0 < <drive-slot> }
                 ^token <> nil)
  -->
  (make operator ^id (genatom) ^activity-phase pending ^status proposed
                 ^problem-space select-drive-space
                 ^parent-space <parent-space>
                 ^conception-space select-drive-space ^method propose-apply
                 ^instance <instance> ^preference acceptable
                 ^subtask primary-task ^token <token1>))
```

In some cabinets there are preferences as to which devices are placed where. For instance, some drives may have limitations for cable routing and can be located only in certain spots; some have removable disks or tapes that can only be easily accessable from the top of the cabinet; and so on. These preferences are indicated by the "drive-space-priority" restriction, which indicates that a certain type of device is allowed in the space and has been assigned a priority number in relation to other devices allowed in that space.

```
(p select-drive-space:propose:110j:exclusive-rackmount-drive-space
; Justification: Rack-mountable devices must be mounted in cabinets so
;                 propose an unused drive-slot in the current cabinet which
;                 is reserved exclusively for the current device.
; Specificities: A box-space set-attribute can be used for a device when
;                 the ^drive-slot attribute has a number assigned to it. It
;                 is unused when it is ^state unused. It is exclusively
;                 reserved for a device when there is a drive-space-priorities
;                 restriction associated with it whose ^device-subtype matches
;                 the devices ^subtype and which has ^extent exclusive.
; Loop Inhibitor: Refraction
; Subgroups: 1. select-drive-space
;                 2. primary-task
;
   (gc ^activity-phase current ^step propose-operator ^instance <instance>
         ^problem-space select-drive-space ^parent-space <parent-space>)
   (device ^activity-phase current ^floor-category rack-mountable
           ^subtype <subtype>)
   (container ^class cabinet ^capacity-phase current ^token <token>)
   (capacity-template ^class cabinet ^token <token> ^box-space <box-space>)
   (set-attribute ^parent-attribute box-space ^pointer <box-space>
                  ^drive-slot <=> 1 ^state <> used ^token { <token1> <> nil })
   (restriction ^scope drive-space-priorities ^token <token1>
                ^device-subtype <subtype> ^extent exclusive)
   -->
   (make operator ^id (genatom) ^activity-phase pending ^status proposed
                  ^problem-space select-drive-space
                  ^parent-space <parent-space>
                  ^conception-space select-drive-space ^method propose-apply
                  ^instance <instance> ^preference acceptable
                  ^subtask primary-task ^token <token1>))
```

In a given run of the system, these two rules could propose two different spaces. As an alternative, a more general rule could have been included in the system to propose all possible spaces. This is not done across the board in XCON for efficiency. In either case, the rule below would be applicable. This rule prefers the space with the priority restriction for the chosen device. This frees an unrestricted slot for another device that may need it or eliminates a space that is not appropriate for this particular device.

```
(p select-drive-space:eliminate:340c:prefer-exclusive-space
; Justification: If more than one mounting space is proposed in the current
;               cabinet and one of them is reserved exclusively for the
;               current device, then prefer it.
; Specificities: A mounting space is exclusively reserved for a device when
;               there is a drive-space-priorities restriction associated with
;               it whose ^device-subtype matches the devices ^subtype and
;               which has ^extent exclusive.
; Loop inhibitor: Removed-wme -- operator
; Subgroups: 1. same-subtask
;
  (gc ^activity-phase current ^problem-space select-drive-space
      ^step eliminate-operator)
  (operator ^activity-phase pending ^status proposed ^token <token>
            ^problem-space select-drive-space ^subtask primary-task)
  {(operator ^activity-phase pending ^status proposed
            ^problem-space select-drive-space ^subtask primary-task
            ^token { <token1> <> <token> }) <operator>}
  (device ^activity-phase current ^subtype <subtype>)
  (restriction ^scope drive-space-priorities ^token <token>
            ^device-subtype <subtype> ^extent exclusive)
  -(restriction ^scope drive-space-priorities ^token <token1>
            ^device-subtype <subtype> ^extent exclusive)
  -->
  (remove <operator>))
```

Implications for Automation.

Many of the problem-solving methods are general enough to be used in multiple instances within a task and in different tasks. The features that realize a method (for instance, the steps and their representational implications) can be explicitly defined and used consistently. The other mechanisms for realizing control can also be standardized. With standardization, a part of each rule could be generated automatically or at least checked by an automated tool for conformance.

7.3.2. Focus of Attention

Focus of attention deals with formalities introduced to identify the set of actions and objects that are focused upon during a span of time in program execution. It may be considered an aspect of search control. It is dealt with separately here to highlight its importance in a system that deals with large quantities of potential candidates. XCON must keep track of choices made, since its main task involves defining complex interrelationships.

Guidelines/Principles.

The following are guidelines and principles used to manage the focus of attention:

- Common means of indicating state information should be defined. This is an area that can approach incomprehensibility if a variety of state indicators are allowed to proliferate over time.

- The location of a particular activity in the abstract map of the system should be determined easily. This is vital in a large, complex application.

- Attention should remain on a problem until it is resolved. This is particularly useful for XCON's task, since it provides some predictability in an area that must remain flexible and variable.

- The mechanisms defined should also enhance efficiency of code execution, since pinpointing the focus of attention limits the possibilities for matching. This is an important consideration for XCON, given its use.

Mechanisms.

The following describe some of the mechanisms used to encourage adherence to the guidelines:

- Defined state attributes are used to limit applicable elements. These are illustrated in the example given below. They are defined consistently and used to indicate the state of an element from within the particular element.

- Defined elements are used to form sets of possible alternatives, pare down appropriate members, and pinpoint the focus of attention. Operators perform this function for the propose-apply method. They are special-purpose elements that may represent other elements, groups of elements, or other entities, such as problem spaces. This is an external mechanism to indicate the state of other elements and entities.

- A specified element is used to locate activity in the higher-level map of the system. In XCON, this is also the control element or element recognized by OPS5 for special, control-related properties.

EXAMPLE: State Indicators.

In any program, it is important to understand where attention is focused at any point in time. Questions such as, "How does the system flow?"; "What happens when?"; and "What object is being focused on?" must be addressed for coding by either a human developer or an automated tool. In a sequential language, some of the control is embedded (that is, the next line of code will execute next) with explicit exceptions (such as calls to subroutines that return to the next sequential line of code and go-to statements). In a pattern-matching language, the focus of attention is revisited, or decided anew, after each rule firing. This allows for flexibility, but a program can also become hopelessly confused, and be confusing to a human. The following mechanism involves special attributes with a set of defined values that indicate state for an element from within that element.

Activity-Phase and Capacity-Phase: The values of these attributes (*virgin, pending, current, inactive, done*) indicate the state of an element at any point in time. A value of *current* indicates that the element is being attended to at that point in time. It indicates a choice or a decision that was made. *Virgin* indicates that the element has not yet been considered or touched by the program. *Pending* is used to narrow a set of contenders, while *inactive* indicates that the element has been temporarily excluded from consideration. Both imply that some activity has occurred but more is still needed. *Done* means that processing the element is complete. Since these values are constants in the code, efficiency of pattern matching is increased.

Implications for Automation.

The mechanisms described are used consistently across varying elements and types of entities. This makes them amenable to future automation, as well as to human comprehension. In addition, the indicator of a problem or constraint violation is represented in a standard way throughout the system, which aids in tracking its resolution. This type of regularity can initially lead to a tool that detects areas where the path to resolution is not fully covered.

7.3.3. Organizational Structures

Organizational structures deal with formalities introduced to provide a framework and a way to refer to collections or groupings of rules and index into them effectively. These categories may, or may not, relate to program control or even functionality. They do require the definition of explicit criteria for membership.

Guidelines/Principles.

The following encourage the explicit categorization of system entities:

- "Have a place for everything and keep everything in its place" is the underlying theme. The notion that "data-driven programming is easy because you can just add rules anywhere" is not manageable in complex, rapidly evolving applications.

- It is important to name groups of rules and explicitly define their criteria for membership. To enforce this guideline, it is useful to define the maximum number of rules allowed to remain in a group with no further partitioning. This limit was set at 26 for XCON, since the unique identifiers for rules within a group are the letters of the alphabet. Groupings are encouraged even when this number has not been reached, if there are apparent divisions.

- A rule should be limited to a single function. A number of programming efforts have come to this conclusion independently. In XCON, the initial trend was to pack a rule with multiple functions. In time, it became difficult to discern distinctions among rules.

Mechanisms.

The following mechanisms are used in the definition of categories:

- Problem spaces are used for task-level groupings. Problem spaces in XCON are grouped using logical criteria relating to the task. Some focus on the configuration of an object (for example, a box or module); others focus on a generic function (for example, performing computations). There are still others in which grouping is important for other reasons (for example, output messages and external routine calls).

- Steps within a problem space partition the rules that can potentially activate at the same time. This grouping mechanism relates to control issues. Rules belonging to the same step cannot have any requirements for sequencing among them.

- Subgroups provide for categorization based on defined criteria within a step of a particular problem space. A Dewey-decimal-like system for knowledge organization is used and described in the example. None of the criteria defined by this mechanism relates to control issues.

EXAMPLE: Subgroups.

The role that knowledge plays in a problem-solving method defines a part of its representation in the system. Representation at the rule level is defined as a rule type (sometimes referred to as a knowledge type), with each rule type associated with a step in a method. Problem-solving methods define a level of representation based on the kind of knowledge they use and the form the knowledge must take for program execution. Within a rule type there may be numerous rules. There are representational issues that deal with the scope of the entire application rather than with just what can co-occur during a single run of the program. This representational complexity, in some cases, includes hundreds of rules of diverse function.

For example, cabling is treated differently in different hardware system types. Although all panel types may not co-occur for any particular configuration, their representational implications for taking advantage of similarities and distinguishing differences must be considered. Similarly, if an application for diagnosing human diseases were expanded to include diseases of other animals, rules that perform the same role may need to be partitioned along other dimensions. For example, differences between doctors and veterinarians, communication paths between patient and healer, or variations of testing procedures could be reflected. Common aspects could be treated generally. This partitioning may relate to types of objects or functions rather than to the role the knowledge plays in the system.

Subgroups were created to organize rules that have something in common. That "something" is explicitly identified and named. This acts as an index into the knowledge base, to identify what already exists and to help a programmer or an automated tool decide where to place something new. Guidelines were developed to define common criteria used in the XCON domain and to lend some regularity across the problem spaces.

Figure 7-2 displays the guidelines used for two rule types from the propose-apply method: eliminate and apply. Rules are assigned a subgroup identification number according to their membership in each subgroup level. The "(optional)"s indicate that the criteria can be specific to the problem space or can remain undefined. When defined, these are filled-in for a particular problem space. Additional subgroups can be defined by a specific problem space. If there are only a few rules in the level 1 group, there is no need to define further levels, and so forth. The number of levels can be increased without affecting the overall organization. Most of XCON's subgroups are defined for three or fewer levels, with a few at four. The accumulation of more than 26 rules in a subgroup requires the definition of another subgroup level or a regrouping at the present level. Category names not in parentheses are criteria to be used as is. They are specific for the configuration of an entity. Other, significantly different tasks, require different groupings.

Implications for Automation.

The subgroup mechanism uses a standard, hierarchical numbering scheme. Some subgroup levels are used consistently across multiple problem spaces. This could help an automated tool understand the types of knowledge that may be needed beyond the level required for control. These mechanisms would also benefit a tool that indexed into the knowledge base in order to communicate with an expert concerning existing knowledge.

7.3.4. Programming Conventions

Programming conventions deal with formalities introduced to insure homogeneity of the code and to use similar means of realizing similar functionality. Many of these were introduced to emulate the uniformity of code that would be produced by an automated generator. Others deal with conventions of representation.

Guidelines/Principles.

The following describe guidelines in the use of programming conventions.

- Explicitly defined conventions and consistent use of them are key. Conventions are defined at a variety of levels from the white-space format of rules to techniques of problem-solving.

Rule Type: ELIMINATE

#	LEVEL 1	LEVEL 2	LEVEL 3
100	Absolute	(optional)	(optional)
200	Diff-problem-spaces	(optional)	(optional)
300	Same-problem-space	absolute	(optional)
310	diff-subtasks	(optional)	
320	diff-instances	(optional)	
330	same-bus	\<bus\>	
340	same-derived-bus	\<bus\>	
350	same-class	\<class\>	
360	same-type	\<type\>	
370	same-name	(optional)	
380	same-subtask	(optional)	

Rule Type: APPLY

#	LEVEL 1	LEVEL 2	LEVEL 3
100	Initialize	(optional)	(optional)
200	Update-status-or-phase	component	(optional)
210	operator	(optional)	
220	restriction	(optional)	
230	template	(optional)	
300	Update-capacity	retrieve-template	(optional)
310	power	(optional)	
320	space	(optional)	
330	load	(optional)	
340	length	(optional)	
350	bus-support	(optional)	
360	bandwidth	(optional)	
400	Update-containership	create-pcon	(optional)
410	text-slots	(optional)	
420	contained	(optional)	
430	containing	(optional)	
440	container	(optional)	
450	image-name	(optional)	
500	Update-connectivity	create-pcon	(optional)
510	from	(optional)	
520	to	(optional)	
530	cable	(optional)	
540	other	(optional)	
600	Update-relative-position	assign-ordinal	(optional)
610	position	(optional)	
700	Finalize	(optional)	(optional)

Figure 7-2: Sample Subgroup Scheme Definition Guides

- Mechanisms, tools, processes, and other·means should be developed to encourage and enforce the adherence to convention. This is important in an environment where expediency is critical.

- The author of the code should not be identifiable based on style idiosyncracies. Creativity should be expressed at the problem-solving level, rather than through the structure of rules.

Mechanisms.

The following mechanisms encourage the realization of the guidelines above:

- Conventions are defined that govern the following areas: the form of the code (for example, format, white-space, names), attribute and value definition, code documentation, and levels of organization. These conventions promote consistency and limit proliferation.

- Tailored automated editors and tools are used to make adhering to conventions easier. Checking mechanisms highlight violations, and processes encourage the following of conventions to become habitual.

- "Programming plans" are defined to implement such common practices as resolving constraint violations or reserving capacity. The processes for configuring similar types of objects are also defined.

EXAMPLE: Rule Naming Conventions.

This example of XCON conventions for rule names is presented to illustrate some of the low-level, seemingly trivial, often overlooked guidelines that are necessary to a large, complex application. In a knowledge-acquisition tool as described in this book, this level of definition would not be necessary as a rule name itself, since the user or expert would not operate at the code level. However, a rule name encapsulates the unique place a rule holds in the knowledge base. A rule generator would need to index into the knowledge base along similar dimensions. A human knowledge engineer also uses the rule name in this sense of indexing, and it is surprisingly critical to define names in a reasonably consistent mode.

In XCON, the rules are named according to the following format:

problem-space:rule-type:number-&-letter:description

The rule name must be re-examined when rule content is changed.

The elements of a rule name are defined as follows:

Problem-space. Problem-space gives the name of the problem space in which the rule is located. This should match the value for the attribute ^problem-space in the control element.

Rule-type. The rule-type must be the name of a defined rule type within a step of a problem-solving method. (See section 7.3.3.)

Number-&-letter. The number is used to group the rules in a rule type to insure that similar rules are kept together. It is a three-or-more-digit number, single-letter combination. The number represents the subgroups to which the rule belongs; each digit representing a different level of subgroup. The letter is used to uniquely identify the rule within its lowest-level subgroup. This designation is used for categorization purposes only and is not reflected anywhere in the body of the rule.

Description. The description specifies the function of the rule and should be generated using the following guidelines:

- For each rule type, a description should be constructed using the format defined for the associated problem-solving method.

- The description should be in action-object form.

- It should be less than 80 characters long, preferably less than 60, with no backslash characters, parentheses, or question marks. The recommended characters include only letters, numbers, dashes, and colons.

- Abbreviations should be avoided.

- The same description should be used to refer to the same thing. Common terms should be used consistently and an attempt should be made to limit the vocabulary where possible.

- References to specific systems or situations should be avoided.

- The number in the **number-&-letter** of the rule name should not be assumed to be a significant part of the description.

The description format for rules in the propose-apply method follow:

- **Propose:** For proposing problem spaces and subtasks, the description should be action-oriented (state where next activity should occur). In a qualifier-entity form it should be object-oriented (state what is being proposed as an alternative; for example, cpu-backplane, lowest-slot, large-backplane, typed-box).

- **Reject:** The description should state the reason for rejection (for example, insufficient-pos-5-power, insufficient-backplane-space, exceeds-ac-loads).

- **Eliminate:** The description should have the form prefer-<object> or eliminate-<object>, where <object> is the name or short description of object chosen (for example, prefer-configure-box, prefer-system-ancestor, remove-higher-slot).

- **Apply:** The description should focus on the change accomplished by the rule, not the situation in which the change occurs (for example, mark-module-configured, update-length-restriction, update-contained-in-location, assign-type-ordinal).

- **Succeed:** The description should state success criteria (for example, no-more-modules, slot-chosen).

Implications for Automation.

Many of these conventions would be evident if the code were produced by a generator. This simulation of automated generation identifies distinctions between things that could be made uniform, things that could be made fairly regular with exceptions, and things that are difficult to describe consistently.

7.4. Scope of Applicability

XCON was recently reimplemented in the RIME methodology, and this version has been in production use since January, 1988. Various possibilities for determining assessment metrics are being explored (see [Soloway 87]), but no quantitative measures have yet been determined. However, evidence indicates the usefulness of the methodology even without the aid of an automated tool. In XCON, RIME has already been shown useful as an aid to program evolution. It has helped XCON's developers deal with a constantly changing system by clearly identifying what exists in a coherent, organized way and providing guidelines and structure for introducing updates. The categorization and explicit levels of abstraction have made it easier to locate code relevant to the updates and to understand the system composition. These are not new concepts (see [Clancey 86]); rather this is an instance that gives credence to their value. XCON is a large, complex, knowledge-intensive expert system application in production mode. There have not been enough examples to distinguish what characteristics make it particularly suited to RIME.

Although the project focused on this reimplementation, with applicability to other systems a byproduct, there have been other attempts to apply the methodology. Other projects have been coded in this style or are now in the process of being converted, including MOLE and KNACK, knowledge-acquisition tools described in chapters 3 and 5. These applications and tools are all implemented in OPS5, although RIME does not assume any of the constructs unique to OPS5 beyond the pattern-matching, rule-based approach.

One application being developed used the RIME methodology from scratch. The nature of its task is significantly different from XCON's. Other problem-solving methods, mechanisms, and so forth were defined for it. Its developers claim that the methodology helped them significantly with program design, as well as development, since they could reuse some of the architectural code, structures, and so forth that were created for XCON. They also found that trying to cast their task in terms of problem-solving methods, problem spaces, and other higher-level abstractions provided a framework for thought that aided the design activities.

In addition, the attempts to code the knowledge-acquisition tools in the RIME methodology appear to be a fruitful path that may permit greater flexibility and allow for alterations and extensions to the tools, as well as to the applications produced. It is not clear yet whether this leads to complications or excessive overhead.

7.5. Future Directions
Because of the focus of the enterprise concerned with configuration at DEC, the shape of the future appears to include multiple, cooperating expert system applications in domains that are related but whose tasks may have very different natures. Since they will need to share parts of their knowledge

bases and communicate with each other and with users, both human and machine, there are needs for both structure and flexibility. There will be greater needs to increase the productivity and effectiveness of the developers as they will be dealing with ever more complex interrelations and the possibility of more widespread effects of any change. Automation is gradually being introduced into the development process and this should accelerate over time. It is likely that automated tools will be developed to encourage and monitor the adherence to the guidelines and structures defined, as well as aiding in those definitions.

RIME itself is still in the process of maturing and needs to be further developed. There is interest in exploring its potential for more widespread use. This will help develop it from varying perspectives and should help in the clarification of when and where such a methodology can be beneficial.

Acknowledgements

The foundations upon which RIME is based are varied. The other members of the RIME project team (Keith Jensen, Diane Muise, Michael Grimes) and I are deeply indebted to the work on SOAR [Laird 87] and especially to the SOAR-related research by Arnold van de Brug [van de Brug 85, van de Brug 86], who created a knowledge-acquisition tool prototype that was a precursor to RIME. In addition to the basic concepts of "problem space" and "operators," we were able to adapt the problem-solving method embedded in SOAR (the Universal Weak method [Laird 83]). We identified with and were encouraged by the work of Bill Clancey [Clancey 86] as he reported similar experiences as a result of his long-term work involved with expanding the scope and exploring other uses for MYCIN's knowledge. Elliot Soloway helped to evaluate our work in terms of basic software-engineering principles [Soloway 87]. The knowledge-acquisition tool work detailed in this book, as well as other work in the space [Chandrasekaran 86, Davis 82], was also extremely valuable. The members of the Configuration Systems Development Group and their management, Virginia Barker and Dennis O'Connor, contributed substantially to the success of the RIME project. Themis Carr, Tom Cooper, David Hartzband, Keith Jonson, Sandy Marcus, David Marques, John McDermott, Elliot Soloway, and Anne VanTine provided helpful comments on earlier drafts of the chapter.

8. Preliminary Steps Toward a Taxonomy of Problem-Solving Methods

John McDermott

Abstract

Although efforts, some successful, to develop expert systems (application systems that can perform knowledge-intensive tasks) have been going on now for almost 20 years, we are not yet very good at describing the variations in problem-solving methods that these systems use, nor do we have much of an understanding of how to characterize the methods in terms of features of the types of tasks for which they are appropriate. This chapter takes a few steps toward creating a taxonomy of methods -- a taxonomy that identifies some of the discriminating characteristics of the methods expert systems use and that suggests how methods can be mapped onto tasks.

8.1. Introduction

The various research efforts described in this book are experiments in automating the programming process by building tools, each of which knows what sort of knowledge is required to solve some class of tasks. The research is interesting to the extent that the scope of at least some of the tools is fairly broad; that is, the kinds of knowledge that a tool knows how to collect and represent are useful for solving a significant number of real tasks in a variety of domains.

This chapter presents problem solving as the identification, selection, and implementation of a sequence of actions that accomplish some task within a specific domain. A problem-solving method provides a means of identifying, at each step, candidate actions. It provides one or more mechanisms for selecting among candidate actions. Finally, it ensures that the selected action is implemented and often provides a mechanism that allows the actual effect of the action to be compared with the expected or desired effect. To a first approximation, a method's control knowledge comprises (1) an algorithm specifying when to use what knowledge to identify, select, and implement actions, together with (2) whatever knowledge the method has for selecting among candidate actions. The knowledge it uses to identify candidate actions and to implement the action selected is not control knowledge. In traditional expert systems terminology, a problem-solving method is called an inference engine. The inference engine comes with all of the control knowledge needed to solve some class of tasks; none of the knowledge in its knowledge base is (supposed to be) control knowledge.

Control knowledge can vary from being extremely unspecific to the actual task at hand to being tightly wrapped around task details. This chapter is an attempt to describe a way of classifying inference engines and the knowledge they use for action selection in terms of the specificity of the control structures to task features. This focus leads to the identification of inference engines that are somewhat limited in scope, but that provide substantial assistance in automating the task types they cover. There are task families for which control knowledge that strongly abstracts from task details is adequate for selecting the next action. The point of this chapter is that to the extent that such task families can be identified, there is a real opportunity for radically simplifying the programming enterprise. In this chapter, I will refer to the knowledge that is specific to a particular task instance as task-specific knowledge. Almost all of the knowledge that a method uses to identify and implement actions is task-specific knowledge. Knowledge used to select among candidate actions that depends on details of particular task instances is also task-specific knowledge. This chapter makes three claims:

- There are families of tasks that can be adequately performed by methods whose control knowledge strongly abstracts from the peculiarities of any of the family members.

- A method whose control knowledge is not very task-specific will use task-specific knowledge for identification and implementation that is highly regular; each piece of task-specific knowledge will play one of a small number of roles; thus the method will provide strong guidance with respect to what knowledge is required to perform a particular task and how that knowledge should be encoded.

- The clarity of these knowledge roles, and thus the strength of the guidance provided by a method, diminishes with the increasing diversity of the information required to identify candidate actions and to define the conditions that must obtain in order for an action to be implemented.

In this chapter, methods that strongly guide knowledge collection and encoding will be called **role-limiting** methods.

During the 1960's, a significant piece of the AI community's attention was devoted to identifying and analyzing what Newell has called the **weak methods** [Laird 83].   The weak methods are called weak because their usefulness is only weakly constrained by task features; each is potentially applicable to a broad set of task types.   They typically achieve this generality with simple control structures that require additional control knowledge to be supplied before the method can be applied.   The Hill Climbing method, for example, requires control knowledge in the form of a task-specific evaluation function that determines whether a candidate action will move the system closer to or farther from a solution.   Since one can imagine a weak method whose control knowledge contains only a small amount of task-specific knowledge (a Hill Climbing method, for example, whose evaluation function consists of comparing the value of just one feature of one class of objects), weak methods would seem to be likely instances of role-limiting methods.   But a weak method is more open with respect to control than a role-limiting method can be; a weak method does not put any limits on the nature or complexity of the task-specific control knowledge it can use.   A role-limiting method can be viewed as a specialization of a weak method that predefines the task-related control knowledge the method can use.

The MYCIN experiments [Buchanan 84], which ran through most of the 1970's, introduced a role-limiting method.   The MYCIN inference engine is an example of a method, heuristic classification [Clancey 84], that is similar to the weak methods in that it is a very simple control structure.   However, it differs from weak methods in that the task-related control knowledge the method uses is included in the definition of the method.   One of the most important insights of the MYCIN project was that, given that no control knowledge needs to be added to the method before it is applied, it should be possible to fully understand the interdependencies between the control knowledge and whatever other knowledge the method will need.   This in turn, can substantially simplify the task of the method user who has to formulate the task-specific knowledge for identification and implementation of actions in a way that allows the control knowledge to operate on it effectively.

The thesis of this book is that role-limiting methods are an important class of methods because they both have a quite broad scope of applicability and also provide substantial help in specifying what knowledge needs to be collected to perform a particular task and how that knowledge can be appropriately encoded. Methods that allow task-specific control knowledge to be added as a knowledge base is built up cannot provide as much help in determining what knowledge needs to be collected or how it should be encoded; this is because the requirements for task-specific knowledge cannot be known until the additional control knowledge is defined, and that is not known at method definition time. We have created support for this thesis by developing automatic knowledge-acquisition tools for collecting and encoding the knowledge required by five different role-limiting methods.

There has not been much attention given to identifying role-limiting methods. Clancey's description of heuristic classification is surely the most complete, but he doesn't attempt to identify others. Chandrasekaran has identified a number of methods for generic tasks [Chandrasekaran 83, Chandrasekaran 86]; however he has not discussed the interdependencies between his methods and the task-specific knowledge they operate on.

The underlying idea here is that if we take seriously the knowledge-base/inference-engine distinction that expert system developers have made so much of, it should be possible to devise a set of role-limiting methods, where each method defines the roles that the task-specific knowledge it requires must play and the forms in which that knowledge can be represented. A review of a number of role-limiting methods in the next section will show the sense in which their task-specific knowledge is highly regular and will show the implications of each piece of knowledge participating in one of a few roles. The methods provide strong guidance. This is what we would expect given that each of the methods is a simple control structure, since the simplicity of the control structure will not allow a knowledge base with little regularity to be effectively exploited. The situation is different with the weak methods. For weak methods, the task-specific evaluation function can be arbitrarily complex, and thus the method can be shaped to exploit knowledge that is highly irregular. A role-limiting method typically consists of a simple loop over a sequence of 5 or 10 steps.

Some of the steps operate on significant bodies of task-specific knowledge, and within a step there is no control; that is, it makes no difference in what order the actions that can be performed are performed.

It is the regularity of the task-specific knowledge that a role-limiting method requires that makes automating the building of expert systems a tractable task. A couple of examples may make this more concrete. Two of the knowledge-acquisition tools discussed in this book are MOLE and SALT. Each program that MOLE creates uses the cover-and-differentiate problem-solving method -- a method suitable for certain types of diagnostic tasks. A MOLE-built program searches a space of possible explanations. The explanation space can be represented by one or more graphs where each node is an event and the unidirectional links represent possible explanatory relationships. The values of some nodes must be provided externally; the values of other nodes can then be inferred. The cover-and-differentiate method assumes that the intial state is a set of one or more symptoms. The method has the following control knowledge:

1. Determine the events that potentially explain (that is, cover) the symptoms.

2. If there is more than one candidate explanation for any event, then identify information that will differentiate the candidates by

   - ruling out one or more of the explanatory connections,

   - ruling out one or more of the candidate explanatory events,

   - providing sufficient support for one of the candidate explanatory events,

   - providing a reason for preferring some of the explanatory connections over others.

3. Get this information (in any order) and apply it (in any order).

4. If step 3 uncovers new symptoms, go to step 1.

This control knowledge is sufficient for performing diagnostic tasks in a wide variety of domains. Most of the task-specific knowledge for action identification and implementation comes into play in steps 1 and 2. In step 1, each symptom that needs to be explained generates the set of events, any of which might explain that symptom. Each piece of task-specific knowledge relevant to this step associates a symptom with an event. The form of each piece of knowledge must be such that touching a symptom returns the set of associated events. In step 2, four kinds of task-specific knowledge are potentially relevant; each of these four kinds of knowledge provide hypothesis differentiation of one of the four types identified above. The form of each piece of knowledge must be such that touching a candidate explanatory event returns a description of the information that will help confirm or disconfirm that event.

Each program that SALT creates uses the propose-and-revise problem-solving method -- a method suitable for certain types of constructive tasks. A SALT-built program searches a space of possible designs. The design space can be represented by a graph where each node is a partial design and the unidirectional links represent possible design extensions. The propose-and-revise method assumes that the initial state is a set of specifications. The method has the following control knowledge:

1. Extend a design and identify constraints on the extension just formed.

2. Identify constraint violations; if none, go to step 1.

3. Suggest potential fixes for a constraint violation.

4. Select the least costly fix not yet attempted.

5. Tentatively modify the design and identify constraints on the modification just formed.

6. Identify constraint violations due to the revision; if any, go to 4.

7. Remove relationships incompatible with the revision.

8. If the design is incomplete, go to 1.

Most of the task-specific knowledge that the method uses comes into play in steps 1, 3, and 5. The knowledge in those three steps play three roles: Each piece of knowledge describes a possible plan extension, defines a constraint, or describes a possible fix for a constraint violation. In step 1, a partial design is extended or a constraint is identified. Either of the first two kinds of task-specific knowledge may be relevant. The first describes a possible design extension; the form of pieces of this kind of knowledge must be such that a partial design can extend itself in some manner. The second kind of task-specific knowledge relevant in this step defines a constraint; the form of pieces of this kind of knowledge must be such that the extension of a partial design identifies that constraint on the partial design. In step 3, a violated constraint associated with a partial design identifies a potential fix. Each piece of task-specific knowledge associates a set of fixes with a constraint and indicates the cost of using each of those fixes to solve the problem; the form of each piece of knowledge must be such that the existence of the constraint violation returns the set of associated fixes. The task-specific knowledge required in step 5 is the same as that required in step 1.

Hopefully these two examples illustrate the nature of the control knowledge that one finds in role-limiting methods. The control knowledge is useful for deciding what to do next only within the context of a particular task type. But the two tasks illustrated here, and the other three illustrated in the next section, are tasks that are performed in a wide variety of domains. Thus the role-limiting methods have a quite broad scope of potential applicability. It is likely to turn out that there are hundreds of role-limiting methods; it is also likely that there will be an even larger number of task types in which the control knowledge required to perform the task adequately can only be acquired as the other task-specific knowledge needed for the task is acquired. Chapter 7, on RIME, addressed the issue of how to provide assistance in defining methods and in imposing structure on task-specific knowledge in situations where role-limiting methods are not applicable.

To lend support to the claim that there are tasks that are difficult to cast in role-limiting methods, we will look briefly at a small piece of XCON (or R1) [McDermott 82]. The version of XCON that has recently been reimplemented using the RIME methodology is organized as problem spaces. One of the problem spaces, Select-Device, has as its overall purpose to determine the next device to configure. The problem space has 46 pieces of task-specific knowledge, 15 of which are pieces of control knowledge; each piece of control knowledge prefers a candidate action over another candidate. Four examples should give some sense of the level of detail in which the control knowledge is immersed:

If two of the candidate actions are
        to configure an RA60 drive
        to configure another type of drive
            that uses the same cabinet type,
Then prefer configuring the RA60 next.

If two of the candidate actions are
        to configure a rack-mountable device
        to configure a free standing tape
            drive or a tape drive that is to be
            bolted to the CPU cabinet,
Then prefer configuring the non-rack-mountable
        device next.

If two of the candidate actions are
        to configure a rack-mountable device
            whose subtype is not RV20A or RV20B
        to configure a different rack-
            mountable device whose subtype is
            not RV20A or RV20B,
    and no cabinet has been selected,
    and the second device is not bundled with
        an available cabinet,
    and there is an available cabinet or tape
        drive in which the devices can be
        placed,
    and it is desirable to place the first
        device in the cabinet before the
        second device,
Then prefer configuring the first device.

```
If two of the candidate actions are
        to configure a box-mountable device
        to configure a different box-mountable
            device,
    and the first device is bundled with the
        system,
    and there is a selected cabinet or box
        in which the devices can be placed,
    and it is desirable to place each of the
        devices in the selected cabinet or
        box,
Then prefer configuring the first device.
```

Because selection of the action to perform next is so intimately tied to the details of the type of system being configured, and because the nature of the considerations that lead to preferring one action over another change as new products are developed, it is not possible to predefine what control knowledge will be required to perform XCON's task. Thus, the task cannot be done with a role-limiting method. XCON's task also exemplifies a task in which the information required to identify candidate actions and to define the conditions under which an action may be implemented is highly diverse. Thus, even if a role-limiting method could be used for the task, within each of the roles that the method would impose there would be substantial diversity, and thus the method would provide less assistance with the collection and encoding of task-specific knowledge than for any of the other tasks discussed in this chapter.

In section 8.2, six knowledge-acquisition tools are described. The first five of these tools each presuppose a particular role-limiting method; each tool elicits information that its method demands and constructs a knowledge base that the method can use. The sixth tool, SEAR, assists the user in defining problem-solving methods and in using the method definition to determine what task-specific knowledge, including control knowledge, needs to be collected and how it should be encoded.

8.2. A Few Data Points

Four of the six knowledge-acquisition tools described in this section
(MOLE, SALT, KNACK, and SIZZLE) are treated in detail in chapters 3
through 6. The other two tools (YAKA and SEAR) do not have chapters
devoted to them because they are not yet sufficiently well-developed to
warrant it. YAKA is included in this section because it is, in many respects,
quite similar to MOLE, and thus can give us some insight into the relative
power and scope of closely related methods. SEAR is included because,
although it is still in the early stages of development, it is closely related to
the RIME methodology introduced in chapter 7.

In order to make it easy to compare the tools presented in this section, the
form of each of the following subsections is identical.

The first part of each subsection begins with a list of what characteristics a
task must have in order for the method presupposed by the tool to be
suitable; this list is followed by another indicating what additional task
characteristics make the method particularly suitable. Then there is a brief
description of the problem-solving behavior of the systems built using the
knowledge-acquisition tool, and this is followed by a few examples of how
these systems perform representative tasks. The first example in each
subsection provides illustrations of each of the necessary and desirable task
characteristics.

The second part of each subsection begins with an identification of the
intended users of the tool. This is followed by a brief description of how the
knowledge-acquisition tool (as opposed to the systems it builds) works and
examples of the kinds of knowledge the tool collects.

8.2.1. MOLE

Possible Tasks.

MOLE is a tool for building diagnostic expert systems whose role-limiting
method is *cover-and-differentiate* (a form of heuristic classification). A task
must have the following characteristics in order for cover-and-differentiate
to be an appropriate method: (1) There is an identifiable set of problem
states or events (for example, symptoms, complaints, abnormalities) each of

which must be explained or accounted for (that is, covered). (2) An exhaustive set of candidate explanations (that is, hypotheses, explanatory events) that cover these events can be statically pre-enumerated. The method is most appropriate for tasks that, in addition, have the following characteristics: (3) There is information that will help differentiate the candidate explanations for each abnormal event. (4) Usually only one candidate explanation is applicable at any given time per event (the single fault assumption).

MOLE includes a performance system ($MOLE_p$) that interprets the knowledge base generated by the knowledge-acquisition tool ($MOLE_{KA}$). $MOLE_p$'s task-specific control knowledge guides it iteratively through the following steps: It asks the user for the complaints that are present. It next activates the candidate hypotheses that will explain these complaints. It then queries the user about the presence or absence of states or events that will help it differentiate these hypotheses.

Examples of MOLE-built systems:

Diagnosing car engine problems. $MOLE_p$ asks the user if certain noticeable malfunctions of a car engine are present (for example, the engine is not running smoothly). If it is told that the engine is not running smoothly, MOLE activates the hypotheses that might explain this abnormality (for example, the engine is overheating, there is incomplete combustion, the valves are bad). MOLE next queries the user about events or states that will differentiate these explanations (for example, incomplete combustion is indicated by black deposits on the spark plugs). If incomplete combustion is the most likely explanation of the engine not running smoothly, its possible causes are activated (for example, a maladjusted carburetor or maladjusted rockers are potential causes of incomplete combustion). MOLE then queries the user about events or states that will differentiate these explanations.

Cover-and-differentiate is an appropriate method for this task because the task has the following characteristics: (1) It is possible to identify a set of complaints that motivate car users to seek help (for example, the car won't start, the engine makes a loud noise when idling). (2) Once a complaint is identified, possible explanations can be statically pre-enumerated (for example, the battery is dead, a fuel line is blocked). (3) The problem-solving process can be naturally represented as a process of differentiating possible explanations of the complaints (for example, knowing that the engine won't crank differentiates in favor of the battery being dead rather than a blocked fuel line as an explanation for why the car won't start). (4) Usually only one actual explanation is necessary per complaint (for example, if it is discovered that the car won't start because the battery is dead, then other explanations are probably irrelevant).

Diagnosing problems in a steel-rolling mill. A steel-rolling mill processes steel by rolling bars of steel into thin sheets. MOLE asks the user if there are any defects in the product (for example, the steel is too narrow or too thin). If it is told that the steel is too narrow, MOLE activates the hypotheses that will explain this abnormality (for example, the steel was too narrow coming out of the preprocessor, the rolls are worn out, or there is too much tension between stands). MOLE next queries the user about events or states that will differentiate these explanations (for example, if there is no oscillation of the roll, then it is probably not worn out). Since MOLE assumes that every abnormal event has a cause, if MOLE can rule out all but one of the explanations of an event, it will accept the remaining explanation. For example, if MOLE can rule out both that the steel is too narrow coming out of the preprocessor and that the roll is worn out, then it will accept as the explanation of the steel being too narrow that there is excessive tension between stands. Acceptance of this hypothesis will in turn activate hypotheses that explain the excessive tension between stands (for example, there is an overload or a looper malfunction).

Diagnosing inefficiencies in a coal-burning power plant. The boiler is the central unit in a coal-burning power plan. Problems rarely prevent the boiler from functioning, but they are major sources of inefficiency that can waste millions of dollars of fuel as well as dump tons of pollutants into the atmosphere. MOLE asks the user if there are any events or states indicating that the plant is working inefficently (for example, the ash is dark). MOLE activates the hypotheses that will explain this state (for example, there is high excess air, low excess air, or large fuel particles). MOLE queries the user about events or states that will differentiate these explanations (for example, the oxygen reading differentiates the high and low excess air hypotheses from the large particles hypothesis). These hypothesized events in turn can be explained by other events (for example, possible explanations for large fuel particles are a pulverizer malfunction and a wrong setting of the pulverizer).

Using MOLE to Develop Application Systems.

Section 8.2.1 described the kinds of tasks that the MOLE performance programs perform and gave an indication of the types of information those performance programs ask their users for. In this section, we look at the knowledge that the performance programs need in order to perform such tasks and indicate how the MOLE knowledge-acquisition tool elicits that knowledge from domain experts. $MOLE_{KA}$ is intended to be used by domain experts who need not know anything about programming. The expert must provide the following types of task-specific knowledge:

- *Complaints* or abnormalities.

- *Explanations* (that is, possible causes) for these complaints.

- *Differentiation* knowledge (that is, information that will help differentiate these possible complaints).

$MOLE_{KA}$ begins by asking the expert to list the complaints or abnormalities that would motivate someone to seek diagnostic help. It next asks for possible explanations for each of these complaints. MOLE then asks whether these explaining events or states in turn have relevant explanations, and so on. Finally, MOLE seeks information that will enable it to differentiate these candidate explanations. This is done both statically and dynamically. Static differentiation looks at the knowledge base and makes sure that each hypothesis can in principle be differentiated from its competitors. Dynamic differentiation compares the diagnosis of the performance system for some case with an expert's diagnosis, and if they differ, elicits information that will help differentiate hypotheses in this situation.

Examples of task-specific knowledge that domain experts provided for the three diagnostic tasks described earlier:

Diagnosing car engine problems:

Complaints: car won't start, engine not running smoothly.

Explanations: the engine not running smoothly is explained by incomplete combustion, engine overheating, or problems with valves, crankshaft, pistons, or cylinders.

Differentiation: carbon deposits on the spark plugs point to incomplete combustion as the problem.

Diagnosing steel-rolling mill problems:

Complaints: steel too thin, too thick, too wide, too narrow.

Explanations: the steel too narrow is explained by the steel entering the rolls being too narrow, a worn out roll, or by too much tension between stands.

Differentiation: an oscillation of the looper roll indicates a worn out roll; a major imbalance between rolls indicates the problem must be either a worn out roll or a tension problem, but the problem is not that the steel is too narrow upon entry.

Diagnosing inefficiencies in a coal-burning power plant:

Complaints: dark ash, high fly ash flow, high bottom ash flow, loss in gas.

Explanations: dark ash is explained by high excess air, low excess air, and large particles; high fly ash flow is explained by high excess air and small particles.

Differentiation: a high or low oxygen reading identifies high or low excess air; the absence of high fly ash flow rules out high excess air.

8.2.2. YAKA

Possible Tasks.

YAKA is a tool for building diagnostic expert systems whose role-limiting method is a combination of *qualitative reasoning* and *cover-and-differentiate.* A task must have the following characteristics in order for this method to be appropriate: (1) There is an identifiable set of problem states or events (for example, symptoms, complaints, abnormalities) each of which must be explained or accounted for (that is, covered). (2) A model of the normal functioning of the system can be provided, and this model can be characterized in terms of qualitative equations between state variables describing components and conduits. The method is most appropriate for tasks that, in addition, have the following characteristics: (3) Candidate explanations that are external to the functional model (faults) can be expressed as disturbances affecting the functioning of a conduit or component, hence changing its equation(s). (4) There is information that will help differentiate candidate faults for each abnormal event. (5) Usually only one fault is applicable at any given time per event.

YAKA includes a performance system (YAKA$_p$) that interprets the knowledge base generated by the knowledge-acquisition tool (YAKA$_{KA}$). YAKA$_p$'s task-specific control knowledge guides it iteratively through the following steps: Given a variable whose value is abnormal at time t, YAKA$_p$ traces back through the equations upon which the variable is dependent until equations are found whose independent variables are all measured. If this set of equations is inconsistent, then YAKA identifies (by a process of substitution) all faults (represented by equations) that potentially account for the inconsistency. On the other hand, if the set of equations is consistent, YAKA treats the measured variables whose values explain the problem as abnormal values and repeats the process. Once a set of candidate faults has been identifed, YAKA makes use of heuristic knowledge that will enable it to differentiate them.

An example of a YAKA-built system:

Diagnosing problems in a refinery process. An oil refinery is quite complex but it can be described in terms of a relatively small number of component and conduit types (for example, pipes, tanks, valves, pumps). The task is to track down where a problem is occuring. Given a symptom at time t such as a low value for the state variable "tank-level", YAKA$_p$ evaluates the equation upon which the value of the tank-level is dependent, $dL/dt = Fin - Fout$, at time $t1 = t$ - time-delay of the equation. If this equation holds, the symptom is caused by an abnormal value in one of the variables it is dependent upon (Fin or Fout), so YAKA repeats the process with this variable. If the equation is violated, the problem is caused by a disturbance preventing the tank from performing its function correctly (for example, a leak in the tank). YAKA generates the fault hypotheses that can affect the tank and tests the equations relevant to these faults (for example, for the leak in the tank, dL/dt < Fin - Fout). The fault hypotheses corresponding to equations that hold are marked as possible; the others are rejected. If there is no hypothesis, YAKA points out that there is a problem "around the tank". In this manner, YAKA generates a set of hypotheses that are plausible explanations for the observed symptom (for example, leak in the tank, leak in the inlet pipe) and then uses a MOLE-like approach to differentiate them.

The method is appropriate for this task because the task has the following characteristics: (1) It is possible to identify a set of complaints that motivate refinery operators to seek help (for example, tank-level too low). (2) It is possible to describe the system in terms of components (for example, tanks) and conduits (for example, pipes), and it is possible to derive from this and a library of generic qualitative equations, a functional model, in terms of qualitative equations (dL/dt = Fin - Fout). (3) Faults can be expressed as disturbances affecting the functioning of a component or conduit; that is, disturbances of its characterizing equation(s) (for example, the leak in the tank is characterized by the new equation: dL/dt < Fin - Fout). (4) There is knowledge available to differentiate the faults (for example, evidence of a leak, liquid on the floor, near the tank). (5) Usually only one fault is applicable (for example, if there is a leak in the tank, then it is unlikely that there is also a leak in the inlet pipe).

Using YAKA to Develop Application Systems.

YAKA$_{KA}$ is intended to be used by domain experts. Two levels of expertise are required; neither requires any knowledge of programming. The first level requires an understanding of qualitative physics as well as a theoretical understanding of the domain in order to build a library of generic qualitative equations and faults. This level of expertise is needed only initially for a given domain. The second level requires no understanding of qualitative physics but requires instead familiarity with the physical structure and functioning of specific applications. The experts must provide the following types of task-specific knowledge:

- A *library* of generic equations and faults (provided by experts with first-level expertise).

- A *structural model* of the system.

- *Refinements* of the functional model generated by YAKA, including cardinal time-delays of the equations, and refinements of the general equations proposed by YAKA.

- Descriptions of possible *faults* in terms of the changes they can induce in the equations.

- *Differentiation* knowledge (that is, information that will help differentiate possible faults having the same direct effect).

YAKA$_{KA}$ uses the structural model plus the library of generic equations to derive a functional model -- a set of equations characterizing the functioning of each component. The expert may need to complete, refine and confirm this set of equations. YAKA provides a step-by-step qualitative simulation algorithm, to help the expert in this process, which includes the acquisition of the cardinal time-delays for the equations. YAKA classifies faults as conduit faults and component faults. It is able to generate the conduit faults and some of the component faults from a library. YAKA asks the expert about the others, and then updates its library. The faults are characterized as disturbances that will affect or replace equations of the normal functioning of components, and thus are represented locally with respect to a component and its connections. Finally, YAKA groups the faults that have the same direct effect and asks the expert for differentiating knowledge.

Examples of task-specific knowledge that domain experts provided:

Diagnosing problems in a refinery process:

Library: dL/dt = Fin - Fout.

Structural model: There is a tank connected to two pipes (conduits) -- one for inlet flow and the other for outlet flow.

Refinement: In the functional model generated by YAKA, the conduits are characterized by variables such as flow-rate and pressure, and the tank by its level, and also by the following qualitative equation:

$$dL/dt = Fin - Fout$$

As a refinement, the expert adds that for this particular tank, this equation has a time-delay of t1.

Faults: a leak in the tank (a component fault), characterized by the following equation:

$$dL/dt < Fin - Fout,$$

a leak in a pipe between the tank and the flow-rate sensor of the inlet pipe (a conduit fault), affecting the value of Fin in the above equation.

Differentiation: liquid around the bottom of the tank.

8.2.3. SALT

Possible Tasks.

SALT is a tool for building constructive expert systems whose role-limiting method is *propose-and-revise*. A task must have the following characteristics in order for propose-and-revise to be an appropriate method: (1) Procedures can be specified to determine a starting point or most preferred, likely value for each piece of the design. (2) For each design constraint, remedies (indicating what to do if the constraint is violated) can be specified in the form of modifications to the design. The method is most appropriate for tasks that, in addition, have the following characteristic: (3) There is not a high level of potential conflict in preferences for alternative design extensions.

A SALT-built system's task-specific control knowledge guides it iteratively through the following steps: It first accepts a set of specifications (which may include a partial design) and proposes additions to the design while checking for constraint violations. If a constraint is violated, the system finds the least costly fix or combination of fixes that will eliminate the violation, and applies them. This propose-and-revise process continues until no more additions can be made to the design and no constraints are violated.

Examples of SALT-built systems:

Configuring an elevator system. Elevator configuration involves designing an elevator system from an initial set of specifications, which include architectural specifications and customer preferences. VT, a SALT-generated system, first verifies the consistency of the input specifications (for example, that the number of front openings plus the number of rear openings equals the total number of openings). It then proposes design extensions (for example, selecting the smallest motor that can supply the required horsepower) until a constraint is violated. It eliminates a violation by implementing the least costly fix or fixes (which are expressed in terms of nonoptimal modifications to previous design extensions).

Propose-and-revise is an appropriate method for this task because the task has the following characteristics: (1) Procedures can be specified for determining an initial value for each piece of the elevator design (for example, use the least expensive piece of equipment that has a chance of being acceptable). (2) Each constraint that may be violated has at least one remedy (for example, equipment can be moved and/or more expensive equipment can be used). (3) The amount of potential conflict in preferences for alternative design extensions is low. Alternatives for individual design parameters can be selected using a single property (for example, minimizing weight) and while preference for alternative remedies to constraint violations involves multiple considerations (for example, minimizing cost and maximizing customer satisfaction) alternatives can be categorized into 12 ordered preference classes.

Task scheduling in an engineering department. Task scheduling involves adding a new job to an existing schedule. The job is specified in terms of its attributes and any constraints on the its schedule (for example, deadlines promised to the customer). The schedule comprises the dates each job will enter and leave each subdepartment and details about how it will be handled in each one. The purpose of Scheduler, a SALT-generated system, is to schedule each job as it comes in with a minimum of disruption to the existing schedule. Scheduler first schedules the job without regard for possible constraint violations (for example, overloads in departments and promised delivery dates not met are ignored). It then examines all the constraint violations, picks the most important one (for example, a promised delivery date not met), implements the least costly fix for that constraint (for example, hurry the job through a particular department), and rebuilds the schedule as before.

Using SALT to Develop Application Systems.

SALT is intended to be used by domain experts who need not know anything about programming, but who do have a formalized grasp of their domain. The expert must provide the following types of task-specific knowledge:

- *Procedures* for obtaining initial values *for pieces of the design.*

- *Procedures for* obtaining any *constraints* on these values.

- Local *remedies* for violated constraints (that is, remedies that do not have to address the possibility that they may cause other constraints to be violated).

SALT begins by asking the user to specify any of the three types of knowledge listed above, in any convenient order. When the user is done, SALT checks that all pieces of the design mentioned by the user have associated procedures (or are inputs), that all constraints that might be violated have remedies, that pieces with multiple procedures have disjoint preconditions, and so forth. SALT also analyzes the knowledge base to ensure that there are no loops among procedures, and if there are, it will ask the user to specify a new procedure for initially estimating one of the pieces and convert its original procedure into a constraint, which then requires remedies.

Examples of task-specific knowledge that domain experts provided:

Configuring an elevator system:

Procedures for pieces of the design: select the smallest motor that can produce horsepower greater than the maximum required horsepower; place the car platform 1.25 inches from the door sill at the front of the shaft.

Procedures for constraints: a model 38 machine can be used only with a 25, 30, or 35 hp motor (for mechanical reasons); if there is no counterweight guard, there must be a minimum of 1 inch between the car platform and the counterweight (due to safety regulations).

Remedies: upgrade to the next larger motor (a more expensive, less optimal choice); select a smaller car platform (which would be a change to the customer's specifications).

Task scheduling in an engineering department:

Procedures for pieces of the design: an order spends two weeks in the Contract Coordination Department; the Contract Coordination Department's load for each week is a weighted sum of all the jobs in that department for that week.

Procedures for constraints: the Contract Coordination Department's maximum load for each week is a weighted sum of each of the people in the department who will be working that week.

Remedies: delay the job's entry into the department until it can handle it, rush the job through a previous department in order to get the job into Contract Coordination before the overload.

8.2.4. KNACK

Possible Tasks.

KNACK is a tool for building expert systems, called WRINGERs, whose role-limiting method is acquire-and-present. A task must have the following characteristics in order for acquire-and-present to be an appropriate method: (1) A report is a suitable means of documenting the task (that is, it is possible to document the task with a report). (2) A relatively small set of concepts cover the substance of what is contained in all of the reports for any particular task. The method is most appropriate for tasks that, in addition, have the following characteristic: (3) A report is an essential means of documenting the task (that is, it is necessary to document the task with a report).

A WRINGER's task-specific control knowledge guides it iteratively through the following steps: It first identifies all relevant pieces of information that are appropriate to acquire next and determines what procedures can be used to gather that information. It then selects one piece of information to acquire next and a strategy for acquiring it. A WRINGER applies the selected strategy and integrates the gathered information with whatever information it already has. This acquisition process goes on until the WRINGER has tried to gather all of the information it thinks it needs. WRINGER then produces a report, which documents the task.

Examples of KNACK-built systems:

Reporting on designs of electromechanical systems that may be suboptimal from a hardening perspective. Nuclear hardening involves the use of specific engineering design practices to increase the resistance of an electromechanical system to the environmental effects of a nuclear event. Designers of electromechanical systems usually have little or no knowledge about the specialized analytical methods and engineering practices of the hardening domain. The purpose of this WRINGER is to assist a designer in presenting given designs of electromechanical systems such that hardening experts have readily available the information they need to evaluate the system from a hardening perspective. The WRINGER first gathers information about the ElectroMagnetic Pulse (EMP) environment (for example, rise time, electrical field). It then asks for the geometry and a description of the major components of the system (for example, cables, equipment, protections). Values for system and environment properties are determined through various analytical methods, depending on the level of description of the system -- the poorer the description is, the more conservative are the underlying assumptions (for example, normal operating environment, screen analysis, resistor analysis). This analysis can continue down to the level of individual semiconductors (for example, bulk resistance of a diode, transfer impedance of a cable). The WRINGER's output is a report about the design of the system.

Acquire-and-present is an appropriate method for this task because the task has the following characteristics: (1) A report is a suitable means of documenting the design of an electromechanical system (for example, a Program Plan is the primary top-level report covering all phases of the design process, a Design Parameters Report presents a detailed system description). (2) The reports are all quite similar and quite focused (for example, 43 concepts cover the substance of what is contained in a Program Plan; 92 concepts cover the substance of what is contained in a Design Parameters report). (3) A report is an essential means of presenting the design of an electromechanical system (for example, government requirements prescribe that the design of an electromechanical system be presented in the form of both a Program Plan and a Design Parameters Report).

Assisting with the creation of a project proposal. A first step in starting a new project is typically the creation of a project proposal. The proposal must be concise and contain all the information management needs to accept or reject the project. The purpose of this WRINGER is to assist a project leader in creating a project proposal such that management has readily available the information needed to make a decision. The WRINGER asks for information about the planned project (for example, objectives, functionality, motivation, research or engineering issues, related issues, methodology, resources, schedule, and tasks). It then produces a proposal.

Assisting with the definition of requirements for software systems. Defining requirements for new software is a complex process. It involves functionally decomposing the software into basic modules, defining the data requirements, and integrating the new software with the existing software environment. The purpose of this WRINGER is to assist a systems analyst in functionally decomposing a high-level description of a planned software system into basic modules and in defining the data requirements for each of the modules. The WRINGER first gathers information about high-level functions (for example, major groups involved, main activities of the groups). It then assists the systems analyst in functionally decomposing that description into basic modules (for example, Determine Drawing Identification, Get Drawing Standards). In a next step the WRINGER assists in defining the data requirements for the modules (for example, input for Get Drawing Standards is model-type; output of Get Drawing Standards is a list of drawing standards). The WRINGER produces a technical document describing the requirements for the software system. This includes an executive summary that presents the information management needs to evaluate whether the planned software will be a valuable enhancement to the existing software environment.

Using KNACK to Develop Application Systems.

KNACK is intended to be used by domain experts who need not know anything about programming. The expert must provide the following types of task-specific knowledge:

- A *domain model*.
- A *sample report*.
- *Sample strategies* for acquiring specific information.

In an initial interaction, KNACK acquires a preliminary model of a domain. The domain model describes the concepts and the vocabulary that experts use in performing their task. KNACK also requires a sample report as an initial input. The sample report is a document that exemplifies the output a WRINGER is expected to produce. Once the sample report is provided and an initial domain model is defined, KNACK interacts with a domain expert to integrate the sample report with the domain model. The integration process generalizes the sample report, making it applicable to different applications. KNACK then instantiates the generalized examples with known concept representatives taken from the domain model and displays several differently instantiated examples for each generalization. The expert edits any examples that make implausible statements. KNACK uses those corrections as additional knowledge to refine its generalizations and the domain model. Once the expert is content with KNACK's understanding of the sample report, KNACK elicits knowledge about how to customize the generalized sample report for a particular application. The expert defines sample strategies that a KNACK-generated expert system, a WRINGER, will use to acquire values instantiating the concepts in the generalized fragments. KNACK displays sample instantiations for review and correction by the expert.

Examples of task-specific knowledge that domain experts provided:

Reporting on designs of electromechanical systems that may be suboptimal from a hardening perspective:

Domain model: cable, enclosure, threat, aperture (concepts); type, resistive component of pin voltage, length of shield, transfer resistance of shield, current on shield (concept characteristics for cable); power cable, signal cable (concept representatives for cable).

Sample report fragment: The power cable penetrates the S-280C enclosure and induces 0.4 volts on the window of this enclosure.

Sample strategy: (Formula) Resistive Component of Pin Voltage = Length of Shield * Transfer Resistance of Shield * Current on Shield

Assisting with the creation of a project proposal:

Domain model: project, objective, task, software (concepts); name, description (concept characteristics for software); KNACK, WRINGER (concept representatives for software).

Sample report fragment: The objective of the NAC WRINGER project is to refine KNACK, a knowledge-acquisition tool currently being developed at CMU, so that it can be used to build expert systems that assist with the design of computer networks.

Sample strategy: (Question) What are the objectives of the NAC WRINGER project?

Assisting with the definition of requirements for software systems:

Domain model: external function, function requirements (concepts); name, processing steps (concept characteristics for external function); define bundle geometry, produce system schematics manual (concept representatives for external functions).

Sample report fragment: Projected impact of requirements for the external function, Define Bundle Geometry: an interface must be built between the electronic/electrical workstation and the software ASGR.

Sample strategy: (Inference) Because Define Bundle Geometry is an external function for the software Electronic/Electrical Workstation, and Define Bundle Geometry must get data from the Electronic/Electrical Workstation, and Define Bundle Geometry is a function of the software ASGR, and there is no interface between ASGR and the Electronic/Electrical Workstation, the impact of Define Bundle Geometry is: an interface must be built between the software Electronic/Electrical Workstation and ASGR.

8.2.5. SIZZLE

Possible Tasks.

SIZZLE is a tool for building expert systems whose role-limiting method is *extrapolate-from-a-similar-case*.   Characteristics that a task must have in order for extrapolate-from-a-similar-case to be an appropriate method are: (1) A large collection of validated cases is available. (2) Experts have a notion of the overall degree of similarity between different cases. (3) Knowledge exists of how to adjust a case solution as a function of changes to the case problem. The method is most appropriate for tasks that, in addition, have the following characteristics: (4) The problem is to determine needed quantities of various resources for some process when the precise nature of the process is not very well understood. (5) The set of factors that need to be considered is very large. (6) The quality of a solution can be characterized as incrementally better or worse, rather than as categorically acceptable or not acceptable, when compared to some other solution.

A SIZZLE-built system's task-specific control knowledge guides it iteratively through the following steps: It asks for enough information about a particular sizing problem to identify other, similar, already-solved problems in a knowledge base of cases. It then uses those differences between the solved and unsolved cases to determine how to extrapolate from the known solution to the new solution.

An example of a SIZZLE-built system:

Sizing the requirements for a computer system. Computer-system sizing involves creating a generic description of a computer system that will provide adequate computational resources for some set of intended uses. Sizer, a SIZZLE-generated system, asks the user to identify how many of various kinds of workers will be using the computer system. Sizer then looks in its knowledge base of cases for the two cases that are most similar to the case at hand. It uses simple techniques to extrapolate from each known solution to create a solutions for the new case. If the two solutions for the new case are very similar, it proposes one of them to the user; If not, it suggests to the user that its knowledge base needs to be more dense in the area of the new case.

Extrapolate-from-a-similar-case is an appropriate method for this task because the task has the following characteristics: (1) Thousands of validated cases are available. (2) Experts have a notion of the overall degree of similarity between different cases (for example, experts can indicate how close two cases are on the basis of how many of various kinds of users will be using the system). (3) Knowledge exists of how to adjust a case solution as a function of changes to the case problem (for example, for a particular class of cases, each additional analyst will require 5 megabytes of disk). (4) The problem is to determine needed quantities of various computing resources, but there is no good model of how the computer is going to be used. (5) The set of factors that would need to be considered to determine how much computing resource each worker in the organization requires is very large. (6) An incremental change to a computing system sizing solution of a given quality results in a solution that is incrementally more or less good, rather than a solution that is categorically acceptable or unacceptable.

Using SIZZLE to Develop Application Systems.

SIZZLE is intended to be used by domain experts who need not know anything about programming. The expert must provide three types of task-specific knowledge:

- A population of *sized cases.*

- Case *indexing knowledge.*

- *Extrapolation knowledge* that will allow a sizer to extrapolate from the solved case to the unsolved case.

SIZZLE permits the expert to build a sizer by specifying sizing cases and user models and indexing into them by means of a discrimination tree of case features. This capability is provided primarily by a rule generator, which translates a source file of case features, cases, and user resource-demand models into rules. Integrated with every such sizer is a mechanism that permits the user to interactively define new sizing cases and to test their effect upon the performance of the system as a whole.

Examples of task-specific knowledge that domain experts provided:

Sizing the requirements for a computer system:

Sized cases: a case includes a description of the types and quantities of users of the system, paired with a characterization of the required computing resources along such dimensions as user disk space, number of disk spindles, and number of mips.

Indexing knowledge: a discrimination tree that classifies cases on the basis of industry and organizational function.

Extrapolation knowledge: computer user demand models that define solution features (for example, total user disk space required) with respect to the number of given types of user (for example, accountants) in the region of the case space in which a sizing case lies.

8.2.6. SEAR

This subsection will differ in format somewhat from the previous five. SEAR, the tool described here, does not presuppose a particular role-limiting method, but instead provides a capability for allowing developers to define a set of methods, some of which might have substantial amounts of task-specific control knowledge and which collectively will be particularly appropriate for some class of tasks. SEAR is intended to be a guide to and an enforcer of the RIME methodology described in chapter 7. SEAR currently provides only very modest assistance to the user of the RIME methodology; however a description of SEAR is included here because of the potentially strong complementarity between SEAR and the other tools described in this chapter.

Possible Tasks.

SEAR is a set of tools for developing higher-level knowledge-acquisition tools as well as applications systems. A task must have the following characteristics in order for SEAR to be an appropriate tool: (1) There is no known role-limiting method suitable for the task that is to be automated. (2) A set of methods for performing the task can be defined. The method is most appropriate for tasks that, in addition, have the following characteristic: (3) A lot of what makes the task challenging is deciding what to do next based on a variety of task details.

A SEAR-built system uses whatever collection of problem-solving methods its developers have defined.

Examples of systems whose developers SEAR assisted:

Configuring a computer system. Computer-system configuration involves two interdependent activities: (1) the customer's order must be determined to be complete; if it is not, whatever components are missing must be added to the order; and (2) the spatial relationships among the components (including those added) must be determined. XCON starts with a set of unrelated components and incrementally builds up the set of relationships among the components, adding components where necessary, until a functional system has been defined. A great deal of XCON's attention is devoted to deciding which extension to make next; because it spends significant energy deciding what to do next, it seldom needs to backtrack.

SEAR is an appropriate knowledge-acquisition tool for this task because the task has the following characteristics: (1) There is no known role-limiting method suitable for the task. The most likely candidate, SALT's propose-and-revise method, appears unsuitable because there is a high level of potential conflict among preferences for alternative design extensions in XCON's task. (2) Six methods have been defined for XCON; the number of steps in each method range from 4 to 10. (3) XCON's most frequently used method, *propose-apply*, is designed for tasks in which substantial amounts of task-specific control knowledge must be brought to bear in order for it to decide what action should be performed next.

Acquiring knowledge for a heuristic classifier. $MOLE_{KA}$ has also been reimplemented using the RIME methodology. As was mentioned above, MOLE begins its knowledge-acquisition efforts by asking the expert to list the typical complaints or abnormalities that would motivate someone to seek diagnostic help. MOLE next asks for possible explanations for each of these complaints. MOLE then asks whether these explaining events or states in turn have relevant explanations, and so on. Finally, MOLE seeks information that will enable it to differentiate, both statically and dynamically, these candidate explanations.

There are two reasons why MOLE is being developed using RIME: (1) As with XCON, there is no known role-limiting method suitable for the task of acquiring knowledge for a heuristic classifier. (2) It seems quite likely that some, if not many, of the systems that MOLE might be used to build will not be able to do the task the real world imposes on them using the particular heuristic classification method MOLE presupposes. Therefore, MOLE is being implemented in RIME to allow the MOLE developer to more easily create method variants.

Using SEAR to Develop Higher-Level Tools and Application Systems.

SEAR is intended to be used by fairly knowledgeable system designers, with strong programming backgrounds, who wish to build an application system or a knowledge-acquisition tool. These users will need to be able to define new methods and specify how knowledge is to be structured for particular domains. The SEAR method-definer tool will allow designers to define and combine problem-solving methods to create a knowledge-impoverished skeleton. Then, people with more modest programming skills can go to work with the rule-definer to add the knowledge necessary for a viable application. Other planned extensions to SEAR include a debugging assistant and a testing assistant.

Currently, the only tool available for use is a method-knowledgeable rule analyzer. This tool checks that an application system's knowledge is represented in a fashion appropriate for the particular problem-solving methods the system uses. Senior developers define the problem-solving methods and define rule types for each method. The SEAR rule analyzer ensures that the rules in these systems follow the requirements specified for the rule types.

8.3. Conclusions

Five role-limiting methods have been identified and briefly described. The scope of applicability of a role-limiting method, because it is a method for performing a particular type of task, is less broad than that of a weak method. But role-limiting methods, unlike weak methods, have little, if any, task-specific control knowledge. This characteristic makes role-limiting methods good foundations on which to build knowledge-acquisition tools, since knowing in advance all of the control knowledge that a method will use gives substantial insight into what kinds of task-specific knowledge will be required and into how that knowledge can be appropriately encoded.

Although several expert systems have been developed using the knowledge-acquisition tools described in this book, we do not yet have even a good guess as to what percentage of tasks can be adequately performed by systems that have no task-specific control knowledge. The RIME methodology was created to deal with building systems whose tasks cannot be performed adequately without task-specific control knowledge. It provides two kinds of assistance: (1) It can help guide the definition of previously undefined role-limiting methods. (2) It can assist with the collection of task-specific control knowledge for tasks that can only be solved effectively (for example, efficiently enough) if a great deal of control knowledge is brought to bear. The rewrite of XCON exemplifies both. Previous reports on XCON [Bachant 84, McDermott 82] have characterized the system as strongly data-driven; the data drove the system in two ways: (1) to apply appropriate task-specific knowledge, and (2) to select among competing pieces of task-specific knowledge. The initial version of XCON did not distinguish between the knowledge required for these two kinds of activities. The RIME methodology forces the developer to clearly distinguish between knowledge to be used to select among candidate actions and knowledge to be used to identify and implement actions.

We have gotten a little ways toward a taxonomy of problem-solving methods -- or at least toward a way of thinking about what a taxonomy might look like. It is possible that as we spend more energy analyzing methods, we will discover that all tasks can be performed adequately with only modest amounts of task-specific control knowledge. I doubt it, however. Systems like XCON and $MOLE_{KA}$ have control knowledge that appears to be very closely tied to the peculiarities of their tasks. It is more likely that a fairly large number of role-limiting methods will be identified, each of which can solve a range of similar problems. These methods will serve as the jumping-off point for a large number of methods that use substantial amounts of task-specific control knowledge whose only common denominator is the underlying role-limiting method. Thus, in addition to the strong assistance role-limiting methods give to automating the collecting and encoding of task-specific knowledge, they also give us the means of developing a helpful taxonomy.

Acknowledgements

Tom Cooper, Larry Eshelman, Serge Genetet, Keith Jensen, Georg Klinker, Herve Lambert, Sandy Marcus, Dan Offutt, and Jeff Stout provided substantial assistance in formulating the tool descriptions in this chapter. Judy Bachant, Rex Flynn, John Laird, David Marques, Tom Mitchell, Allen Newell, Elliot Soloway, and Bill Swartout provided extremely helpful comments on earlier drafts.

References

[Abrett 87]   Abrett, G., and M. Burstein.
                   The KREME knowledge editing environment.
                   International Journal of Man-Machine Studies
                       27(2):103-126, 1987.

[Bachant 84]   Bachant, J., and J. McDermott.
                   R1 revisted: Four years in the trenches.
                   AI Magazine 5(3):21-32, 1984.

[Boose 84]   Boose, J.
                   Personal construct theory and the transfer of human
                       expertise.
                   In *Proceedings of the Fourth National Conference on
                       Artificial Intelligence.* Austin, Texas, 1984.

[Boose 87]   Boose, J., and J. Bradshaw.
                   Expertise transfer and complex problems: Using
                       AQUINAS as a knowledge acquisition workbench for
                       expert systems.
                   International Journal of Man-Machine Studies
                       26(1):3-28, 1987.

[Brown 87]   Brown, D.
                   Failure handling in a design expert system.
                   Computer-Aided Design 17(9):436-441, 1987.

[Buchanan 84]   Buchanan, B., and E. Shortliffe.
                   *Rule-Based Systems: The Mycin Experiments of the
                       Stanford Heuristic Programming Project.*
                   Addison-Wesley, Reading, Massachusetts, 1984.

[Carbonell 85]   Carbonell, J.
                   *Derivational Analogy: A Theory of Reconstructive
                       Problem Solving and Expertise Acquisition.*
                   Technical Report, Carnegie Mellon University,
                       Department of Computer Science, 1985.

[Chandrasekaran 83]
                   Chandrasekaran, B.
                   Towards a taxonomy of problem solving types.
                   AI Magazine 4(1):9-17, 1983.

[Chandrasekaran 86]
            Chandrasekaran, B.
            Generic tasks in knowledge-based reasoning: High-level
                building blocks for expert system design.
            IEEE Expert 1(3):23-29, 1986.

[Charniak 83]   Charniak, E.
            The Bayesian basis of common sense medical diagnosis.
            In *Proceedings of the Third National Conference on
                Artificial Intelligence.* Washington, D.C., 1983.

[Clancey 83]   Clancey, W.
            The advantages of abstract control knowledge in expert
                system design.
            In *Proceedings of the Third National Conference on
                Artificial Intelligence.* Washington, D.C., 1983.

[Clancey 84]   Clancey, W.
            Classification problem solving.
            In *Proceedings of the Fourth National Conference on
                Artificial Intelligence.* Austin, Texas, 1984.

[Clancey 85]   Clancey, W.
            Heuristic classification.
            Artificial Intelligence 27(3):289-350, 1985.

[Clancey 86]   Clancey, W.
            From Guidon to Neomycin and Heracles in twenty short
                lessons.
            AI Magazine 7(3):40-77, 1986.

[Cohen 83]   Cohen, P., and M. Grinberg.
            A theory of heuristic reasoning about uncertainty.
            AI Magazine 4(2):17-24, 1983.

[Davis 79]   Davis, R.
            Interactive transfer of expertise: Acquisition of new
                inference rules.
            Artificial Intelligence 12(2):121-157, 1979.

[Davis 82]   Davis, R., and D. Lenat.
            Knowledge-Based Systems in Artificial Intelligence.
            McGraw-Hill, New York, New York, 1982.

[Dechter 85]   Dechter, R., and J. Pearl.
                 The anatomy of easy problems: A constraint-satisfaction
                     formulation.
                 In *Proceedings of the Ninth International Joint
                     Conference on Artificial Intelligence.* Los Angeles,
                     California, 1985.

[Dechter 87]   Dechter, R., and J. Pearl.
                 The cycle-cutset method for improving search
                     performance in AI applications.
                 In *Proceedings of the Third Conference on Artificial
                     Intelligence Applications.* Orlando, Florida, 1987.

[Diederich 87]   Diederich, J., I. Ruhmann, and M. May.
                 KRITON: A knowledge acquisition tool for expert
                     systems.
                 International Journal of Man-Machine Studies
                     26(1):29-40, 1987.

[Dietterich 82] Dietterich, T.
                 Learning and inductive inference.
                 In P. Cohen and E. Feigenbaum (editors), *The Handbook
                     of Artificial Intelligence.* Morgan Kaufmann, Los
                     Altos, California, 1982.

[Doyle 79]   Doyle, J.
                 A truth maintenance system.
                 Artificial Intelligence 12(3):231-272, 1979.

[Doyle 85]   Doyle, J.
                 Reasoned assumptions and pareto optimality.
                 In *Proceedings of the Eighth International Joint
                     Conference on Artificial Intelligence.* Los Angles,
                     California, 1985.

[Eshelman 86]   Eshelman, L., and J. McDermott.
                 MOLE: A knowledge acquisition tool that uses its head.
                 In *Proceedings of the Fifth National Conference on
                     Artificial Intelligence.* Philadelphia, Pennsylvania,
                     1986.

[Eshelman 87a]   Eshelman, L., D. Ehret, J. McDermott, and M. Tan.
                 MOLE: A tenacious knowledge acquisition tool.
                 International Journal of Man-Machine Studies
                     26(1):41-54, 1987.

[Eshelman 87b]   Eshelman, L.
                   MOLE: A knowledge acquisition tool that buries
                       certainty factors.
                   In *Proceedings of the Second Knowledge Acquisition for
                       Knowledge-based Systems Workshop*. Banff, Canada,
                       1987.

[Forgy 81]   Forgy, C.
                   The OPS5 Users Manual.
                   Technical Report, Carnegie Mellon University,
                       Department of Computer Science, 1981.

[Fox 83]   Fox, M., S. Lowenfield, and P. Kleinosky.
                   Techniques for sensor-based diagnosis.
                   In *Proceedings of the Eighth International Joint
                       Conference on Artificial Intelligence*. Karlsruhe,
                       West Germany, 1983.

[Freuder 82]   Freuder, E.
                   A sufficient condition for backtrack-free search.
                   Journal of the Association for Computing Machinery
                       29(11):24-32, 1982.

[Gale 87]   Gale, W.
                   Knowledge-based knowledge acquisition for a statistical
                       consulting system.
                   International Journal of Man-Machine Studies
                       26(1):55-64, 1987.

[Gruber 87a]   Gruber, T., and P. Cohen.
                   Design for acquisition: Principles of knowledge-system
                       design to facilitate knowledge acquisition.
                   International Journal of Man-Machine Studies
                       26(2):143-159, 1987.

[Gruber 87b]   Gruber, T.
                   Acquiring strategic knowledge from experts.
                   In *Proceedings of the Second Knowledge Acquisition for
                       Knowledge-based Systems Workshop*. Banff, Canada,
                       1987.

[Harman 86]   Harman, G.
                   Change in View: Principles of Reasoning.
                   The MIT Press, Cambridge, Massachusetts, 1986.

[Herman 86]   Herman, D., J. Josephson, and R. Hartung.
                   Use of DSPL for the Design of a Mission Planning
                        Assistant.
                   Technical Report, Ohio State University, Department of
                        Computer and Information Science, 1986.

[IntelliCorp 87]   IntelliCorp.
                   KEE 3.0 Training Manual.
                   IntelliCorp, Mountain View, California, 1987.

[Kahn 84]   Kahn, G., and J. McDermott.
                   The MUD system.
                   In *Proceedings of the First IEEE Conference on Artificial*
                        Intelligence Applications. Denver, Colorado, 1984.

[Kahn 85a]   Kahn, G., S. Nowlan, and J. McDermott.
                   Strategies for knowledge acquisition.
                   IEEE Transactions on Pattern Analysis and Machine
                        Intelligence 7(5):511-522, 1985.

[Kahn 85b]   Kahn, G., S. Nowlan, and J. McDermott.
                   MORE: An intelligent knowledge acquisition tool.
                   In *Proceedings of Ninth International Conference on*
                        Artificial Intelligence. Los Angeles, California, 1985.

[Kahn 87a]   Kahn, G.
                   TEST: A model-driven application shell.
                   In *Proceedings of the Sixth National Conference on*
                        Artificial Intelligence. Seattle, Washington, 1987.

[Kahn 87b]   Kahn, G., E. Breaux, P. DeKlerk, and R. Joseph.
                   A mixed-initiative workbench for knowledge acquisition.
                   International Journal of Man-Machine Studies
                        27(2):167-179, 1987.

[Kahn 87c]   Kahn, G.
                   From application shell to knowledge acquisition System.
                   In *Proceedings of Tenth International Joint Conference*
                        on Artificial Intelligence. Milan, Italy, 1987.

[Kahn 87d]   Kahn, G., E. Breaux, R. Joseph, and P. DeKlerk.
                   An intelligent mixed-initiative workbench for knowledge
                        acquisition.
                   International Journal of Man-Machine Studies
                        27(2):167-179, 1987.

[Klinker 87a]   Klinker, G., J. Bentolila, S. Genetet, M. Grimes, and
J. McDermott.
KNACK -- Report-driven knowledge acquisition.
International Journal of Man-Machine Studies
26(1):65-79, 1987.

[Klinker 87b]   Klinker, G., C. Boyd, S. Genetet, and J. McDermott.
A KNACK for knowledge acquisition.
In *Proceedings of Sixth National Conference on Artificial
Intelligence.* Seattle, Washington, 1987.

[Klinker 87c]   Klinker, G., S. Genetet, and J. McDermott.
Knowledge acquisition for evaluation systems.
In *Proceedings of the Second Knowledge Acquisition for
Knowledge-based Systems Workshop.* Banff, Canada,
1987.

[Laird 83]   Laird, J., and A. Newell.
A Universal Weak Method.
Technical Report, Carnegie Mellon University,
Department of Computer Science, 1983.

[Laird 87]   Laird, J., A. Newell, and P. Rosenbloom.
SOAR: An architecture for general intelligence.
Artificial Intelligence 33(1):1-64, 1987.

[Lenat 86]   Lenat, D., M. Prakash, and M. Shepherd.
CYC: Using common sense knowledge to overcome
brittleness and knowledge acquisition bottlenecks.
AI Magazine 6(4):65-85, 1986.

[Marcus 85]   Marcus, S., J. McDermott, and T. Wang.
Knowledge acquisition for constructive systems.
In *Proceedings of Ninth International Conference on
Artificial Intelligence.* Los Angeles, California, 1985.

[Marcus 87]   Marcus, S.
Taking backtracking with a grain of SALT.
International Journal of Man-Machine Studies
26(4):383-398, 1987.

[Marcus 88a]   Marcus, S., J. Stout, and J. McDermott.
VT: An expert elevator configurer that uses knowledge-
based backtracking.
AI Magazine 9(1):95-112, 1988.

[Marcus 88b]   Marcus, S.
                  A knowledge representation scheme for acquiring design
                      knowledge.
                  In C. Tong and D. Sriram (editors), *Artificial Intelligence
                      Approaches to Engineering Design*. Addison-Wesley,
                      Reading, Massachusetts, forthcoming, 1988.

[McDermott 82]   McDermott, J.
                  R1: A rule-based configurer of computer systems.
                  Artificial Intelligence 19(1):39-88, 1982.

[McDermott 86]   McDermott, J.
                  Making expert systems explicit.
                  In *Proceedings of Tenth Congress of the International
                      Federation of Information Processing Societies*.
                      Dublin, Ireland, 1986.

[Miller 82]   Miller, R., H. Pople, and J. Myers.
                  INTERNIST-1, an experimental computer-based
                      diagnostic consultant for general internal medicine.
                  New England Journal of Medicine 307(8):468-476, 1982.

[Mitchell 85]   Mitchell, T., S. Mahadevan, and L. Steinberg.
                  LEAP: A learning apprentice for VLSI design.
                  In *Proceedings of the Ninth International Joint
                      Conference on Artificial Intelligence*. Los Angeles,
                      California, 1985.

[Mittal 86]   Mittal, S., and A. Araya.
                  A knowledge-based framework for design.
                  In *Proceedings of the Fifth National Conference on
                      Artificial Intelligence*. Philadelphia, Pennsylvania,
                      1986.

[Musen 87]   Musen, M., L. Fagan, D. Combs, and E. Shortliffe.
                  Using a domain model to drive an interactive knowledge-
                      editing tool.
                  International Journal of Man-Machine Studies
                      26(1):105-121, 1987.

[Neches 84]   Neches, R., W. Swartout, and J. Moore.
                  Enhanced maintenance and explanation of expert systems
                      through explicit models of their development.
                  In *Proceedings of IEEE Workshop on Principles of
                      Knowledge-Based Systems*. Denver, Colorado, 1984.

[Newell 81]   Newell, A.
                   The knowledge level.
                   AI Magazine 2(2):1-20, 1981.

[Omohundro 87]   Omohundro, S.
                   Efficient algorithms with neural network behavior.
                   Complex Systems 26(1):273-347, 1987.

[Pearl 86]   Pearl, J.
                   Fusion, propagation and structuring in belief networks.
                   Artificial Intelligence 29(3):241-288, 1986.

[Pople 82]   Pople, H.
                   Heuristic methods for imposing structure on ill-structured
                       problems.
                   In P. Szolovits (editor), *Artificial Intelligence in
                       Medicine.* Westview Press, Boulder, Colorado, 1982.

[Schank 82]   Schank, R.
                   *Dynamic Memory: A Theory of Reminding and Learning
                       in Computers and People.*
                   Cambridge University Press, Cambridge, England, 1982.

[Schank 86]   Schank, R.
                   *Explanation Patterns: Understanding Mechanically and
                       Creatively.*
                   Lawrence-Erlbaum Associates, Hillsdale, New Jersey,
                       1986.

[Shafer 76]   Shafer, G.
                   A Mathematical Theory of Evidence.
                   Princeton University Press, Princeton, New Jersey, 1976.

[Shortliffe 76]   Shortliffe, E.
                   Computer-Based Medical Consultation: Mycin.
                   Elsevier, 1976.

[Smith 85]   Smith, R., H. Winston, T. Mitchell, and B. Buchanan.
                   Representation and use of explicit justifications for
                       knowledge base refinement.
                   In *Proceedings of the Ninth International Joint
                       Conference on Artificial Intelligence.* Los Angeles,
                       California, 1985.

[Smith 86] Smith, S., M. Fox, and P. Ow.
Constructing and maintaining detailed production plans: Investigations into the development of knowledge-based factory scheduling systems.
AI Magazine 7(4):45-60, 1986.

[Soloway 87] Soloway, E., J. Bachant, and K. Jensen.
Assessing the maintainability of XCON-in-RIME: Coping with the problems of a VERY large rule-based system.
In *Proceedings of the Sixth National Conference on Artificial Intelligence.* Seattle, Washington, 1987.

[Stallman 77] Stallman, R., and G. Sussman.
Forward reasoning and dependency-directed backtracking in a system for computer-aided circuit analysis.
Artificial Intelligence 9(2):135-196, 1977.

[Stefik 81a] Stefik, M.
Planning with constraints (MOLGEN: Part 1).
Artificial Intelligence 16(2):111-140, 1981.

[Stefik 81b] Stefik, M.
Planning and meta-planning (MOLGEN: Part 2).
Artificial Intelligence 16(2):141-170, 1981.

[Stout 88] Stout, J., G. Caplain, S. Marcus, and J. McDermott.
Toward automating recognition of differing problem-solving demands.
International Journal of Man-Machine Studies , forthcoming, 1988.

[Sussman 80] Sussman, G., and G. Steele, Jr.
CONSTRAINTS -- A language for expressing almost-hierarchical descriptions.
Artificial Intelligence 14(1):1-39, 1980.

[Swartout 83] Swartout, W.
XPLAIN: A system for creating and explaining expert consulting systems.
Artificial Intelligence 21(3):285-325, 1983.

[Szolovits 78] Szolovits, P., and Pauker, S.
Categorical and probabilistic reasoning in medical diagnosis.
Artificial Intelligence 11(1, 2):115-144, 1978.

[van de Brug 85] van de Brug, A., J. Bachant, and J. McDermott.
Doing R1 with style.
In *Proceedings of the Second IEEE Conference on Artificial Intelligence Applications.* Miami, Florida, 1985.

[van de Brug 86] van de Brug, A., J. Bachant, and J. McDermott.
The taming of R1.
IEEE Expert 1(3):33-38, 1986.

[vanMelle 81] van Melle, W., A. Scott, J. Bennet, and M. Peairs.
The EMYCIN manual.
Technical Report, Stanford University, Heuristic Programming Project, 1981.

[Waterman 85] Waterman, D.
A Guide to Expert Systems.
Addison-Wesley, Reading, Massachusetts, 1985.

[Weiss 78] Weiss, S., C. Kulikowski, S. Amarel, and A. Safir.
A model-based method for computer-aided medical decision-making.
Artificial Intelligence 11(1, 2):145-172, 1978.

Index